To Improve the Academy

To Improve the Academy

Resources for Faculty, Instructional, and Organizational Development

Volume 21

Catherine M. Wehlburg, Editor
Texas Christian University

Sandra Chadwick-Blossey, Associate Editor
Rollins College

ANKER PUBLISHING COMPANY, INC.

Bolton, Massachusetts

To Improve the Academy
Resources for Faculty, Instructional, and Organizational Development

Volume 21

ISBN 1-882982-55-X

Composition by Deerfoot Studios
Cover design by Boynton Hue Studio

Anker Publishing Company, Inc.
176 Ballville Road
P.O. Box 249
Bolton, MA 01740-0249 USA

www.ankerpub.com

To Improve the Academy

To Improve the Academy is published annually by the Professional and Organizational Network in Higher Education (POD) through Anker Publishing Company, and is abstracted in ERIC documents and in Higher Education Abstracts.

Ordering Information

The annual volume of *To Improve the Academy* is distributed to members at the POD conference in the autumn of each year. To order or to obtain ordering information, contact:

Anker Publishing Company, Inc.
P.O. Box 249
Bolton, MA 01740-0249
Voice   (978) 779-6190
Fax   (978) 779-6366
Email   info@ankerpub.com
Web   www.ankerpub.com

Permission to Copy

The contents of *To Improve the Academy* are copyrighted to protect the authors. Nevertheless, consistent with the networking and resource-sharing functions of POD, readers are encouraged to reproduce articles and cases from *To Improve the Academy* for educational use, as long as the source is identified.

Instructions to Contributors for the Next Volume

Anyone interested in the issues related to instructional, faculty, and organizational development in higher education may submit manuscripts. Manuscripts are submitted to the current editors in December of each year and sent through a blind review process. Correspondence, including requests for information about guidelines and submission of manuscripts for Volume 22, should be directed to:

Catherine M. Wehlburg
Director, Center for Teaching Excellence
Texas Christian University
Box 298970
Ft. Worth, TX 76129
Voice   (817) 257-7104
Fax   (817) 257-5913
Email   c.wehlburg@tcu.edu

Mission Statement

Approved by the Core Committee on March 24, 1991:

The Professional and Organizational Development Network in Higher Education (POD) fosters human development in higher education through faculty, instructional, and organizational development.

POD believes that people have value, as individuals and as members of groups. The development of students is a fundamental purpose of higher education and requires for its success effective advising, teaching, leadership, and management. Central to POD's philosophy is lifelong, holistic, personal, and professional learning growth, and change for the higher education community.

The three purposes of POD are:

1)   To provide support and services for its members through publications, conferences, consulting, and networking.

2)   To offer services and resources to others interested in faculty development.

3)   To fulfill an advocacy role, nationally, seeking to inform and persuade educational leaders of the value of faculty, instructional, and organizational development in institutions of higher education.

Membership, Conference, and Programs Information

For information contact:

Frank and Kay Gillespie, Executive Directors
The POD Network
P.O. Box 9696
Fort Collins, CO 80525
Voice   (970) 377-9269
Fax   (970) 377-9282
Email   podnetwork@podweb.org

Chapter Contributors

Michael Anderson, University of Nebraska, Lincoln
Virginia Baldwin, University of Nebraska, Lincoln
Laurie Bellows, University of Nebraska, Lincoln
Josef Broder, University of Georgia
Sheryl Burgstahler, University of Washington
Laura Bush, Arizona State University
X. Mara Chen, Salisbury University
Milton D. Cox, Miami University
Joseph R. Danos, Delgado Community College
Deborah DeZure, University of Michigan
Michele DiPietro, Carnegie Mellon University
Alan E. Guskin, Antioch University
William K. Jackson, University of Georgia
Patricia Kalivoda, University of Georgia
Delores Knipp, United States Air Force Academy
Carolin Kreber, University of Alberta
Alan Kindler, University of Toronto
Ellen M. Lawler, Salisbury University
Devorah A. Lieberman, Portland State University
Barry Maid, Arizona State University
Barbara J. Millis, United States Air Force Academy
Edward Nuhfer, University of Colorado at Denver
Candyce Reynolds, Portland State University
Douglas Robertson, Eastern Kentucky University
Duane Roen, Arizona State University
Kathleen S. Smith, University of Georgia
Richard G. Tiberius, University of Toronto
John Teshima, University of Toronto
Elichia A. Venso, Salisbury University
Edward Zlotkowski, Bentley College

Table of Contents

Section III: Student-Centered Faculty Development

Section IV: Philosophical Issues in Faculty Development

Preface

The 2001 POD Conference was held only one month after the tragic events of September 11. These events and their aftermath were discussed in many different ways by POD members before, during, and after the conference. The impact that those of us working in higher education have on society cannot be overlooked, and this fact became apparent in the reaction of our educational community to these events. Section I of this volume contains chapters that focus on the events of September 11, 2001, and the overarching theme of internationalization within our educational community. Sections II and III contain chapters that are more "traditional" within faculty development and focus on faculty roles within a student-centered philosophy. The chapters in Section IV grapple with some deeply rooted philosophical issues and how newer technologies may affect higher education.

The continuing high quality of *To Improve the Academy* requires that excellent manuscripts be submitted by members of the higher education community. I would like to thank the authors whose articles are contained within this volume. In addition, I would like to thank the work done by the reviewers for Volume 21. These include Phyllis Blumberg, Lesley Cafarelli, Nancy Diamond, Karen Gustavson, Judith Miller, Edward Nuhfer, Donna Qualters, Michael Rodgers, Lynn Sorenson, and Linda von Hoene. I would like to add special thanks to Sandra Chadwick-Blossey, Associate Editor. She not only reviewed and edited manuscripts, she also offered support and wonderful ideas throughout this process. Finally, I would like to thank Carolyn Dumore and the staff at Anker Publishing for their tireless answering of questions and their wonderful technological expertise.

Much of the work on this volume was done while I was Associate Vice President for Academic and Student Affairs at Stephens College. I wish to extend my appreciation to members of the Stephens College community, without whose support I would not have been able to edit this volume. As with many small colleges, Stephens College has a very limited number of individuals directly involved with faculty development and there are no staff members whose time is allocated to faculty development. As a result, many of my colleagues have helped in a variety of ways. Robert S. Badal, Provost, has been (and continues to be) encouraging of my work with POD. In addition, both Deborah Hume and Lois Bichler have been tremendously supportive of faculty development and my work with this year's edition. I would also like to thank Rosemary Barrow and Jim Hertel, faculty members within my department, for taking over some of the psychology department's administrative work so that I could focus on this year's volume.

Finally, I would like to thank my family, George, Trevor, and Brooke, for their unwavering love, support, and encouragement.

Catherine M. Wehlburg
Stephens College
Columbia, Missouri
April 2002

Introduction

The chapters in this volume of *To Improve the Academy* reflect the current practice of faculty development in higher education and highlight the need to be aware of our continuously changing world. The events of September 11, 2001, have affected all of us in so many ways, personally and professionally. The role that faculty development plays can become even more important to our campus communities as the connections between real life and the classroom emerge.

Section I: Faculty Development and Its Role in Institutional and National Crisis explores not only the events of September 11, but also the bigger picture of the changing face of higher education in the United States. Edward Zlotkowski's chapter reminds us of the critical importance of civic engagement in higher education. He discusses the role that faculty development could play in the promotion of connecting learning to real-world problems and concerns. No longer can we assume that learning for "its own sake" is sufficient.

In Chapter 2, Michele DiPietro describes the results of a faculty survey he conducted following the events of September 11, 2001. The results of this survey will benefit all as we look to find the teachable moment. The events of September 11 are just one example of how the real world affects higher education and demonstrates how important it is for faculty to be able to tie information from their relatively narrow field of study to broader concerns.

Deborah Dezure's chapter looks at how faculty developers need to reflect on global competencies as becoming an even more important part of higher education as we continue to move into the 21st century. Her call to action is one to which we should all listen.

Section II: Faculty Focus in Faculty Development addresses issues that are central to the "faculty" part of faculty and organizational development. This section contains chapters that range in topics, but all focus on what a faculty member might need for enhanced development. The first chapter in this section, by Edward Nuhfer and Delores Knipp, describes the knowledge survey. This type of survey has been used successfully to understand a student's mastery of course learning objectives. By learning what students already know at the beginning of a course, the instructor can better provide information during the course to increase student learning and student satisfaction. This proactive method of understanding student learning can also be used at the end of a course for a more direct assessment of student learning.

Another faculty development tool described in this section is that of a teaching academy which affects faculty development at the organizational level. Patricia Kalivoda, Josef Broder, and William Jackson describe the process of developing and implementing a Teaching Academy at the University of Georgia in Chapter 5. In addition to the academy development process, other faculty recognition tools are described.

Faculty development does not always involve workshops and brown bag lunches. Barbara Millis encourages us to use cooperative games with faculty in Chapter 6. Not only does she discuss the educational purpose of using games as a learning tool, she also describes two games that have been used for faculty development: the faculty scavenger hunt and Bingo. Using games with our faculty may bring back some of the joy of learning and be a new way to present material and engage faculty.

In Chapter 7, Milton Cox discusses the faculty learning community as one tool for faculty development. Not only can faculty enjoy the company of their peers outside the traditional disciplinary lines, but they can actually discuss pedagogy and learn from each other. This chapter outlines the faculty development tools that have been developed over the last 23 years that led to the successful connection between the scholarship of teaching and learning and faculty learning communities at Miami University.

Of course, faculty development does not just focus on full-time, fully degreed faculty members. Many in faculty development work with teaching and research assistants. In Chapter 8, Kathleen Smith describes a teaching assistant (TA) support program at the University of Georgia and the longitudinal case study assessment of this program. The results of this assessment helped to identify and enhance the program. The knowledge gained concerning the job market for TAs is useful to all those in faculty and organizational development.

The final chapter in this section describes a cooperative venture between a large university and a smaller community college. Laurie Bellows and Joseph Danos created an online workshop on syllabus construction that was available to faculty at both institutions. This online workshop was asynchronous and had 103 faculty members participate during one of the four presentations of this three-week workshop. This chapter discusses what worked and what did not in using an online instructional development workshop. Their results will benefit many faculty developers as technology becomes more and more a part of how information is delivered.

In Section III: Student-Centered Faculty Development, the teacher-student relationship and the crucial (but sometimes forgotten) role that students play in the teaching/learning process is discussed. Individual differences among students make teaching a challenge, as we all know. Looking at these challenges as opportunities for growth is crucial to the field of faculty and organizational development. In Chapter 10, Sheryl Burgstahler's article has a focus on the professional development needs of faculty concerning the accommodations made for students with disabilities. Faculty developers are faced with offering options for faculty working with students with disabilities and this chapter can help us to educate members of our institutional communities.

Douglas Robertson's chapter looks at learner-centered teaching and the inherent risks to educational integrity that are a part of this concept. The contradictory demands that are placed on instructors (trying to both facilitate learning for the student and also evaluate the student) are not always identified in an explicit manner. This can undermine the integrity of the educational process for both the teacher and student.

Even though there is risk in teaching with a student/learner-centered approach, the benefits are extraordinary. Richard Tiberius, John Teshima, and Alan Kindler explore pivotal moments that can occur in a teacher-student relationship. These moments can have a powerful educational affect. However, teachers do not often know how to recognize these moments when they occur and so a potentially meaningful opportunity is lost. Discovering how to recognize them and, even more important, how to create these moments are certainly an important part of faculty development and of higher education.

These powerful moments of meeting do not just occur between a teacher and a single student. The increasing use of learning communities points to the effectiveness of creating and using these moments in small groups. Candyce Reynolds discusses how the use of learning communities can affect student learning. Specifically, student mentors are used at Portland State University to encourage students to connect with other students as well as with faculty. In addition, the mentor process has helped faculty to better understand student perspectives and issues since students are more likely to share personal information with another student. The feedback to faculty from the student mentors has enabled the faculty at Portland State University to make better educational decisions about assignments, course structure, and overall student learning.

The final chapter in this section also discusses student perspectives. Mara Chen, Ellen Lawler, and Elichia Venso conducted a study to discover students' opinions about college teaching and learning. The results of this survey can be generalized and used on most campuses to encourage faculty to reevaluate their current teaching strategies and take into consideration student input. Some of the findings are eye-opening and create the opportunity for rich discussion about what we think we know about students.

The final section, Section IV: Philosophical Issues in Faculty Development, contains chapters that move our focus from specific faculty and organizational development tools to the bigger picture. Devorah Lieberman and Alan Guskin discuss the role that faculty development plays in higher education. How those in the field of faculty, instructional, and organizational development deal with new educational environments, budgetary concerns, and accountability issues will certainly impact higher education. How this plays out is yet to be seen, but the issues raised by Lieberman and Guskin are thought-provoking and will lead to much discussion in the future.

Some of these issues will take creativity and imagination to solve. Chapter 16, by Michael Anderson and Virginia Baldwin, encourages us to look more closely at how we define "teachers" and involves a creative collaboration. Their chapter is a case study involving collaboration among faculty development professionals and information specialists. These types of collaboration may be one way to stress the importance of faculty development by involving more of the campus community.

Given the recent shift from a teacher-centered model to a student-centered model, how often have we really asked faculty to think about their role, not just in terms of behavior but in terms of values and beliefs? Carolin Kreber discusses the role of the belief system and the critical importance of life-long learning in Chapter 17.

In the final chapter in this section, Laura Bush, Barry Maid, and Duane Roen connect Boyer's classic work on the scholarship of teaching with Glassick, Huber, and Maeroff's work on assessing scholarship. Using the frame of e-learning, the model that they discuss can be used in most teaching contexts in higher education, and this is useful in and of itself. However, the application of this model to the use of technology gives even more focus to the bigger picture and the future of faculty and organizational development in higher education.

The connection between what happens in the classroom and real-world experiences is becoming even stronger. The grounding of academic theory must occur in the context of experience. Faculty and organizational development must continue to play a crucial role in developing the many kinds of scholarship that will benefit not only higher education but the broader society as well.

Catherine M. Wehlburg
Stephens College
Columbia, Missouri
April 2002

Section I

Faculty Development and Its Role in Institutional and National Crisis

1

September 11, 2001, as a Teachable Moment

Edward Zlotkowski
Bentley College

The Opening Plenary at the 2001 POD Conference was given by Edward Zlotkowski. Using the reactions to the events of September 11, 2001, as an example, he urged those in higher education to search out opportunities for academically based civic engagement and to focus on Boyer's concept of the scholarship of engagement.

INTRODUCTION

On September 11, 2001, late in the afternoon, an email message went out from the undergraduate dean of my institution (C. Hadlock, personal communication, September 11, 2001). It began as follows:

> To follow up on [the college president's] message, most of the faculty I have talked to agree that we will all find various kinds of benefits in further discussion of today's events in classes tomorrow... Students who typically see teachers as presenters of academic material in a narrow discipline have much to learn from witnessing our universal concern for the issues raised by the tragedy...
>
> Therefore, I would encourage everyone to make an effort to raise some of these issues for discussion. There is no single discipline that owns the subject of human tragedy, nor is there any faculty member who would not have valuable points of view to share with his or her classes.

That the dean should publicly recognize the "narrow" disciplinary identities most faculty offer their students and the way in which such identities are immediately challenged by events of "universal concern" struck me as both admirable and sad. Was this also the identity I shared with my students? Did the way in which I typically presented my material leave them feeling disconnected from universal concerns?

Two days later another message (J. Morone, personal communication, September 13, 2001) with a very similar theme was sent from our president. Again, faculty were encouraged "if possible to connect the events around us to the content of your subject and discipline." Recognizing that some faculty might well be "uncomfortable about this, or . . . not sure how to proceed," he suggested they contact the undergraduate dean, their chair, or a "colleague who might be able to help." It seems as though the dean's encouragement had not had the desired results.

> I've received a number of emails from faculty reporting that they had wonderful sessions yesterday. Unfortunately, I've also received emails from students expressing disappointment that their professors barely mentioned what was going on around us before launching into their scheduled lectures. Our job as educators today and tomorrow and for quite some time to come is to help our students, as best we can, to make sense of all this. And for every discipline, surely there are connections that can and should be made between the tragedy our students are living through and the subjects we teach.

It would be for me hard to find a casual document that so clearly suggested what is wrong with contemporary American higher education. The gap between faculty performance and student expectations, the recognition that our job as educators now demands more than business as usual, the almost plaintive suggestion that surely there are connections between what we live and what we teach—these all suggest what the late Donald Schon (1995) called "the dilemma of rigor or relevance" (p. 28). It is a dilemma that has been growing in visibility over the past ten years, a dilemma the events of September 11 and their aftermath powerfully drive home.

THE POST–COLD WAR ACADEMY

Whether or not most academics now recognize it, the end of the Cold War may emerge as a watershed event not just in international relations but also in American higher education. While the Clark Kerr (1963, 1994) of the early

1960s "was generally optimistic about the workings of the knowledge process" (p. 155), celebrating the triumph of what he called the "multiversity" as an "imperative rooted in the logic of history" (p. 5), the Kerr of the early 1990s had "more reservations" (p. 155):

> New knowledge, like addictive drugs, can have bad as well as good effects. And new knowledge has limits to its curative effects, as in directly controlling the population explosion or the eruption of ethnic and religious fundamentalism. Knowledge is not clearly all good, and certainly not the one and only "one good." The university, consequently, needs to be more careful in what it does and less arrogant about what it claims it can do. So many of us should have realized all of this more fully so much earlier. We were too euphoric. (p. 155)

This new recognition that knowledge for its own sake—still the mantra of most elite institutions—is not the unambiguous, self-sufficient good many academics like to assert it is and that university-generated knowledge cannot even begin to address many of our most important social problems may have been long overdo, but it was the end of the Cold War that allowed it to surface. As R. C. Lewontin (1997) points out,

> Although the power to command ... favorable conditions of employment [as a result of government investment in research] accrues at first-hand to established academics in the natural and some of the social sciences, primarily at large research universities, it has changed the relationship between institutions and academics generally. . . . Lower teaching loads in science have meant lower teaching loads in the humanities. (p. 130)

Indeed, the availability of research money did more than tip the balance toward research and away from students. It also reinforced a trend evident from the earliest decades of the modern university to substitute disciplinary stature for local engagement (Lewontin, 1997). Government funding and an assumption of national importance aided and abetted a "guild mentality" that Kerr (1963, 1994) characterizes as "isolationist toward society, devoted to producer as against consumer sovereignty, and committed more to guild rules than to quick adaptation to popular demand" (p. 73).

For many faculty, this guild mentality is still a boon devoutly to be wished, but, unfortunately for them, neither governmental largesse nor public attitudes make its future prospects bright. Frank Newman (2000), Director of the Futures Project: Policy for Higher Education in a Changing World, notes that

> over the long history of higher education, universities and colleges—both state-owned and private—have held a privileged position because they have focused on the needs of society rather than self-gains. They have, in turn, been given special responsibilities. As higher education becomes more closely linked to for-profit activities and market forces, its special status is endangered. (p. 16)

What exactly are the special responsibilities American higher education has assumed now that the ideological contest with the former Soviet Union has been won, and the technological superiority the academy helped the country achieve is no longer needed in quite the same way? Speaking to a gathering of Jesuit educators at Santa Clara University in fall 2000, Peter-Hans Kolvenbach, the order's Superior General, commented on some of the ramifications of this change:

> This valley [Silicon Valley], this nation and the whole world look very different from the way they looked twenty-five years ago. With the collapse of Communism and the end of the Cold War, national and even international politics have been eclipsed by a resurgent capitalism that faces no ideological rival. (p. 5)

As a result,

> all American universities, [Jesuit] included, are under tremendous pressure to opt entirely for success [in the sense of placing graduates in high-paying jobs]. But what our students want—and deserve—includes but transcends this "worldly success" based on marketable skills. (Kolvenbach, 2000, p. 6)

This is the same emphasis on private gain Newman (2000) warns against. Indeed, it is the very same phenomenon Boyer (1996) warned against in one of his very last publications.

In an essay published posthumously in the inaugural issue of the *Journal of Public Service and Outreach,* Boyer (1996) anticipated precisely the analysis made by Newman and Kolvenbach. After lamenting the faculty's increasingly evident intellectual insularity, he identifies a second, related trend:

But, what I find most disturbing ... is a growing feeling in this country that higher education is, in fact, part of the problem rather than the solution. Going still further, that it's become a private benefit, not a public good. Increasingly, the campus is being viewed as a place where students get credentialed and faculty get tenured, while the overall work of the academy does not seem particularly relevant to the nation's most pressing civic, social, economic, and moral problems. (p. 14)

The suggestion that higher education may now be part of the problem rather than the solution has several dimensions. First and foremost, it implies the lack of a guiding public purpose just alluded to. However, it also implies an at least implicit collaboration with elitist, anti-democratic forces and purely market-driven mechanisms. Recent studies indicating that the most accurate predictor of a college education is family income, the increasing interchangeability of university presidents and corporate CEOs (Lind, 1995), the growing reliance of many higher education institutions on poorly compensated part-time instructors as well as the wage-scale differential between those instructors and the academic "stars" who move from institution to institution selling their reputations to the highest bidder all suggest that the academy's own operations are far closer to a corporate model than the trumpeted ideal of a community of scholars would lead the public to suspect.

But the disturbing situation Boyer (1996) refers to has its roots in something far deeper than such cross-sector institutional parallels; it also reflects the intellectual assumptions that continue to ground most faculty work—in practice, if not in theory. Harry Boyte (2000), among others, has identified this set of assumptions with the still powerful legacy of positivism:

The ideal of the detached scholar, teacher, and outside expert has roots in the impact of German universities on American scholars in the late nineteenth century, as the Princeton historian Daniel Rodgers has described in *Atlantic Crossings*. American economic graduate students learned an ethos of scientific "objectivity" and a model of policy making in private consultation with political leadership, far removed from public involvement. The ethos of detachment was further fed by an uncritical celebration of science, and especially by the philosophers of positivism, who argued that science rested on the discovery of permanent, atemporal standards of rationality that could be found and then applied. (p. 46)

Hence, "everywhere the sense of detachment and the stance of 'objectivity' which are positivism's legacy lead to isolation and competition" and encourage professionals to "imagine themselves outside a shared reality with their fellow citizens" (p. 50).

It is also to this legacy that Sullivan (n.d.), in a recent essay entitled "Institutional Identity and Social Responsibility," attributes what he calls the "default program of instrumental individualism" (p. 8) that defines most of the contemporary academy's work:

> In the absence of an updated version of its founding conception of itself as a participant in the life of civil society, as a citizen of American democracy, much of higher education has come to operate on a sort of default program of instrumental individualism. This is the familiar notion that the academy exists to research and disseminate knowledge and skills as tools for economic development and the upward mobility of individuals. This "default program" of instrumental individualism leaves the larger questions of social, political, and moral purpose out of explicit consideration. (p. 2)

In adopting the phrase "*default* program" [emphasis added], Sullivan succinctly captures both the pervasiveness and the insidiousness of the academy's lack of a defining public vision: the failure of most faculty to pursue work that clearly articulates and advances some sense of the public good perforce results in teaching and scholarship that reinforces a dysfunctional status quo—regardless of an activity's particular content or focus. As Boyte (2000) notes, "Positivism structures our research, our disciplines, our teaching, and our institutions long after it has been discredited intellectually. It is like a genie that academia let loose long ago, now lurking below the surface and threatening our destruction" (p. 48).

Hence, it is hardly surprising that the faculty response to the events of September 11, 2001, should have been in many instances disappointing. Although more and more faculty recognize the importance of paying more attention to civic engagement, most continue to see this attention as somebody else's business. According to research conducted by the Higher Education Research Institute (1999),

> Faculty are increasingly likely to believe that American colleges and universities are committed to involving students in community service. ... Between 1989 and 1998, the percent of faculty who believe that their institution places a priority on facilitating student involvement in

community service has grown from 23 to 36 percent" (Community Service and Social Activism section, ¶ 1). However,

> Despite the faculty's growing awareness of their institution's commitment to community service, such trends are not evident with respect to the faculty's personal commitment to community service and social activism. Since 1989, *a declining percentage of faculty* are personally committed to such goals as influencing the political structure, influencing social values, and cleaning up the environment.... And although 54 percent of faculty believe that "community service should be given weight in college admissions" (up from 47 percent in 1995), *there has been essentially no change in faculty's own commitment to "instill in students a commitment to community service" and to "prepare students for responsible citizenship."* [emphasis added] (Higher Education Research Institute, 1999, Community Service and Social Activism section, ¶ 2)

Under such circumstances, it should not be surprising that even when faced with a public event of historic proportions, many faculty are simply unable—psychologically, conceptually, pedagogically—to make a meaningful connection between that event and their professional work. Indeed, the very idea of doing so must seem to many of them rather unprofessional! (See, for example, Howard, 2001.) To respond to a public event means to be willing to suspend, to bracket the "real" work of a class, to siphon precious time and energy away from the primary work at hand: a distanced, detached consideration of largely prepackaged, self-referential material. The idea that there exist natural "connections that can and should be made between [what] our students are living through and *the subjects we teach*" [emphasis added] (J. Morone, personal communication, September 2001) must seem, at best, puzzling. What more can one demand from faculty than that they be willing to make time for conscientious "personal" reactions?

The Engaged Campus and the Scholarship of Engagement

It is in response to this disabling and ultimately dysfunctional professional disengagement from public life that the civic engagement movement of the last decade has taken shape. And again it was Boyer (1996) who helped give us our conceptual bearings. In the same posthumous essay in which he warns against higher education's becoming a purely "private benefit" (p. 14), he also reviews the four kinds of scholarship proposed in *Scholarship Reconsidered* (1990), namely, the scholarships of discovery, integration, teaching, and application. His discussion of the last of these eventually brings him to the conclusion "that in the century ahead, higher education in this country has an urgent obligation to become more vigorously *engaged* in the issues of our day" [emphasis added] (p. 17). Soon the phrase "scholarship of application" disappears, only to be replaced by the phrase "scholarship of engagement" (p. 18), and it is with this concept that the essay ends:

> Increasingly, I'm convinced that ultimately, the scholarship of engagement also means creating a special climate in which the academic and civic cultures communicate more continuously and more creatively with each other, helping to enlarge what anthropologist Clifford Geertz describes as the universe of human discourse and enriching the quality of life for all of us. (p. 20)

This conviction that a scholarship of engagement ultimately aims at nothing less than "enriching the quality of life for all of us" finds its institutional equivalent in something Boyer (1994) had described two years earlier as the "New American College":

> This New American College would organize cross-disciplinary institutes around pressing social issues. Undergraduates at the college would participate in field projects, relating ideas to real life. Classrooms and laboratories would be extended to include health clinics, youth centers, schools, and government offices. Faculty members would build partners with practitioners who would, in turn, come to campus as lecturers and student advisers. (p. A48)

For like the scholarship of engagement, the New American College "would be committed to improving, in a very intentional way, the human condition" (Boyer, 1994, p. A48). Like the scholarship of engagement, it would redefine academic excellence, embracing social relevance without abandoning intellectual rigor. In the little more than five years since Boyer left us with these guiding formulations, a small but increasing number of individual teacher-scholars as well as an ever more significant number of academic institutions have attempted to explore and embody the vision Boyer sketched.

It is not possible in an essay of this length even to begin to do justice to the breath and depth of the civic engagement movement as it has developed in the academy over the past ten years. Hence, a few suggestive indicators will have to suffice. Over the last three years alone, Campus Compact, the only national higher education organization whose sole purpose is to promote public and community service, particularly academically based service, grew by 30% to over 750 member colleges and universities (Campus Compact, 2001). During approximately the same period of time, the American Association for Higher Education (AAHE) completed a series of 18 monographs on service-learning in the academic disciplines (Zlotkowski, 1997–2000). It was the largest publishing venture in AAHE's history, and in the end drew upon the work of over 400 teacher-scholars from many different sectors of American higher education. The last few years have also seen major engagement initiatives launched by the New England Research Center for Higher Education, the Council of Independent Colleges, the American Association of Community Colleges, the National Association of State Universities and Land-Grant Colleges, and over half a dozen national disciplinary associations. Indeed, in direct response to Boyer's New American College vision, a group calling itself the Associated New American Colleges was formed.

What has made possible much of this work is generous funding from a host of public and private sources. Although many associate federal sponsorship of national and community service programs with the Clinton administration, it was actually the first George Bush that laid the foundation for them with his Commission on National and Community Service in 1990. Clinton then built upon and expanded this foundation into the Corporation on National Service (CNS). Learn and service funding, though limited in the context of the overall CNS program, has been especially important in helping colleges and universities develop institutional structures capable of facilitating and sustaining academic engagement efforts. Funds made available through the Community Outreach Partnership Centers (COPC) Program at the Department of Housing and Urban Development, initiated in 1994, have played a similar role. It is one indication of the growth of national interest in engagement initiatives that bipartisan efforts are currently underway to increase federal funding for community-based student work.

Private foundations have also stepped up the plate. The Pew Charitable Trusts awarded Campus Compact several million dollars to develop a pyramid of service-learning, with programming specifically designed for institutions and faculty at different levels of experience with engaged work. Ford, Kellogg, Kettering, and Lilly have funded a complementary set of initiatives around community partnering and civic discourse. The Atlantic Philanthropies have invested in a variety of efforts related to higher education reform and civic renewal.

FACULTY CONSIDERATIONS

By this point, I think it should be clear why academic renewal through civic engagement is ultimately a faculty affair. As a Campus Compact report authored by Tim Stanton (1990), then associate director of the Haas Center at Stanford University, made clear, faculty participation in engagement, "in supporting student service efforts and in setting an example of civic participation and leadership through their own efforts" (p. 1), is critical to any strategy to promote effective and sustainable academic-civic partnerships.

And yet, despite this seemingly self-evident fact, many schools have, nonetheless, set about trying to claim Boyer's mantel without addressing the serious faculty development issues that mantel implies. Presidential proclamations laced with statistics on the number of student volunteer hours provided to the community, economic measures to benefit housing stock in local neighborhoods, new "urban research" institutes, strong community service traditions maintained through religious affiliations or specially endowed philanthropic halls or houses, donations of sporting equipment and not-quite cutting-edge technology to local youth groups—these initiatives, as valuable and as admirable as they are, cannot by themselves constitute the kind of academic engagement Boyer envisioned and American society needs. They are the equivalent of those personal and private expressions of comfort and grief that appeared everywhere across American campuses in the wake of September 11. While meaningful and even necessary, such expressions failed to draw upon the academy's core function: the creation and dissemination of knowledge. Leaving rank-and-file faculty free to close the classroom or the office door and to continue with business as usual, they can actually divert attention from what is in many instances a serious lack of vision and a distressing failure of nerve.

One of the few university presidents to recognize and address the critical importance of developing an ethos of engagement in and through the work of mainstream faculty is Judith Ramaley, who first at Portland State University and later at the University of Vermont sought to implement Boyer's vision in a comprehensive, sustainable way. In an article titled "Nurturing the 'Engaged University,'" Ramaley (2000) shares some of what she has learned about the process of winning faculty support for "activities that promote civic responsibility and sustain campus-community engagement" (p. 12).

She begins by noting that, in her experience, "10 to 15 percent of the faculty or staff on campus already have a broad repertoire of interests . . . consistent with the full realization of engagement." A second group, roughly double in size, has "a genuine interest in new ways of doing things but want clear signals [of support] ... if they venture into new territory, in this case, literally, into the community." Group three, approximately the same size as group two, see the new agenda as a fad or institutional whim, "certain [to] disappear when the new president/provost/dean moves on to greener pastures." Finally, there is "a small number (maybe 10 percent) of the faculty or staff ... certain that the new agenda or the new modes are not legitimate faculty work" (Ramaley, 2000, p. 50).

According to Ramaley (2000), each of the last three groups has its own distinctive "energy barrier" which must be addressed if its members are to get on board:

> The boundary between the committed [group one] and the cautious [group two] is defined by a *disciplinary barrier* and discipline-based definitions of research and scholarship ... The border between the cautious and the skeptical [group three] is maintained by the lack of convincing evidence that the new ways or the new agenda works better than the old one ... The resisters [group four] are protected by a fear of the risk of change itself. ... Different strategies are needed to overcome each barrier. (p. 12)

My own experience in working with faculty from hundreds of institutions largely confirms this analysis. On every campus there is a core of faculty already aware of the significance and the potential of community-based academic work. Furthermore, in many cases, this core is composed largely of, on the one hand, young, tenure-track or part-time faculty and, on the other, senior professors. Those faculty closest to a tenure application and decision are most conspicuously missing.

By far the largest group of faculty I encounter belong to group two: their openness to change and/or their sense that change is needed sparks a degree of genuine interest. However, what they need to move forward is a sense that others in their field have already demonstrated the feasibility and value of acting on that interest. It was for this group in particular that AAHE's 18-volume series on service-learning in the academic disciplines (Zlotkowski, 1997–2000) was created, and it is this group that has profited most from AAHE and Campus Compact's efforts to support engaged scholarship in and through the national disciplinary societies.

It is when a dean or an academic vice president makes mandatory departmental representation at a presentation or workshop on engagement that I most often encounter members of group three. Quite legitimately, they demand to see "proof" that community-based work has real academic value.

Fortunately, thanks to the work of a growing number of researchers (Astin, Vogelgesang, Ikeda, & Yee, 2000; Eyler & Giles, 1999; Harkavy, Puckett, & Romer, 2000) that proof is increasingly easy to produce. Still, the fact that these "skeptics" seem largely uninterested in research that suggests serious epistemological and pedagogical questions regarding traditional classroom practices may render their calls for a culture of evidence somewhat disingenuous. In any event, it is those faculty from this group who, through some circumstance, are able to experience personally the heightened sense of significance and efficacy community-based work brings that become its most enthusiastic proponents. As for faculty from group four, I myself have had relatively little contact with them since they lack sufficient interest to initiate contact on their own and possess sufficient power not to need to do so to please others.

THE POD CONNECTION

By this point, I imagine it is clear to most readers how POD members could contribute significantly to the civic renewal of American higher education. As the professionals responsible for faculty development, they are well positioned to collaborate with Campus Compact and AAHE both in bringing the engagement-related resources developed thus far to the faculty on their campuses and in creating additional resources based on their own expertise. Indeed, without access to the professional and organizational opportunities POD members represent, advancing the national engagement agenda will be slow and difficult. On most campuses there currently exists a complete disconnect between faculty development activities and efforts to promote a scholarship of engagement. A collaborative agenda could begin by addressing several essential tasks.

First and foremost, faculty need to understand more clearly the difference between ordinary civic contributions and the scholarship of engagement. As Boyer (1996) noted in the same essay in which he introduced the scholarship of engagement,

> When we speak of applying knowledge we do not mean "doing good," although that's important. Academics have their civic functions, which should be honored, but by scholarship of application we mean having professors become what Donald Schon of MIT has called "reflective practitioners," moving from theory to practice, and from practice back to theory, which in fact makes theory, then, more authentic... (p. 17)

Since then, many individual colleges and universities have gone on to draw essentially the same distinction (New England Resource Center for Higher Education, n.d.). Especially important in this regard are 1) the distinction between the more or less routine application of existing knowledge (a form of consulting) and the generation of new knowledge through a theory-practice dialectic, and 2) the distinction between community service, even if sponsored by a course, and academically rigorous service-based learning or service-learning. So long as faculty continue to conflate generic public assistance with the development of greater conceptual understanding through activities that benefit the public, challenges to the professional legitimacy of the scholarship of engagement will continue to distract attention from its creative utilization.

Closely related to this primary distinction is the ability to identify engagement opportunities that speak appropriately to the focus of a faculty member's expertise. It was to jumpstart this activity, at least with regard to teaching, that the AAHE monograph series (Zlotkowski, 1997–2000) was created, and it remains the single most useful resource available to faculty developers working with particular disciplinary constituencies. Indeed, to build on a faculty development strategy developed by a longtime POD member, Deborah DeZure (1996), Coordinator of Faculty Programs at the University of Michigan, one can easily imagine an entire program built around departmental workshops. As DeZure (1996) writes:

> While useful in many ways ... centralized [faculty development] services are often underused by faculty, rejected by many as too remote from their disciplinary teaching concerns. For many faculty, *teaching* means *teaching history* or *teaching music* or *teaching biology.* For them, instructional development should become more disciplinary, engaging these faculty by exploring issues of teaching in the context of their departmental expectations and their disciplinary values and modes of discourse. (p. 9)

Drawing upon the monograph series and other engaged resources created by the national disciplinary associations, one could effortlessly adapt DeZure's strategy to introduce the scholarship of engagement to faculty in every academic area, if not every academic department.

Few researchers have studied the academic department more thoroughly than Jon Wergin (2001), Professor of Educational Studies at Virginia Commonwealth University. Recently, Wergin turned his attention to the issue of effective faculty incentives, only to conclude that talk of special, extrinsic incentives can be misleading:

> More than forty years of research on faculty motivation has resulted
> in some remarkably consistent findings. Over and over again this re-
> search has found that those of us who choose to be faculty are driven
> by a relatively small number of motives: autonomy, community,
> recognition, efficacy. (p. 50)

Viewing this list from the standpoint of the scholarship of engagement
(in all its forms), one can conclude that items one and two should not represent barriers to such work since autonomy, which Wergin (2001) glosses as
"the freedom to grow in ways that contribute to the common good" (p. 50),
is not threatened and community is probably enhanced. However, recognition and efficacy do represent barriers, and of the two it is recognition that is
most often discussed.

Although no one who has spent much time with faculty interested in engaged work can deny that institutional recognition, especially as it applies to
tenure and promotion, is an issue of fundamental concern, there is probably
little that most POD members can do about it. Over the last five years, more
and more colleges and universities wishing to move in an engaged direction
have begun revising their tenure and promotion guidelines to recognize community-based work. However, efficacy, the sense that one is being effective,
rarely comes up directly in conversations with would-be engaged faculty, and
yet, it can be no less decisive than recognition. Indeed, according to Blackburn
and Lawrence (1995), " . . . self-efficacy . . . mattered more than any other variable in any category [of factors affecting faculty motivation]. It was significant
in 26 instances at one time or another in every institutional type and academic
discipline" (p. 281).

Very few of today's faculty have had, in the course of their ordinary graduate school and post-graduate work, any opportunity to develop either the
awareness or the skills necessary for effective community outreach. While
many of the skills they have developed remain relevant, when community enters the picture, the picture becomes especially complex. It is here that POD
members could make a major contribution to the scholarship of engagement,
first, by helping to identify what the additional skills are that it requires, and,
second, by designing strategies and programs that allow faculty to develop
those skills. Here, it seems to me, one finds ample room for theoretical and op-
erational innovation. What do successful academy-community partnerships
look like, and how does one form them? What models are available? How does

one document community-based work? How does one assess its success from an academic, public, and institutional standpoint? What is the role of reflection in learning to learn from experience? How does one lead student reflection? How does one deal with the "messiness" inherent in such work?

Until now, there has been relatively little effort to train faculty to do work that more and more institutions are coming to regard as important. Dale Rice at Eastern Michigan University, Bob Bringle and Julie Hatcher at Indiana University–Purdue University Indianapolis, and a few others have pioneered faculty development models in theory and/or in practice (Bringle & Hatcher, 1995; Rice & Stacey, 1997; Zlotkowski, 1998). In 1992, Portland State University (Driscoll, 1998) began working toward an organizational structure that would allow faculty development, community partnerships, and assessment to share the same space and support each other. Unfortunately, despite the university's widely acknowledged success, few other institutions have succeeded in learning from its example. POD involvement could help change that.

Conclusion

Gene Rice, Director of AAHE's Forum on Faculty Roles and Rewards, and Ernest Boyer's collaborator in redefining legitimate faculty work, has often recalled how heretical the idea of faculty development seemed in the early 1970s. The scholarship of engagement currently occupies a similar position, and, if the comparison holds true, may in 20 years seem as self-evident as faculty development does now. At least we can hope that is the case. In 1998, a special task force of the American Political Science Association (APSA) released a statement on civic education in the 21st century. It reads in part:

> We start with the evidence suggesting mounting political apathy in the United States. . . . Long-term efforts to reverse [this] must obviously address many possible causes. We do, however, take as axiomatic that current levels of political knowledge, political engagement, and political enthusiasm are so low as to threaten the vitality and stability of democratic politics in the United States. (p. 636)

While this warning directs itself explicitly to forms of political engagement, other formulations in the document make clear that it is concerned with civic engagement in a broad as well as a narrow sense. Certainly its summary response speaks to that broader sense of engagement; namely, that there is an urgent need to "[t]each the motivation and competence to engage actively in public problem solving" (p. 636). This was precisely what most of my

Bentley College colleagues did not know how to do in the days immediately following September 11. We have little reason to believe faculty at other institutions were any more prepared to move beyond general discussions and expressions of personal concern. To be sure, these are important. But by themselves they will not lead to academic renewal or higher education reform.

Over the past decade AAHE and Campus Compact have made a major investment in helping both faculty and institutions learn to practice and to teach public problem solving—the scholarship of engagement. It is my sincere hope that members of POD will regard publication of this essay as an invitation to join that effort.

REFERENCES

American Political Science Association (APSA). (1998). Task force on civic education in the 21st century: Expanded articulation statement: A call for reactions and contributions. *PS: Politics and Political Science, 31* (3), 636.

Astin, W. A., Vogelgesang, L. J., Ikeda, E. K., & Yee, J. A. (2000). *How service learning affects students.* Los Angeles, CA: University of California at Los Angeles, Higher Education Research Institute.

Blackburn, R. T., & Lawrence, J. H. (1995). *Faculty at work: Motivation, expectation, satisfaction.* Baltimore, MD: The Johns Hopkins University Press.

Boyer, E. L. (1990). *Scholarship reconsidered: Priorities of the professoriate.* Princeton, NJ: The Carnegie Foundation for the Advancement of Teaching.

Boyer, E. L. (1994, March 9). Creating the new American college. *The Chronicle of Higher Education*, p. A48.

Boyer, E. L. (1996). The scholarship of engagement. *Journal of Public Service & Outreach, 1* (1), 11–20.

Boyte, H. C. (2000). The struggle against positivism. *Academe, 86,* 46–51.

Bringle, R. G., & Hatcher, J. A. (1995). A service-learning curriculum for faculty. *Michigan Journal of Community Service Learning, 2,* 112–122.

Campus Compact. (2001). *A conceptual framework for building the pyramid of service-learning and civic engagement: Creating an engaged campus.* Providence, RI: Campus Compact.

DeZure, D. (1996). Closer to the disciplines: A model for improving teaching within departments. *AAHE Bulletin, 48* (6), 9–12.

Driscoll, A. (1998). Comprehensive design of community service: New understanding, options, and vitality in student learning at Portland State University. In E. Zlotkowski (Ed.), *Successful service-learning programs: New models of excellence in higher education* (pp. 150–168). Bolton, MA: Anker.

Eyler, J., & Giles, D. E., Jr. (1999). *Where's the learning in service-learning?* San Francisco, CA: Jossey-Bass.

Harkavy, I., Puckett, J., & Romer, D. (2000). Action research: Bridging action and Research. *Michigan Journal of Community Service Learning*, special issue, 113–118.

Higher Education Research Institute (HERI). (1999). *National norms: 1998–1999 HERI faculty survey report*. Los Angeles, CA: University of California at Los Angeles Graduate School of Education and Information Studies. Retrieved April 16, 2001 from http://www.gseis.ucla.edu/heri/heri.html

Howard, D. L. (2001, September 20). Teaching through tragedy. *The Chronicle of Higher Education*. Retrieved April 2, 2001, from http://chronicle.com/jobs/2001/09/2001092001c.htm

Kerr, C. (1963, 1994). *The uses of the university*. Cambridge, MA: Harvard University Press.

Kolvenbach, Rev. S. J. (2000, October). *The service of faith and the promotion of justice in American Jesuit higher education*. Paper presented at the Conference on Commitment to Justice in Jesuit Higher Education, Santa Clara University, CA.

Lewontin, R. C. (1997). The Cold War and the transformation of the academy. In A. Schiffrin (Ed.), *The Cold War and the university: Toward an intellectual history of the postwar years* (pp. 1–34). New York, NY: The New Press.

Lind, M. (1995). To have and have not: Notes on the progress of the American class war. *Harper's, 250* (1741), 35–47.

New England Resource Center for Higher Education. (n.d.). Program on faculty professional service and academic outreach. *Boston, MA: University of Massachusetts, Boston.*

Newman, F. (2000). Saving higher education's soul. *Change, 33,* 16–23.

Ramaley, J. A. (2000). Embracing civic responsibility. *AAHE Bulletin, 52* (7), 9–13.

Rice, D., & Stacey, K. (1997). Small group dynamics as a catalyst for change: A faculty development model for academic service-learning. *Michigan Journal of Community Service Learning, 4,* 64–71.

Schon, D. A. (1995). The new scholarship requires a new epistemology. *Change, 27* (6), 27–34.

Stanton, T. K. (1990). *Integrating public service with academic study: The faculty role.* Providence, RI: Campus Compact.

Sullivan, W. M. (n.d.). *Institutional identity and social responsibility.* Washington, DC: Council on Public Policy Education.

Wergin, J. F. (2001). Beyond carrots: What really motivates faculty. *Liberal education, 87*(1), 50–53.

Zlotkowski, E. (Ed.). (1997–2000). *AAHE series on service-learning in the disciplines.* Washington, DC: American Association for Higher Education.

Zlotkowski, E. (1998). A service learning approach to faculty development. In J. P. Howard & R. Rhodes (Eds.), *Service learning pedagogy and research* (pp. 81–89). San Francisco, CA: Jossey-Bass.

Contact:

Edward Zlotkowski
MOR 328
Bentley College
175 Forest Street
Waltham, MA 02452-4705
Voice   (781) 891-2592
Email   ezlotkowski@bentley.edu

Edward Zlotkowski is a Professor of English at Bentley College, a Senior Associate at the American Association for Higher Education (AAHE), and a Senior Faculty Fellow at Campus Compact. In 1990, he founded the Bentley Service-Learning Project, an institution-wide program that has involved in its work all of the college's undergraduate academic departments, more than a quarter of its full-time faculty, and several thousand students. In 1995, he was named a senior associate at AAHE and in that capacity has served as general editor of a monograph series exploring the relationship between service-learning and academic disciplines/disciplinary areas. In 1999, he was named a senior faculty fellow at Campus Compact, responsible for developing professional development opportunities in service-learning for provosts and deans as well as a series of summer institutes for engaged academic departments. He has published and spoken extensively on a wide range of service-learning topics and regularly uses a service-learning approach in his own teaching.

2

The Day After: Faculty Behavior in Post–September 11, 2001, Classes

Michele DiPietro
Carnegie Mellon University

What is the best thing to do in the classroom in the face of a tragedy like the terrorist attacks of September 11, 2001? What should instructors do to help students, if anything? This article describes the results of a faculty survey at Carnegie Mellon University. Faculty reported what actions they took in the classroom to help their students (or their rationales for not mentioning the attacks), and their degree of confidence on the effectiveness of their behaviors. Statistical techniques are used to assess the significance of some trends, and implications for faculty developers are discussed in light of cognitive, motivational, and developmental theories.

INTRODUCTION

On September 11, 2001, after the World Trade Center towers collapsed, many colleges across the nation canceled classes and organized a series of events in condemnation of terrorism and in support of the victims. Carnegie Mellon University canceled classes around 11:30 a.m. and held a candlelight vigil that night, followed by a peace rally (both events were sponsored by the office of student affairs) and a teach-in ("A Time to Learn: Professors Explain the Crisis," sponsored by the office of the vice provost for education), both on September 17. In addition, some departments and colleges sponsored their events. As helpful as these events were, they left the faculty with no answers about the dilemma of how to open their classes in the days immediately after the attacks. Howard (2001) poignantly describes this tension, saying that "Professionalism generally upholds the importance of the job over personal concerns . . . But humanity demands the expression and acknowledgement of feelings over logic and analysis" (online).

The literature on crisis intervention has suggestions for campus administrators and crisis intervention teams (Asmussen & Creswell, 1995; Hurst, 1999; Larson, 1994; Siegel, 1994), but does not address individual classroom responses. I therefore decided collect data to see how Carnegie Mellon faculty handled the return to class. The purpose of the survey was threefold:

- To identify a list of best practices

- To build a model of how faculty reactions were influenced by other variables such as teaching experience, gender, discipline, size of class, and type of students taught

- To raise awareness among faculty that there are many possible ways of addressing the issue, within or outside the curriculum, and that some of them can be very low-risk and still beneficial to students

For the first objective, I realized from the outset that in order to assess the effect of any practices I would need a companion survey for students. I decided to wait until the end of the term so they could comment on long-term effects. The results of that survey will be discussed elsewhere.

For the second objective, I collected all the covariates that seemed relevant: I asked for instructor gender, years spent teaching, whether or not the person was an international faculty, department, type of class taught (large lecture, small lecture, discussion, lab/studio, project), and prevalent audience (freshmen, sophomores, juniors, seniors, graduates, or mixed).

For the third objective, I structured the survey as a list of possible reactions rather than an open-ended question. The list ranged from minimal reactions, such as briefly acknowledging the event and moving on, having a minute of silence, or handing out phone numbers to the Red Cross or other charities, to more extensive ones, such as having a class discussion of the events and students' reactions to them, or incorporating the attacks in the curriculum. The list included an "Other" category so that faculty could write about interventions not included in the list. To ensure I was incorporating all perspectives on appropriate ways to hold class, I also asked the faculty who didn't do anything different in their class to explain their rationale for doing so. This question was presented in the form of a list as well, with possible answers being:

- Wasn't comfortable

- Asked students if they wanted to do anything differently and they said no

- Wanted to provide a sense of normalcy/routine

- Didn't know what would be effective/advisable

- Not my role

Again, I included an "Other" category for rationales not included in the list (the full survey is in Appendix 2.1).

RESULTS

The survey was administered by email to 756 instructors, with a cover letter explaining that the end product of the study would be a compilation of individual responses. After a follow-up email message, 153 instructors replied, corresponding to a return rate of 20%. After discarding the respondents who weren't teaching during that term, there were 143 responses. From a strictly statistical point, the sample was self-selected, and therefore possibly biased; furthermore, the return rate was not ideal. I knew that by administering the survey to all faculty (instead of randomly selecting a subgroup and following up persistently), the return rate would drop, but this was an accepted tradeoff in the spirit of raising awareness among the faculty.

Composition of the Sample

Respondents included faculty from all seven colleges and departments, including some special programs such as ROTC. Of the 143 teaching respondents, 46 were women (32%) and 97 (68%) were men. A subset of 21 instructors, or 15%, was international. The sample provides a reasonable cross-section of faculty with respect to years of teaching experience, as can be seen from Figure 2.1. The distributions for class size and prevalent audience are shown in Table 2.1. Reactions in the classroom varied: 15 instructors, or 10.5% of the respondents, carried on with business as usual; the remaining 89.5% reacted with an array of approaches. Those reactions, and the rationales for not reacting will be discussed below.

FIGURE 2.1

Histogram for Years of Teaching Experience in the Sample

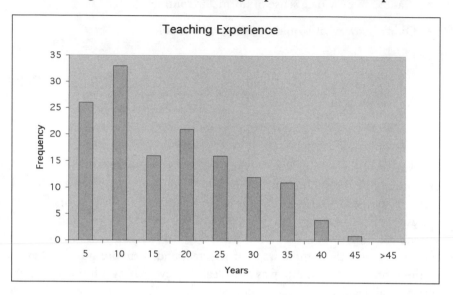

TABLE 2.1

**Distribution of Class Size and Prevalent Audience
in the Sample (N=143)**

Class Size	Frequency	Prevalent Audience	Frequency
Large Lecture	29	Freshmen	23
Small Lecture	67	Sophomores	19
Discussion	34	Juniors	8
Lab/Studio	22	Seniors	17
Project	11	Graduates	31
		Mixed UG	35
		Graduates and Mixed UG	14

Reactions in the Classroom

Table 2.2 reports the frequency distribution of the 128 instructors who chose to address the attacks in the classroom. Most options that I provided in the survey where checked by some instructors, except "Bring a counselor to class,"

"Class fundraising," and "Talk to Student Affairs/Teaching Center for strategies on how to handle class." One faculty member, however, wrote that she had contacted Counseling Services prior to class for suggestions. It may be worth noting that although Counseling Services set up a special September 11 support group for students, they later reported there have not been any takers.

TABLE 2.2

Frequency and Percent Distribution of Faculty Reactions in the Classroom (N=128)

Reactions to 9/11 attacks	Frequency	Percentage
Excuse students/Offer extensions if assignments were due	72	56%
Acknowledge the class needs to go on with the material but reassure class that if students are too distressed to process the information there will be other opportunities down the road	64	50%
Have a brief discussion in class	55	43%
Ask students if their families and friends were physically affected	51	40%
Offer to talk privately with anybody who might want to	37	29%
Incorporate the attacks in the curriculum	36	28%
Devote the class after the attacks to discussion	31	24%
Mention Counseling Services	21	16%
Mention ways people can help (give out Red Cross number, other charities, blood donation centers, etc.)	15	12%
One minute of silence	9	7%
Alert TAs to be extra tactful in recitations/office hours	6	5%
Decide to do a project as a class (quilt, fence painting,* etc.)	3	2%
Read a passage from an inspirational book	2	1.5%
Other	30	23%

*Painting the fence is a Carnegie Mellon tradition to demonstrate for various causes.

Most options are self explanatory, but it is worth noting that the three instructors who checked the answer "Decide to do a project as a class" were from the drama, art, and design departments; the projects were about creating art as a means to express feelings related to the attacks. Because the categories "Incorporate the attacks in the curriculum" and "Other" involve a variety of responses, they will be treated separately below.

Incorporating the Attacks in the Curriculum

The distribution by departments of the 36 professors who incorporated the attacks in the curriculum is reported in Table 2.3. These kinds of reactions can be placed in two main groups. The first group tried to tie the events into the topics in class. For instance, one philosophy instructor devoted two lectures and two recitations to the events. The discussions spanned women in Afghanistan issues, race issues and human rights, globalization issues, political situation in the Middle East, terrorism versus freedom fighters debate, and war. An English professor tried to discuss the events, but the discussion was stilted. Nevertheless, the topic spontaneously resurfaced every four classes or so, in a more integrated fashion. One history professor talked about the internment of Japanese-Americans during WWII in the wake of Pearl Harbor, and drew some parallels with the current situation. One professor of biology and health engineering participated in the teach-in event mentioned earlier with a session on bio-terrorism, which was then incorporated in her class as extra credit. Two professors of environmental and behavioral decision making approached the issue from a risk and risk-perception perspective. One instructor of naval science had a discussion on terrorism and cyber-terrorism and related a personal account of living with terrorism on a daily basis abroad.

The second group used the attacks as a motivating example for a variety of purposes. One drama professor used the attacks as a point of reference to give context to a tragic event in a script. Several professors of modern languages (on specific suggestion of their department head) tackled the issue from a cultural differences framework, and used magazine articles in the target language to provide different perspectives on the issue while still practicing the language. Two professor of statistics talked about using statistics to understand social phenomena: One looked at census data on the Arab-American population in the United States; the other had an exam question about using Bayes's theorem to reassess the validity of ethnic and religious profiling to identify terrorists. Instructors outside these two groups also had a variety of reactions. For instance, two professors of information systems and decision science started study groups on the issue, where 15 students have met on an ongoing basis and undertaken research projects to present to the class. In addition, some graduate students decided to change their research direction and work on something that could make a difference. One professor, who teaches a robotics class with applications in search and rescue, made the students sit in silence for five minutes—"an eternity." Then he urged them to think how much worse it would be for the trapped survivors.

TABLE 2.3

Distribution by Department of Instructors Who Incorporated the Attacks in the Curriculum (N=36)

Department	Frequency	Department	Frequency
Modern Languages	4	Engineering and Public Policy	2
Drama	3	Philosophy	2
English	3	Psychology	2
School of Industrial Administration	3	ROTC	2
Heinz School of Public Policy and Management	3	Social and Decision Sciences	2
History	3	Art	1
Architecture	2	Chemistry	1
Design	2	Statistics	1

Open-Ended Responses

The "Other" category elicited several responses. Many professors made a brief statement. A professor gave smaller assignments for the next three weeks, and thought that the students appreciated having more time to cope with their own stress and emotions. A professor in the Heinz School of Public Policy and Management distributed copies of the Bill of Rights and the class discussed what makes America special and what problems events like that of September 11 pose, especially with the Fourth Amendment. A biology professor did not address the class immediately after, but when the students scored badly on a quiz (September 21) she told them that they are all very smart and the results were not indicative of the material. She admitted to having great difficulty maintaining focus, and suspected they had the same problem in the aftermath. She ventured that the difficulty might be compounded by the stress caused by limited-time exams. Then she proceeded to retest them (optionally, with only the better grade passing through) on the next Sunday, with 50% time increase, and reported that the results went "way up." She also continued giving them more time for subsequent quizzes. Many students in the School of Industrial Administration, which consistently places graduates in Wall Street or the World Trade Center, were worried about the well being of alumni and their future job prospects; therefore, some professors had periodic updates (six of our alumni perished in the World Trade Center). One professor has the vice president of students in her class, and invited him to give updates on the campus climate and campus events related to the attacks. Another professor, whose teaching assistant (TA) was once a victim of a serious seven-day hijacking, invited the TA to talk to the class about his experience as a terrorist victim. Some professors teaching early classes on September 11 decided to cancel them. After the administration canceled all classes, one professor talked to students individually to make sure they had a safe place to go and people to be with, with special care for international students. A professor of civil and environmental engineering made the weekly quiz more straightforward than usual, thinking that the students were in no shape for the standard "think and pull together disparate concepts" quiz. A professor of business administration sent email to all of his students with his thoughts on the matter and best wishes for the students and their families. Several professors were involved in planning or presenting at the teach-in, and they involved their students or rescheduled class to allow their students to attend. One instructor who teaches all international students talked to them about safety issues, especially for those of Middle Eastern descent. One English instructor came to class with spiral notebooks for everybody, and encouraged the students to write, immediately and in the days to come, to document the defining moment for their generation.

Rationales for Not Reacting
The results for the 15 faculty who did not address the issues in class are reported in Table 2.4. It is interesting to note that although the question was stated as "If you didn't do any special activity, why not?" many faculty who did address the attacks in their class answered this question as well. In this case, their answer may reflect a rationale for not doing more than what they did, or a way to express their uneasiness. The people who did not do any activity in the classroom fall in three specific categories. The instructors in the first category strongly believe that they should not intervene, unless the students show explicit and persistent signs of distress. They do not want to overreact, are against "psychotherapeutic prayer" and do not believe that students need any

help in dealing with such events, except for pathologies. One professor in particular is involved in the evaluation of psychotherapy, and he asserted that there is no evidence that these kind of interventions work; on the contrary, they might do damage. In general, they seem to believe the best form of support is not emotional but intellectual, with programs about Muslims, Arab history, and so on. They also believe that the best way to help students is to foster a sense of normality and get back to usual activities as soon as possible. Another nuance of this approach is to treat students like adults. One professor wrote: "We all have a job to do, this wasn't changed by 9/11." As a compounding factor, some professors felt it was not their role, especially when teaching graduate students and/or in fields not immediately connected to terrorism.

TABLE 2.4
Distribution of Rationales for Not Mentioning the Attacks in Class

Rationale	Faculty who did not address attacks (N=15)	Faculty who addressed attacks (N=128)	Total
Wasn't comfortable	3	3	6
Asked students if they wanted to do anything differently and they said no	3	4	7
Wanted to provide a sense of normalcy/routine	5	26	31
Didn't know what would be effective/advisable	3	11	14
Not my role	3	8	11
Other	4	4	8

By contrast, the instructors in the second category are very unsure what to do. They also want to foster a sense of normalcy, but they do not know what is effective or advisable; in addition, some are unsure of their role. A couple said they would have liked a list of suggestions like the one on the survey on the day of the attacks, just to have options; some asked to be informed of the results of the survey, to see what everybody else did. Some faculty admitted to feeling unprepared to deal with the events. One professor wrote that he had a few Muslim students in his class and felt quite confused, unprepared, and afraid he would hurt people; additionally, as a Jewish person who personally experienced war, he did not want to share those experiences in public, but was afraid the discussion might go in that direction. So he did not say anything. One other professor admitted to feeling himself "still a bit numb." A new instructor in design said he would have loved to lead a discussion but "didn't have a clue" how to do so. He was afraid contrasting views might emerge, resulting in a tense situation.

The third group did not do anything different in class because they asked the students what they wanted to do, and the students said they were comfortable going on with the material as planned. This group is very small, only three instructors. It appears that they held class in the afternoon or on Thursday, and the students, having already discussed the tragedy, felt ready to move on with the material. Finally, one professor reported he had too much to cover and could not take time out of the busy course schedule.

Self-Assessment of Activities
When faculty members were asked to assess their in-class choice, some respondents launched into a long explanation of the effects of their activity, others skipped the question. I coded all responses into the categories "Very effective," "OK," "Not at all effective," and "Don't know." Clearly, even some faculty who chose not to address the tragedy felt very strongly about their strategy, so the tally for this question includes anybody who provided an answer. Only 76 instructors answered this question, which means that 47% of the sample did not answer it. Of the 76 respondents, 40 thought their strategy was very effective (53%), 20 thought it was OK (26%), 14 didn't know (18%), and two thought it was not at all effective (3%). One of the two faculty in the last category acknowledged the event, granted homework extensions, asked about family and friends, and had a statement about the necessity to move on with the very activities that terrorism seeks to disrupt. The other faculty member also granted extensions and inquired about students' families and friends, and then he had a brief discussion and offered to talk privately with students.

Campus Response
The overwhelming majority of the respondents were very pleased with how the university responded to the events. They felt that the university addressed the tragedy in an effective way, but without going overboard, and managed to

bring things back to normal in a timely fashion. Most faculty felt that the attempt to learn from this event (via the teach-in) was the most effective response. They also welcomed the prayer vigil and peace rally as good moments for the students to express their feelings. Some faculty commented that those activities helped them as well as students. Some faculty would have liked more advertisement for these events, so they could have canceled class and allowed students to participate. Two instructors would have liked a workshop from the teaching center on how to deal with the events in the classroom. One point raised by several faculty is the need to pay more attention to the students, especially international students or those who might be targeted. Some Pittsburghers can be narrow-minded, they felt, and the students should have been warned in advance of this fact, rather than having to find out by themselves. Some faculty also reported student accounts of having been harassed, on and off campus.

STATISTICAL ANALYSIS

It is apparent that the sample is biased. Most of the people who responded decided to address the attacks in the classroom and felt very strongly about doing so. However, judging from informal conversations with students, it appears that the classes where they talked about the tragedy were the exception rather than the rule. The student survey will be able to assess this claim, but it is also worth noting that a significant group of faculty wrote that their students were grateful to them because no other faculty had addressed the attacks in their classes. Because of the bias, not many findings can be generalized to the larger campus population. However, it is possible to determine some associations that are statistically significant in the sample.

Student audience and reactions. I hypothesized that instructors teaching first-year students would be more likely to address the events in the classroom, and those teaching graduate students less likely. A binomial test for the difference of percentages revealed that the percentage of instructors who addressed the attacks in graduate classes is significantly smaller than in all other classes (p-value=0.018). No significance was found for first-year students.

Class size and reactions. I hypothesized that large classes would make it more difficult for instructors to talk about September 11, but no statistical difference was found.

Gender and reactions. No difference was anticipated with respect to gender, and none was found.

International faculty and reactions. I was not sure how this variable would correlate with classroom reactions, but a binomial test showed that international instructors are much less likely to address the attacks (p-value =0.0009).

Teaching experience and reactions. I anticipated that faculty with less teaching experience would be less comfortable addressing these kinds of issues. To test this hypothesis, I used logistic regression. The results revealed that teaching experience influences neither the probability of addressing the attacks nor the level of intervention (low-risk minutes of silence and other time-limited approaches versus intensive class-long discussions or class projects, etc.).

Confusion and gender. Many instructors expressed some confusion and uneasiness, in the form of being unsure about effective/advisable behaviors, being uncomfortable or unsure of their role, or even in the ability to evaluate the effects that their behaviors had on students. A chi-square test for independence reveals that gender is related to confusion in the sense that male instructors are more confused than females (p-value=0.017). I did not anticipate this association and cannot offer an explanation for it.

Confusion and international faculty. A chi-square test for independence shows that international faculty are much more confused than American faculty (p-value=0.006) in terms of their role, appropriateness, and effectiveness of their behavior.

Confusion and reactions. A chi-square test for independence shows that faculty confusion is not related to the kind of action (or lack thereof) the faculty took in the classroom (p-value=0.18).

IMPLICATIONS FOR FACULTY DEVELOPMENT

Both the qualitative comments and the quantitative data analysis point to implications for faculty developers in several areas, which I have identified as best practices, instructor's role, international faculty, cognitive and motivational considerations, developmental considerations, and emotions in the classroom.

Best Practices

I entered this study unsure of what practices would be best and applicable to any class. At the end of this work, I am still unsure. The student survey will provide another side of the story, especially in terms of how well faculty actions were received. Nevertheless, the students' opinion cannot be the last word on the matter. People are not always able to evaluate what is best for them, and this is true especially in times of crisis. I wanted the survey to be distanced in time from the events, so that the students would be able to think more objectively, but four months might not be enough. Oweini (1998) interviewed people who had been college students during the civil war in

Lebanon (1975–1991), where due to the ongoing nature of the conflict, the college tried to foster a business-as-usual atmosphere. The subjects reported high levels of anxiety and fear during their college years, but reflecting on their situation years later, they realized they had been able to cope successfully with the war, especially thanks to their network of social support. On the other hand, the stream of grateful student emails that many faculty who addressed the terrorist attacks in the classroom reported in the survey makes a good case for some kind of intervention. Brownstein (2001) cites the case of Northern Ireland, where students simply learned to go on, but at the same time acknowledges the coping value of public grieving events like the peace garden at the University of Maryland, College Park.

How can faculty developers help in the face of tragedy? I argue that helpful developers have to be humble in the first place. Tiberius (2001) and Kegan (1994) remind us that we must be able to step outside our belief systems and see the value of other people's philosophies. Reading the responses of the survey, I realized that all five perspectives of Pratt and Associates (1998) are present in my sample. I have the "transmission" professor for whom "it's definitely not my role, especially with MBAs," the "apprenticeship" scientist whose experiment with his freshmen was disrupted on September 11, the "developmental" teacher who engaged the students in long discussions of political, social, economic, and religious reasons behind terrorism, the "nurturing" instructor who claimed that the university must act *in loco parentis* and comfort the students, and the "social reform" faculty who organized teach-ins and peace rallies. All claim good reasons for their behaviors, and my obligation is to help them be more effective inside their own paradigm.

Instructor's Role

As a faculty developer, I have an even bigger obligation to those instructors who were unsure of their role. As reported previously, 10% of the respondents felt unsure about what would be effective in the classroom; others wanted to discuss the events in class but were not comfortable. Another 10% was not able to assess the usefulness of what they had tried in the classroom, and two instructors decided what they did had no impact whatsoever. One instructor, who minimally addressed the events and then moved on, wrote that at the time he was sure that was his role, but now he is not so sure anymore, and another one admitted that he simply did not think of all the options he had, and that the list provided with the survey would have been very helpful at the time. Remember also the two instructors who wished there was a workshop they could go to. All these situations are great openings for faculty developers, who can be extremely helpful in facilitating the reflective process leading to a decision, or discovery, about one's role as an educator.

International Faculty

It is important to remember that a subset of the struggling faculty are international scholars who were too paralyzed to do anything in the classroom, and even if they did, felt very unsure about their (possibly negative) impact. It is not clear from the survey why this is the case. Is it a role problem? Is it a matter of not knowing the rules of the game in the American classroom? Is this a case of low-context versus high-context cultures (Hall, 1976)? Whatever the answer, this subgroup clearly needs and wants some support.

Cognitive and Motivational Considerations

The first option as a possible reaction was designed to test the understanding of the mind's working: "Acknowledge the class needs to go on with the material but reassure the class that if students are too distressed to process the information there will be other opportunities down the road." Hamilton (1982) and Arnsten (1998) present a review of cognitive theories and studies that demonstrate that in times of stress the focus of the working memory narrows to the stressful events and neglects routine ones. This process will likely affect retention and recall down the road. Only 50% of the people in the sample understand this concept, which means that our effort to educate instructors about learning theories is not done yet. The function of emotions over judgment and motivation is also well established in the literature (Hammond, 2000). Frijda (1988) reminds us that "the action readiness of emotions tends to occupy center stage . . . It tends to override other concerns, other goals, and other actions. It tends to override considerations of appropriateness or long-term consequence" (p. 355).

When dealing with the aftermath of traumatic events, the average undergraduate would find it very hard to concentrate or study, even though the midterm is coming up, as in the case reported by the biology professor. Professors are likely to be more effective in their classroom if their strategies take these considerations into account.

Developmental Considerations

Developmental theory tells us that in times of crisis people tend to look for easy answers and retreat into the dualistic stage. We saw this happen with some students who wanted to "round up all the foreigners" and "bomb Afghanistan back into the Stone Age." Perry (1999) warns us that when [retreat] occurs, it tends to take a dramatic form. It appears to require fight ... The dichotomous structure itself divides the world into good and bad, we and they, friend and foe—and this on absolute grounds ... threatened by a proximate challenge, this entrenchment can call forth in its defense hate, projection, and denial of all distinctions but one. (p. 205)

I firmly believe that the educator's role in institutions that claim to promote critical thinking is to intellectually engage the students to remain in the complexity of the situation rather than to escape into a world of sweeping generalizations, and to use the tools of the discipline to stay engaged. The professor of statistics who made the students apply Bayes's theorem to evaluate the usefulness of ethnic and religious profiling is a fine example of engagement through the discipline. Conversations about how to facilitate the transition of students into further developmental stages can be very productive in our work with faculty.

Emotions in the Classroom

Several instructors wanted to discuss the issues in class, but were afraid of the emotionality of the topic and of different viewpoints, especially in classes with international students. Those instructors can benefit from workshops or individual conversations about handling controversial topics, perhaps through cooperative controversies (Bredehoft, 1991) or other forms of structured discussion.

CONCLUSION

The events of September 11, 2001, presented faculty developers with an incredible opportunity to make a difference with faculty. If we rise to the occasion and find the teachable moment, we can be of invaluable help in a new world struggling for meaning.

ACKNOWLEDGMENTS

Special thanks to Anne Fay for her assistance in preparing the survey, and to Terri Huston and Ammon Ripple for their thorough feedback and overwhelming support.

REFERENCES

Arnsten, A. F. (1998, June 12). The biology of being frazzled. *Science, 280,* 1711–1712.

Asmussen, K. J., & Creswell, J. W. (1995). Campus response to a student gunman. *Journal of Higher Education, 66*(5), 575–591.

Bredehoft, D. J. (1991). Cooperative controversies in the classroom. *College Teaching, 39*(3), 122–125.

Brownstein, A. (2001, October 29). College board conference reflects a new concern for colleges and students: Terrorism. *The Chronicle of Higher Education Career Network.* Retrieved November 4, 2001 from http://chronicle.com/free/2001/10/2001102904n.htm

Frijda, N. H. (1988). The laws of emotion. *American Psychologist, 43,* 349–358.

Hall, E. T. (1976). *Beyond culture.* New York, NY: Doubleday.

Hamilton, V. (1982). Cognition and stress: An information processing model. In L. Goldberger & S. Breznitz (Eds.), *Handbook of stress: Theoretical and clinical aspects* (pp. 105–120). New York, NY: Free Press.

Hammond, K. R. (2000). *Judgments under stress.* New York, NY: Oxford University Press.

Howard, D. L. (2001, September 20). Teaching through tragedy. *The Chronicle of Higher Education Career Network.* Retrieved September 22, 2001 from http://chronicle.com/jobs/2001/09/2001092001c.htm

Hurst, J. C. (1999). The Matthew Shepard tragedy: Management of a Crisis. *About Campus, 43,* 5–11.

Kegan, R. (1994). *In over our heads: The mental demands of modern life.* Cambridge, MA: Harvard University Press.

Larson, W. A. (Ed.). (1994). *When crisis strikes on campus.* Washington, DC: Council for Advancement and Support of Education.

Oweini, A. (1998). How students coped with the war: The experience of Lebanon. *Journal of Higher Education, 69*(4), 406–423.

Perry, W. J. (1999). *Forms of intellectual and ethical development in the college years* (Reprint). San Francisco, CA: Jossey-Bass.

Pratt, D. D., & Associates. (1998). *Five perspectives on teaching in adult and higher education.* Malabar, FL: Krieger.

Siegel, D. (1994). *Campuses respond to violent tragedy.* Phoenix, AZ: Oryx.

Tiberius, R. G. (2001). A brief history of educational development: Implications for teachers and developers. In D. Lieberman & C. Wehlburg (Eds.), *To improve the academy: Vol. 20. Resources for faculty, instructional, and organizational development* (pp. 20–37). Bolton, MA: Anker.

Contact:

Michele DiPietro
Eberly Center for Teaching Excellence
Carnegie Mellon University
5000 Forbes Avenue, WH 425
Pittsburgh, PA 15213
Voice   (412) 268-1287
Fax   (412) 268-5701
Email   dipietro@stat.cmu.edu

Michele DiPietro is Assistant Director at the Eberly Center for Teaching Excellence and an Instructor in the Department of Statistics at Carnegie Mellon University. His main role is to create, conduct, and evaluate all graduate student programs at the center, and in particular to expand the center's focus on diversity. He also teaches graduate classes in the Department of Statistics and in the Computational Finance distance learning program, with sections in Pittsburgh, New York City, London, Frankfurt, and Bangalore.

Appendix 2.1

Faculty Survey on Reactions to the 9/11 Terrorist Attacks

The Eberly Center for Teaching Excellence is interested in finding out how faculty and students responded to the 9/11 attacks in and out of class.

Background Information
Please check the box that applies to you, or fill in the blanks.

Gender: ☐ Male ☐ Female

Department: _____

Years spent teaching: _____   ☐ Check if international faculty

Type of class(es) taught during Fall 2001 or First Fall Mini:

☐ Discussion   ☐ Small lecture (<50)   ☐ Large lecture (>50)

☐ Lab/Studio   ☐ Project

Audience:

☐ Mostly freshmen   ☐ Mostly sophomores   ☐ Mostly juniors

☐ Mostly seniors   ☐ Mixed undergraduates   ☐ Graduates

Reactions to 9/11 Attacks
Please check the boxes relative to the things you have done *in class* to help students.

☐ Acknowledge the class needs to go on with the material but reassure class that if students are too distressed to process the topic there will be other opportunities to review it down the road

☐ One minute of silence

☐ Mention Counseling Services

☐ Bring a counselor to class to help students process their feelings

☐ Excuse students/offer extensions if assignments were due

☐ Offer to talk privately with anybody who might want to

☐ Have a brief discussion in class

☐ Devote the whole first class after the attacks to discussion

☐ Incorporate the attacks in the curriculum

☐ Decide to do a project as a class (quilt, fence painting, etc.)

☐ Read a passage from an inspirational book

☐ Talk to Student Affairs/Teaching Center for strategies on how to handle class

☐ Alert your TAs to be extra tactful in recitations/office hours

☐ Mention ways people can help (give out Red Cross number, other charities, blood donation centers, etc.)

☐ Class fundraising

☐ Ask students if their families and friends were physically affected

☐ Other (please explain): _____

How effective do you think the activity(ies) was(were)? _____

If you didn't do any special activity, why not? Check all that apply:

☐ Wasn't comfortable

☐ Asked students if they wanted to do anything differently and they said no

☐ Wanted to provide a sense of normality/routine

☐ Didn't know what would be effective/advisable

☐ Not my role

☐ Other (please explain): _____

Please check the boxes relative to any *university-wide activities* you attended:

☐ Prayer Vigil (evening of the attacks)

☐ A Time to Learn: Professors Explain the Crisis

☐ Peace Rally (Monday afternoon, by the Fence)

☐ Other (please explain): _____

How effective do you think the activity(ies) was(were)? _____

Do you have any suggestions/comments for how the university can help the students deal with natural and political tragedies in the future?

3

Internationalizing American Higher Education: A Call to Thought and Action

Deborah DeZure
University of Michigan, Ann Arbor

In the wake of the World Trade Center disaster, many faculty developers are asking themselves what they do to promote international peace and understanding. But even before these events, there has been an indication that there was a pressing need to focus on global competencies as an important part of higher education for the 21st century. The purpose of this essay is threefold: 1) to summarize the research on the status of internationalization on American campuses, 2) to make the case for the active involvement of faculty developers in internationalizing higher education, and 3) to offer strategies with which we can begin or expand our efforts.

INTRODUCTION

In the wake of the World Trade Center disaster, many faculty developers are asking themselves what they can do in the context of their professional roles to promote international peace and understanding, beginning on their own campuses. But even before September 11, 2001, it was clear there was a pressing need to focus on global competencies as a critical feature of higher education for the 21st century (Cornwell & Stoddard, 1999; Hayward, 2000; Hayward & Siaya, 2001; Institute of International Education, 2000). These reports on the status of internationalization in American higher education now take on even more urgency, deserving our attention and careful analysis. They offer insights into key areas that need our expertise and leadership. They can also help us to conceptualize and shape the role we can play in promoting internationalization and intercultural competencies.

This is not a sea change for us. In the last decade, faculty developers across the United States understood and acted upon the need to promote diversity and multicultural competencies to support democratic pluralism, primarily in the context of American society. But we are now a world at war: It is clear that the stakes are very high, and the need is urgent to expand the diversity mandate to include global dimensions. The purpose of this essay is threefold: 1) to summarize the research on the status of internationalization on American campuses, 2) to make the case for the active involvement of faculty developers in internationalizing higher education as a natural extension of our ongoing work and commitments, and 3) to offer strategies with which we can begin or expand our efforts.

WHY SHOULD WE SUPPORT INTERNATIONALIZATION?

Michael McPherson, President of Macalester College, sponsored a full page message in the *New York Times* titled, "International Education. Now More Than Ever" (2001, p. A30). It captures many of the reasons why internationalization is so critical for higher education:

> Education remains the most important vehicle we have for promoting international understanding. We should be encouraging American students to learn all they can about the lives and histories of people around the world. We should encourage young people to study abroad—and not only in the more familiar territory of England and France, but in Eastern Europe, Asia, Africa and Latin America as well.
>
> By the same token, we must keep the doors of American education open to students from all corners of the world. . . . I see first hand the growth both in understanding and curiosity about the world that happens for American students as they engage their colleagues from abroad. Meanwhile our international students experience not only a broad liberal arts experience . . . but they also acquire a deeper understanding of our complex, dynamic, and yet far from perfect country. Real education is the enemy of fanaticism and of complacency . . .
>
> The events of September 11 have shattered forever the illusion, still cherished by too many Americans, that we stand at some distance from the world. We are, it must now be clear, for better and for worse, and quite inescapably, part of the world. However tempting it may be to try to withdraw into ourselves, our best—our only—hope is to engage the world in all its cultural and religious and human variation and to join in the struggle to improve it. (2001, p. A30)

While the primary goal of McPherson's essay was to urge restraint in limiting visas for foreign students, he touches upon many of the reasons why globalization is particularly important to us now at this crossroads in our history. (See also Commission on International Education, 1997; Cornwell & Stoddard, 1999; Hanson & Meyerson, 1994.)

Defining Terms

"Internationalization" is the term that is widely used to refer to four dimensions of American higher education: 1) foreign language study, 2) study abroad, 3) global, diaspora, and area studies, and 4) presence of international students. Additional important dimensions include the presence of international faculty on campus and the involvement of American faculty in teaching and research abroad or with international collaborators (Gaff, Ratcliff, & Associates, 1997; Hayward, 2000; Mestenhauser & Ellingboe, 1998). More broadly defined, internationalization refers to efforts to integrate global perspectives and intercultural competencies in higher education.

Goals and Outcomes

Global competencies are increasingly identified as a valued goal of liberal learning, but currently few American students develop intercultural competence during college. The majority of colleges and universities include the following among their goals for general education: sensitivity to diversity, multicultural and intercultural competencies, and civic, global, and environmental responsibility and engagement (Gaff, 1999; Gaff et al.,1997; Ratcliff, Johnson, La Nasa, & Gaff, 2001; Schneider & Shoenberg, 1998). A recent national survey by the American Council on Education indicates very high levels of public support for internationalizing American higher education, with a majority of respondents indicating that students should study abroad and learn foreign languages (Hayward & Siaya, 2001). Nonetheless, Fred Hayward, author of the *Internationalization of U.S. Higher Education: Preliminary Status Report 2000,* concludes that "in spite of an apparent growing national interest in international education, relatively few undergraduates gain international or intercultural competence in college" (2000, p. 1).

The Evidence

Res ipsa loquitur, that is, the facts speak for themselves. Foreign language enrollments as a percentage of total higher education enrollments have decreased from 16% in the 1960s to 8% in 2000. These enrollments are concentrated in a few languages (55% Spanish, 17% French, 8% German, 6% inclusive of all

Asian languages, fewer than 2% Middle Eastern, and .15% African). This is in sharp contrast to other developed countries where foreign language study is emphasized (Hayward, 2000; Shoenberg & Turlington, 1998).

Participation in study abroad is equally limited. Despite data from incoming first-year students that they hope to study abroad, only 3% of American students do study abroad, comprising 0.8% of total enrollments per year. Students now select shorter programs of study abroad, with the number of students studying for more than a semester abroad falling from 18% in 1985 to 10% in 1997 (Hayward, 2000). These shorter experiences reflect numerous factors: more graduation requirements that are more prescribed and sequenced as well as higher costs (Gaff, 1999; Gaff et al., 1997; Ratcliff, Johnson, La Nasa, & Gaff, 2001). These shorter experiences, while better than nonparticipation, often rely on intercultural shorthand and cultural reductionism that fails to produce intercultural competencies (Cornwell & Stoddard, 1999; Dobbert, 1998). Nonetheless, these experiences include a broader array of disciplines and different countries than previously. Participants come primarily from majors in the social sciences and humanities—with little ethnic or economic diversity (Hayward, 2000).

The data on international content of courses are more elusive and difficult to assess. Much like data on multiculturalism, it is easier to identify a course designated as a diversity course requirement than it is to identify courses and programs that infuse multicultural content and perspectives throughout the curriculum. Even among courses that infuse global perspectives, there is a significant difference in content and impact between courses and programs that use an additive approach to global content (e.g., adding an international unit or speaker) and those that truly transform the curriculum in substantive ways (Cornwell & Stoddard, 1999; Mestenhauser & Ellingboe, 1998). Studies by Davis (1995), Edwards, Jr. (1996) and Klein (1999) summarize trends in interdisciplinary studies in American higher education, indicating that there has been a dramatic increase in interdisciplinary offerings in the last decade, many of which have global dimensions. These include world, global, and international studies; peace and justice studies; ethnic, cultural, diaspora, and area studies; and environmental studies, among others.

Nonetheless, Hayward (2000) concludes that

> Broad curricular internationalization is lacking: postsecondary graduates are poorly informed about other countries, people and events; and offerings by institutional type are uneven, with two-year institutions providing far fewer international education opportunities than their four-year counterparts. Competency represents an even more

pressing concern with one study indicating that less than 7% of all higher education students meet even basic standards of "global preparedness." . . . College students consistently perform more poorly on global competency and geography surveys than do students from other developed countries. The authors of a global understanding measure concluded that only a very small proportion of American students command a level of knowledge necessary for even an adequate understanding of global situations and processes. (p. 2)

International students accounted for 3% of undergraduates and 11% of graduate students in the United States in 1998–1999, more international students than any other country—most of them from Asia (Hayward, 2000). International students provide a vital element in globalizing American campuses, but recent efforts (since September 11, 2001) to ensure tighter controls on visa oversight may reduce the number of international students who will be able to study in the United States in the coming years.

Like the number of international students, the presence of international scholars on American campuses is also on the rise, hosting 70,000 international faculty and researchers in 1998–1999, an increase of 21% in five years. The majority of these were in the sciences, with 42% from Asia.

Admission and graduation requirements in foreign language study are an indicator of the importance to which institutions value intercultural competencies. Over the past 30 years, the number of four-year colleges and universities that require a foreign language for admission dropped from 34% in 1965 to 20% in 1995. Among colleges that require a foreign language for graduation, 90% require a language for humanities majors, 75% for social science majors, 20% for business majors, and 17% for education majors. Only 17% of institutions have a foreign language graduation requirement for all students.

The number of faculty teaching foreign language is declining nationally. In addition, a 1991 study of projected faculty retirements indicates that "area studies faculty, especially those in Soviet, Eastern European and Asian Studies will not be replaced at self-sustaining rates" (Hayward, 2000, p. 3).

On a more positive note, in the last decade most colleges and universities have designated administrative or faculty support for internationally oriented activities like study abroad and foreign student services (Hayward, 2000). Student affairs professionals and those involved in residential life and the co-curriculum have also actively promoted language study by designing living-learning communities centered around foreign language and cultural themes.

Over the last decade, federal funding for globalization of American higher education has decreased, including funds for faculty research, educational and cultural exchanges, and language study. There are pockets of support, such as the Department of Education Fulbright-Hays Programs and President Clinton's April 2000 "Memorandum on International Education Policy," identifying the need for university-level internationalization efforts. It is likely that the events of September 11 will lead to increased federal funding, but it is unclear which dimensions of international education will be priorities. It appears that one priority may be foreign language study to prepare graduates for roles in the foreign and diplomatic service, global business, and national security agencies and the military. In the days following the attacks on the Pentagon and World Trade Center, the CIA and other governmental agencies were actively seeking individuals with fluency in Arabic. One radio commentator noted that in 2000, the United States produced only one graduate with a major in Arabic and prior to September 11, no United States university offered a course in Pashto, the language spoken by half of all Afghans (Shadid, 2002, A4). By February 2002, the United States had committed an additional $20.5 million for 2002, and a proposed $4 million more in 2003, doubling the size of fellowships for study of Arabic, Persian, Pashto, Uzbek, and Urdu. The United States will fund four new academic centers to study Russia, the Middle East, Central Asia, and South Asia. While many academics are celebrating the influx of funds to foreign language and area studies, others are concerned about the role that the Department of Defense will play in campus language programs and tying these programs to national security needs (Shadid, 2002).

Evidence is only anecdotal that the private sector is eager to recruit graduates with intercultural competencies as well as foreign language fluency (Hayward, 2000), but they are often mentioned by multinational corporations as skills that are highly valued among employers.

Hayward (2000) concludes, "The challenge to higher education is clear. We need to increase the participation of students in international programs, reshape and internationalize the curriculum and co-curriculum, and develop a comprehensive international agenda for undergraduates across the curriculum" (p. 4).

WHAT CAN FACULTY DEVELOPERS DO TO PROMOTE INTERNATIONALIZATION?

Based on the evidence, the picture is sobering, but provocative. The situation can be compared to the dualism of the ancient Chinese symbol for crisis, composed of two ideographs—one meaning danger and the other meaning opportunity. The symbol reminds us that inherent within the most difficult challenges there are opportunities for change and growth. As troubling as these reports are, they identify several specific dimensions of internationalization that we can address, and they can serve to provoke both thought and action. What then can faculty developers and campus leaders do to redress these trends?

Where to Begin

For faculty developers who are new to their campuses or have not had much involvement with globalization on campus, a good place to begin is with a needs assessment developed in collaboration with key stakeholders, including administrators, faculty, students, and those already engaged in international efforts.

Designate an advisory group, steering committee, or task force on globalization. Strategic efforts aimed at systemic change may require participation of a steering committee, advisory group, or task force, at least in its initial stages. Such a group might include campus leaders (administrators and faculty), campus experts in aspects of international education (e.g., study abroad, foreign languages, relevant departments such as area studies, foreign student services, admissions, registrar, multicultural affairs, student affairs, academic advising, etc.), and individuals interested in pursuing a global agenda for the institution. Collectively, they should have the authority and legitimacy to develop and disseminate a needs assessment survey and be empowered to use the data that is collected—either to formulate recommendations or to develop, design, implement, or evaluate them.

Conduct a needs assessment on globalization. As with many campus change initiatives, a needs assessment or faculty development audit on campus globalization may be helpful to clarify the priorities, needs, and current level of activity, interest, and expertise. A needs assessment is the first step in raising levels of awareness and is strategically and politically sound to establish legitimacy for subsequent efforts.

Consider surveying the entire campus community, not only targeted groups such as international faculty or students. It is helpful to collect data from specific groups, but if globalization is intended to be a campus-wide commitment, then all members of the community should be included.

Gather available data on campus globalization. It is helpful to identify and gather the data that is already available about globalization initiatives on campus. This data might include demographic information on international faculty and students, including retention data; registration information on study abroad, language study, and courses that feature global content; faculty collaborations with international partners, and funded grants and activities related to international and inter-cultural efforts, among others.

Gather information on resources and best practices from higher education organizations whose missions and expertise include globalization, including for example, the Association of American Colleges and Universities, American Council on Education (ACE), Carnegie Foundation, Kellogg, the Institute of International Education, and NAFSA. Funding agencies like the Fund for the Improvement of Post-Secondary Education (FIPSE), that have long-standing commitments to funding innovations in international education also offer expertise and exemplary models.

In 2000, ACE and the Carnegie Corporation of New York launched a new initiative titled "Promising Practices: Institutional Models of Comprehensive Internationalization," recognizing the achievements of eight institutions that have integrated international activities into their mission, curriculum, and student life. They include Appalachian State University, Beaver College, Dickinson College, Indiana University, Kapi'olani Community College, Missouri Southern State, SUNY Binghamton, and Tidewater Community College (McDonough & Hayward, 2000). All of these institutions offer benchmarks and best practices (see also Johnston, Jr. & Edelstein, 1993).

A case in point: A needs assessment of international faculty. Five years ago, in my role as director of faculty development at a large public comprehensive university and with the support of the provost, a colleague and I conducted a needs assessment survey of the international faculty, comprising 10% of the tenured and tenured track faculty at the institution. The findings revealed widespread and long-standing feelings of marginalization, isolation, and de-legitimization, much like the experiences revealed by American faculty of color and women faculty. There were notable differences between the campus experiences of Asian/Pacific Rim and European faculty and between international faculty trained in the United States and those trained in their countries of origin. Nonetheless, the vast majority expressed disappointment and consternation at their exclusion from the intellectual life of the university. They indicated they were rarely or never invited to share their insights about their cultural heritage with students or their colleagues. Campus-wide panels rarely included their voices or perspectives. As one faculty member wrote, "I've been on this campus for 20 years, and this survey is the first time anyone has asked about my needs or my willingness to share what I know and what I think." Many international faculty expressed anger and frustration at student resistance to their instruction, based on what they felt were ethnic biases. Others felt marginalized by colleagues in their departments who excluded them from department decision-making and leadership opportunities and excluded them from discussion in department meetings.

In response to the survey results, the teaching center supported the creation of an international faculty network, providing opportunities for them to socialize and network and to identify areas of common concern, bringing them to the attention of the campus leaders who were empowered to assist them. The needs assessment provided important insights to shape faculty development support and leverage change.

Expand on experiences with diversity and multiculturalism. Build on the efforts and insights of campus initiatives to promote diversity and multicultural education by expanding the goals to include global curricula and intercultural competencies. Cornwell and Stoddard (1999) make the case for integrating efforts to promote diversity and internationalization in higher education, but they note that these movements developed along parallel streams that have not converged in the past, reflecting the history of American isolationism. The process of integrating multiculturalism and internationalization may present significant challenges, but should be worth the effort nonetheless. Broadly defined, diversity learning includes efforts as varied as multicultural curriculum development, inclusive instructional and assessment methods; experiences with diversity in the co-curriculum; and orientation, mentoring, and networking for faculty, particularly persons of color and women, among others. By extension, internationalizing the campus might include the following efforts: curriculum transformation efforts to infuse global perspectives; internationalizing teaching methods, materials, and assessments to address the needs of international students and nonnative speakers; support for international faculty and international graduate teaching assistants through workshops and services to promote English language fluency and knowledge of American cultural norms; networking opportunities for international faculty and students and their families; and venues to enable international faculty and students to share their cultural experiences and perspectives beyond their disciplinary expertise. (See also Achterberg, 2002; Smith, Byrd, Nelson, Barrett, & Constantinides, 1992.)

A recent study (Humphreys, 2000) on the status of diversity requirements in undergraduate education indicates that 62% of colleges and universities require a diversity course requirement or plan to do so in the next year. While different curricular models are used, the majority of institutions have a diversity course requirement in which students select one or two courses from a list of options. While most of these courses focus on race, ethnicity, gender, class, and sexual orientation in the context of American society, some diversity course options do focus on intercultural issues. While the model of requiring a single diversity course is not a panacea, it has proven to be a productive educational experience that promotes multicultural awareness and competencies. But no single course can carry the full weight of teaching these complex goals. Ideally, these competencies are taught and reinforced throughout the curriculum and co-curriculum.

Similarly, if an additional diversity course requirement on global issues were to be added to the curriculum, it would be important that those skills also be infused throughout the collegiate experience.

One final note on diversity courses: These requirements were adopted at different rates across different regions of the United States (Humphreys, 2000). It can be anticipated that local and regional values will influence the readiness of institutions to embrace requirements for global coursework.

Explore how international education can support other campus initiatives. This might include, for example, service-learning, interdisciplinarity and integrative learning, learning communities, distance learning and other forms of instructional technology, and assessment of student learning outcomes, each of which offers opportunities for international perspectives and experiences.

Increasingly, academic service-learning is being embedded in study abroad programs, such as the program at Worcester Polytechnic Institute in which upper-division students work on group projects under the mentorship of a faculty sponsor to provide service to international communities (Vaz, 2000). Within the United States, many academic service-learning projects take students into local communities in which they can use and develop their intercultural skills and foreign language abilities as they assist communities (DeZure, 2000; Zlotkowski, 2000). As noted above, interdisciplinary studies and learning communities are proliferating, with many of these efforts focusing on international themes and problems of interest worldwide, for example, global warming, AIDS and other global public health issues, and terrorism (DeZure, 1998–1999; Edwards, Jr., 1996; Smith & McCann, 2001).

And last but not least, instructional technology has enabled cost-effective ways to connect students to the world through online discussions via the Internet with people around the world, both synchronous and asynchronous discussions. One innovative example of distance learning is an engineering course, "Global Product Realization," offered by the University of Michigan in collaboration with the Technical University of Delft and the Seoul National

University in South Korea. The course involves students and faculty interacting in real time at sites in Korea, the Netherlands, and Michigan. Working in cross-cultural groups called "global product teams," students design, develop, and present products that must be culturally and technically viable in all three countries (Majher & Kuharevicz, 2001).

Work with student affairs specialists to explore common concerns that might promote dialogue between American and international faculty and students, both in and outside of the classroom (Achterberg, 2002; Dalton, 1999; Hoffa & Pearson, 1997). The co-curricular dimension of internationalization is very significant and should not be overlooked, particularly in light of the expertise of student affairs staff in providing support to international students and promoting study abroad and other intercultural experiences. Based on Hayward's (2000) data, the majority of campuses now have designated faculty and staff who work with study abroad and other international initiatives, offering campus experience and expertise.

Help faculty integrate international elements in their scholarship. Work with faculty who are pursuing the scholarship of engagement, the scholarship of teaching, and the scholarship of discovery to explore how they might integrate international perspectives in their work. Provide grants to stimulate interest and bring grantees together to share their efforts and to develop a network of faculty engaged in global activities.

Expanding and Maximizing Current Efforts

Many faculty developers are already actively engaged in supporting one or more aspects of internationalization on their campuses. Many developers were directly involved in responding to campus needs immediately following the World Trade Center disaster. They developed and disseminated guidelines for classroom and campus discussions about the event; they sponsored discussions and teach-ins; and they endeavored to support international faculty, students, and staff lest they become targets of misguided frustration and anger (Cook, 2001; Ehrlich, 2001; Kardia, Bierwert, Cook, Miller, & Kaplan, 2002).

Prior to September 11, many faculty developers were already active in many aspects of internationalization. These include 1) support for international faculty through orientation sessions, workshops, and networking groups, 2) support for international graduate student teaching assistants, 3) support for all faculty through workshops on the instructional needs of international students and more generally on how to ensure an inclusive and culturally sensitive learning environment, and 4) curricular planning to integrate global perspectives, content, and skills for faculty teaching in the United States and abroad, among others.

For developers already actively involved in internationalizing their campuses, the question is not where should I begin, but what more can I do and how can I do it more effectively?

Integrate and aggregate efforts. One option is to identify the range of campus activities already in place and to make them more visible and integrated, enabling them to function synergistically. The sum can be greater than its parts. All too often faculty development efforts occur as isolated activities, known only to participants and their direct sponsors. When packaged and promoted in the aggregate, they are more likely to create the critical mass of activity and momentum that will foster institutional recognition and commitment (DeZure, 2000).

Assess the impact. A second option is to focus on assessment of the global initiatives on your campus to determine their impact on participants and on the campus culture more broadly. While many schools now identify global and intercultural competence as a learning outcome for general education and the collegiate experience, very few institutions have assessed whether their students attain those goals.

Build cross-institutional collaborations. A third option for faculty developers who have well-developed global initiatives is to seek out and participate in cross-institutional and cross-organizational collaborations, often with external funding.

Combine initiatives in creative ways. A fourth option is to combine campus initiatives in novel ways. Much of the cutting-edge work in global education involves new combinations of instructional innovations. These include, for example, the integration of academic service-learning with study abroad, learning communities focused on global themes, or the use of instructional technology and distance learning to engage students around the world in problem-based learning. The Global Intercultural Experiences Program at the University of Michigan provides undergraduate work-study students with opportunities to do research with faculty abroad. Participating faculty receive grants to support their research and participating students receive stipends. This model addresses one of the long-standing challenges of study abroad to increase the ethnic and economic diversity of participants.

CONCLUSION

Faculty development is a field charged with maintaining the delicate balance between leadership and service. We have a leadership role in shaping the vision for teaching and learning on our campuses. We do that by keeping our eyes on the national and international educational horizons for innovations and winds of change, by keeping abreast of best practices and what research has to tell us about effective teaching and learning, and by sharing these with our campuses. But we are also charged with providing service and being field-responsive to our campus and its varied constituencies. We do that by assessing campus needs; anticipating what it will take to promote and support change within the institutional context; providing training and development when needed; and putting into place those structures, opportunities, and rewards that will enable faculty and administrators to engage in change and to succeed. We have to calibrate the larger vision with the campus realities. Internationalizing higher education is one of those larger visions worthy of our time, efforts, and expertise as change agents. To reiterate the words of President McPherson (2001): "International Education. Now More Than Ever" (p. A30). It is more than a media sound bite. It is a call to thought and action.

REFERENCES

Achterberg, C. (2002). Providing a global perspective. *About Campus, 6* (6), 17–24.

Commission on International Education. (1997). *Educating for global competence: America's passport to the future.* Washington, DC: American Council on Education.

Cook, C. E. (2001, November 18). Center gives teachers guidelines for discussing terrorism. *Ann Arbor News,* p. B2.

Cornwell, G. H., & Stoddard, E. W. (1999). *Globalizing knowledge: Connecting international and intercultural studies.* Washington, DC: Association of American Colleges and Universities.

Dalton, J. C. (1999). Beyond borders: How international developments are changing student affairs practice. *New Directions for Student Services, No. 86.* San Francisco, CA: Jossey-Bass.

Davis, J. R. (1995). *Interdisciplinary courses and team teaching: New arrangements for learning.* Phoenix, AZ: American Council on Education/Oryx Press.

DeZure, D. (1998–1999). Interdisciplinary teaching and learning. *Teaching Excellence Essays: Toward the Best in the Academy, 10* (3). Stillwater, OK: Professional and Organizational Development Network in Higher Education.

DeZure, D. (Ed.). (2000). *Learning from Change: Landmarks in teaching and learning in higher education from Change magazine (1969–1999).* Sterling, VA: Stylus.

Dobbert, M. L. L. (1998). The impossibility of internationalizing students by adding materials to courses. In J. A. Mestenhauser & B. J. Ellingboe (Eds.), *Reforming the higher education curriculum: Internationalizing the campus* (pp. 53–68). Phoenix, AZ: American Council on Education/Oryx Press.

Edwards, A. F., Jr. (1996). *Interdisciplinary undergraduate programs: A directory* (2nd ed.). Acton, MA: Copley.

Ehrlich, C. (2001, November 9). Engineers evaluate their responsibilities. *The Michigan Daily*, p. 3.

Gaff, J. G. (1999). *General education: The changing agenda.* Washington, DC: Association of American Colleges and Universities.

Gaff, J. G., Ratcliff, J. L., & Associates. (1997). *Handbook of the undergraduate curriculum: A comprehensive guide to purposes, structures, practices and change.* San Francisco, CA: Jossey-Bass.

Hanson, K. H., & Meyerson, J. W. (1994). *International challenges to American colleges and universities: Looking ahead.* Washington, DC: American Council on Education/Oryx Press.

Hayward, F. M. (2000). *Internationalization of U.S. higher education: Preliminary status report 2000.* Washington, DC: American Council on Education.

Hayward, F. M., & Siaya, L. M. (2001). Public experience, attitudes, and knowledge: A report of two national surveys about international education. Washington, DC: American Council on Education.

Hoffa, W., & Pearson, J. (1997). *NAFSA's guide to education abroad for advisers and administrators.* Washington, DC: NAFSA Association of International Educators.

Humphreys, D. (2000). National survey finds diversity requirements common around the country. *Diversity Digest.* Retrieved from http://www.diversity web.org/Digest/f00/survey.html

Institute of International Education. (2000). *Open doors 2000.* New York, NY: Institute of International Education.

Johnston, J. S., Jr., & Edelstein, R. J. (1993*). Beyond borders: Profiles in international education.* Washington, DC: Association of American Colleges and Universities.

Kardia, D., Bierwert, C., Cook, C. E., Miller, A. T., & Kaplan, M. L. (2002, February/January). Discussing the unfathomable: Classroom-based responses to tragedy. *Change, 34* (1), 18–23.

Klein, J. T. (1999). *Mapping interdisciplinary studies.* Washington, DC: Association of American Colleges and Universities.

Majher, P., & Kuharevicz, N. L. (2001, January 15). Engineering's innovative global product development course taught simultaneously on three continents. *The University Record*, 1–2. McDonough, T., & Hayward, F. (2000, October 20). ACE, Carnegie select eight institutions with outstanding international programs. *ACENews*. Retrieved from http://www.acenet.edu/news/press_release/2000/10 october/carnegie.html

McPherson, M. (2001, December 9). International education. Now more than ever. *New York Times*, p. A30.

Mestenhauser, J. A., & Ellingboe, B. (1998). *Reforming the higher education curriculum: Internationalizing the curriculum*. Phoenix, AZ: American Council on Education/Oryx Press.

Ratcliff, J. L., Johnson, L. D., La Nasa, S. M., & Gaff, J. G. (2001). *The status of general education in the year 2000: Summary of a national survey*. Washington, DC: Association of American Colleges and Universities.

Schneider, C. G., & Shoenberg, R. (1998). *Contemporary understandings of liberal education*. Washington, DC: Association of American Colleges and Universities.

Shadid, A. (2002, February 26). 'Arc of crisis' study funds hiked: U.S. adding language training centers for strategically important areas. *Ann Arbor News*, p. A4.

Shoenberg, R. E., & Turlington, B. (1998). *Next steps for languages across the curriculum: Prospects, problems, and promise*. Phoenix, AZ: American Council on Education/Oryx Press.

Smith, B. L., & McCann, J. (2001). *Reinventing ourselves: Interdisciplinary education, collaborative learning, and experimentation in higher education*. Bolton, MA: Anker.

Smith, R. M., Byrd, P., Nelson, G. L., Barrett, R. P., & Constantinides, J. C. (1992). Crossing pedagogical oceans: International teaching assistants in U.S. undergraduate education. *ASHE-ERIC Research Reports, Vol. 21, No. 8*. Washington DC: ERIC Clearinghouse on Higher Education.

Vaz, R. F. (2000). Connected learning: Interdisciplinary projects in international settings. *Liberal Education, 86* (1), 2–9.

Zlotkowski, E. (1997–2000). *AAHE series on service-learning in the disciplines*. Washington, DC: American Association for Higher Education.

Contact:

Deborah DeZure
Coordinator of Faculty Programs
Center for Research on Learning and Teaching (CRLT)

University of Michigan
3300 SEB
610 East University Street
Ann Arbor, MI 48109-1259
Voice   (734) 936-1135
Fax   (734) 647-3600
Email   ddezure@umich.edu

Deborah DeZure is Coordinator of Faculty Programs at the Center for Research on Learning and Teaching (CRLT) at the University of Michigan. Deborah edited *Learning from Change: Landmarks in Teaching and Learning from Change Magazine (1969–1999)* (2000, Stylus Publications in collaboration with AAHE) and *To Improve the Academy* (1997) and published numerous book chapters and articles in journals such as *Academe, Change, AAHE Bulletin, Thought and Action,* and publications of the NCTE. Deborah is a Contributing Editor of *Change* and serves on the editorial boards of *Journal of Excellence in College Teaching, Issues and Inquiry in College Teaching, Issues in Interdisciplinary Studies,* and the *Michigan Journal of Community Service Learning.* She is also chair of the POD National Outreach Sub-committee. Previously, Deborah was Director of the Faculty Center for Instructional Excellence at Eastern Michigan University, where she was also Education Consultant to the President.

Section II

Faculty Focus
in Faculty Development

4

The Knowledge Survey: A Tool for All Reasons

Edward Nuhfer
University of Colorado at Denver

Delores Knipp
United States Air Force Academy

Knowledge surveys provide a means to assess changes in specific content learning and intellectual development. More important, they promote student learning by improving course organization and planning. For instructors, the tool establishes a high degree of instructional alignment, and, if properly used, can ensure employment of all seven best practices during the enactment of the course. Beyond increasing success of individual courses, knowledge surveys inform curriculum development to better achieve, improve, and document program success.

INTRODUCTION

An increasing number of students in diverse disciplines at our institutions now take knowledge surveys at the beginning and end of each course. A survey consists of course learning objectives framed as questions that test mastery of particular objectives. Table 4.1 displays an excerpt from a knowledge survey from an introductory course in environmental geology. Six survey items represent a unit lesson on asbestos, together with the header that provides directions for responding to the survey. These six items, taken from a 200-item knowledge survey, range from simple knowledge to evaluation of substantial open-ended questions. Students address the questions, not by providing actual answers, but instead by responding to a three-point rating of one's own confidence to respond with competence to each query (see "Instructions" in

Table 4.1). Knowledge surveys differ from pre-test/post-test evaluations because tests, by their nature, can address only a limited sampling of a course. In contrast, knowledge surveys cover an entire course in depth. While no student could possibly allocate the time to answer all questions on a thorough knowledge survey in any single exam sitting, they can rate their confidence to provide answers to an extensive survey of items in a very short time span. Sequence of items in the survey follows the sequence in which the instructor presents the course material.

A well-designed survey will contain clear, unifying concepts that are fleshed out with the more detailed content needed to develop conceptual learning. The content items in Table 4.1 also develop central unifying concepts about the nature of science and scientific methods (see Table 4.3). Knowledge surveys can present the most complex of open-ended kinds of problems or issues, and they can assess skills as well as content knowledge.

TABLE 4.1

Excerpt of Six Items from a 200-Item Knowledge Survey

Item #	Bloom Level	Content topic: asbestos hazards
20	1	What is asbestos?
22	2	Explain how the characteristics of amphibole asbestos make it more conducive to producing lung damage than other fibrous minerals.
23	3	Given the formula $Mg_3Si_2O_5(OH)_4$, calculate the weight percent of magnesium in chrysotile.
24	4	Two controversies surround the asbestos hazard: (1) it's nothing more than a very expensive bureaucratic creation, or (2) it is a hazard that accounts for tens of thousands of deaths annually. What is the basis for each argument?
25	5	Develop a plan for the kind of study needed to prove that asbestos poses a danger to the general populace.
26	6	Which of the two controversies expressed in item 24 above has *the best* current scientific support?

Excerpt from a Knowledge Survey

INSTRUCTIONS: This is a knowledge survey, not a test. The purposes of this survey are to (1) provide a study guide that discloses the organization, content and levels of thinking expected in this course and (2) help you to monitor your own growth as you proceed through the term. Use the accompanying Form Number 16504 answer sheet provided. **Be sure to fill in your name and student ID number on the front left of the form. This requires both writing your name in the spaces in the top row and filling in the bubbles corresponding to the appropriate letters.** You may use pen or pencil to mark your responses, so long as the pen or pencil is not one with red ink or lead.

In this knowledge survey, don't actually try to answer any of the questions provided. Instead rate (on a three-point scale) **your confidence to answer the questions with your present knowledge.** Read each question and then fill in an A, B or C in the A through E response row that corresponds to the question number in accord with the following instructions:

Mark an "A" as response if you feel confident that you can now answer the question sufficiently for graded test purposes.

Mark a "B" response to the question if you can now answer at least 50% of it or if you know precisely where you could quickly get the information needed and could return here in 20 minutes or less to provide a complete answer for graded test purposes.

Mark a "C" as response to the question if you are not confident that you could adequately answer the question for graded test purposes at this time.

Do your best to provide a totally honest assessment of your present knowledge. When you mark an "A" or a "B," this states that you have significant background to address an item. You should consider it fair if your professor asks you to d emonstrate that capability by actually answering the question. This survey will be given again the last week of the semester. Keep this survey and refer to the items to monitor your increasing mastery of the material through the semester.

Note: Students respond in accord with instructions for either a bubble sheet (as above) or a web-based format. The instructions for completion are generic for most courses; the actual items shown here are from a lower division course in environmental geology.

Figure 4.1 shows the pre- and post-course results from the 200 items in the same semester-long course. The values plotted are the class average of responses to each item, and only the students who completed both pre- and post-surveys are included. When needed, the instructor can call up the data at the level of each individual student. The figure provides insights that global summative student evaluations would never reveal, such as better pacing (see caption) as a key to improve learning when the instructor again teaches the course.

FIGURE 4.1

Pre- and Post-Course Results of a Knowledge Survey

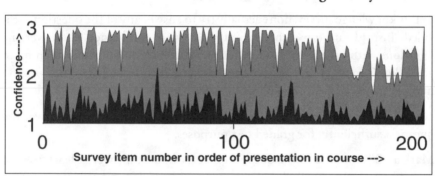

(From Nuhfer, 1996)

Note: Ordinate scales are from 1 (low confidence) to 3 (high confidence). The survey elicited confidence ratings to 200 items (abscissa) in the order in which students encountered items in the course. The sample items 20–26 provided in Table 4.1 are from this same course. The lower darker area (on this and all similar figures in this chapter) reveals the class averages on confidence to address each item at the start of class; the upper shaded area displays the ratings to the same items at the end of class. The course, instructor, and learning experience all received "A" ratings from students on summative evaluations, but lower learning did occur in the final two weeks of classes when the final topic on coastal hazards was hurriedly covered. The right side of the graph (approximately items 170–200) reveals this learning gap. Better pacing eliminated this gap when the instructor next taught the course.

The Need for a More Direct Assessment of Learning

Knowledge surveys address learning in specific detail, as opposed to the common global summative item: "Evaluate this course as a learning experience." Summative student ratings are frequently used to evaluate professors for rank, salary, and tenure. Summative ratings are measures of students' general satisfaction, which results from a mix of content learning, cognitive development, and affective factors. The most thorough research on the relationship between content learning and summative ratings produced a correlation coefficient derived by meta-analysis of r = 0.43 (Cohen, 1981). That relationship is strong enough to prove that, in general, students learn more from professors whom they rate highly, but it is too weak to allow learning in any single class to be assessed by inference based on student ratings of the class, the individual professors who taught it, or the overall learning experience. Researchers such as Feldman (1998) have shown that educational practices that produce the most learning are not exactly the same as those that produce the highest student ratings. Because student ratings alone cannot reliably reveal learning outcomes produced by individual instructors or courses, good assessment requires a more direct assessment of learning. We believe knowledge surveys, properly used, serve this purpose. Knowledge surveys were created to allow instructors to prove that their courses produced specific changes in students' learning and to disclose the detailed content of a course to students (Nuhfer, 1993, 1996). Tobias and Raphael (1997) grasped the usefulness of the tool and included it as a best practice in their book. Knowledge surveys do achieve their original purposes, but employment of this tool encourages further instructional improvements that are discussed in this chapter.

DISCUSSION

Knowledge Surveys that Enhance High-Level Thinking

When instructors develop sophistication with knowledge surveys, they can code each item according to levels of reasoning, such as those of Bloom (1956) (see Tables 4.1 and 4.2). This coding allows an instructor to see the course as a profile of levels of inquiry addressed (Figure 4.2) and verify that the course plan accords with the original intentions of the instructor and the purposes of the course. As noted by Gardiner (1994), most testing pinpoints low-level content knowledge, even though most instructors really aspire to teach some higher-level critical thinking. If an instructor includes critical thinking as her or his course objective, and the detailed knowledge survey reveals overt emphasis on mere memorization, then recognizing this discrepancy is empowering. Such revelations allow course redesign that will ensure the desired critical thinking experiences.

Interpretations of graphs like Figure 4.2 require care. Although 54% of knowledge survey items for this lower division course addressed the lowest Bloom levels, this does not imply that 54% of course time was spent addressing lower levels. In fact, high-level open-ended questions require disproportionately

TABLE 4.2

The Six Levels of Bloom's Classic Taxonomy of Educational Objectives Together with Question Prompts that Commonly Elicit a Response at a Particular Reasoning Level

This Bloom reasoning level is probably addressed...	...if the query sounds like:
1. **Recall** (remember terms, facts)	"Who...?" or "What...?"
2. **Comprehension** (understand meanings)	"Explain." "Predict." "Interpret." "Give an example." "Para phrase..."
3. **Application** (use information in new situations)	"Calculate." "Solve." "Apply." "Demonstrate." "Given ___. Use this information to..."
4. **Analytical** (see organization and patterns)	"Distinguish..." "Compare" or "Contrast" "How does ___ relate to___?" "Why does ___?"
5. **Synthesis** (generalize/ create new ideas from old sources)	Design..." "Construct..." "Develop." "Formulate." "What if..." "Write a poem." "Write a short story..."
6. **Evaluation** (discriminate and assess value of evidence)	"Evaluate." "Appraise." "Justify which is better. " "Evaluate ___ argument, based on established criteria."

more time to confront than do simple recall knowledge items. Figure 4.2 verifies that students encountered no less than (they actually encountered more) 28 analytical, 16 synthesis, and 16 evaluation challenges in this course. Yet, students can do synthesis and evaluation poorly (see Nuhfer and Pavelich, 2001), thus operating at the lower levels of the Perry (1999) model or the reflective judgment model (King & Kitchener, 1994). If one wants to use such a presentation like Figure 4.2 to prove that students truly mastered some critical thinking in this course, then one must disclose the rubrics used to evaluate students' answers to representative high-level items. (Rubrics are the disclosed criteria that instructors use for evaluation of a test question or project.) When instructors present rubrics along with evidence like Figure 4.2, the assertion that students addressed high-level challenges with high levels of sophistication is hard to refute. Table 4.2 near the end of this chapter provides rubrics for a few such questions.

FIGURE 4.2

Levels of Thinking Represented in a Knowledge Survey

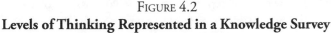
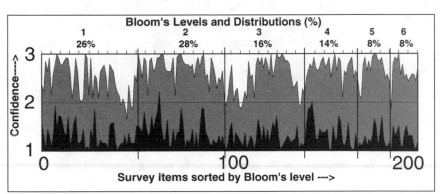

Note: Data are from the same environmental geology class and knowledge survey shown in Figure 4.1, but here have been rearranged to present the course outcomes as a profile of levels of educational objectives (Bloom, 1956) encountered in the course. The graph reveals that reduced learning in the final two weeks (Figure 4.1) occurred in material typified by the lower Bloom's levels.

Does Increased Confidence Reveal Increased Learning?

The video, *Thinking Together: Collaborative Learning in Science* (Derek Bok Center, 1993), from Harvard University shows a brief paired-learning exercise in Dr. Eric Mazur's introductory physics class. The students confront a problem, answer a multiple-choice question about the problem, and rate the confidence that their own answer is correct. The students then engage in paired discussion to convince the partner that one's own answer is correct. Thereafter, the entire class debriefs and summarizes results. In that video, a bar graphic displays a positive relationship between confidence and correctness. Mazur (personal communication, November 29, 2001) revealed that there is no strong correlation initially between correctness and confidence to answer correctly, but overall class confidence rises significantly as discussion of the problem proceeds and greater understanding results.

We have observed overt overconfidence expressed on knowledge surveys given at the start of a class by one or two students enrolled in about 10% of courses we have examined. Such students may appear in any level course, but are more frequently freshmen with undeveloped self-assessment skills. However, the aberrations contributed by occasional individuals never affect a class average in a significant way. To date, every class average we have examined has invariably been a very good representation of that class's knowledge and abilities. The confidence rating to address content does indeed parallel ability to address it in an exam situation (Figure 4.3), especially when a teacher designs effective teaching/learning experiences for the topic. Learning gaps revealed in post-course surveys reflect strong concurrence among nearly all students of little confidence to address an item. Interviews with professors who use knowledge surveys show that they nearly always know what produced a so-designated gap. Often a gap reveals a topic not covered or one that was inadequately addressed (see caption, Figure 4.1).

The best results occur when survey items clearly frame specific content, and students take the survey home to complete it with plenty of time for self-reflection. Instructors should refer frequently to the survey throughout the course and remind all students to monitor their progress. Like any tool, a user's ability to be effective with it increases with practice and experience. Based on our work with individual faculty, the first knowledge survey an instructor creates tends to consist almost entirely of recall and comprehension items, even though the instructor aspires to instill critical thinking skills in the course. Some items may not be so clearly stated as to elicit students' focused reflection upon the intended knowledge or skill. In fact, lack of clarity or direction may contribute to the isolated incidents of overt overconfidence noted above. Initial surveys tend to be constructed without deep reflection on more central unifying concepts, global outcomes, or the function of the course in a larger curriculum. A developer can truly help an instructor to improve a course by making queries about course purpose and instructor's intentions for outcomes. This helps the instructor to frame such outcomes as survey items and to organize lower-level items as a way to develop larger general outcomes.

Once the content and learning goals have been clearly laid out and organized in writing, the instructor can more clearly concentrate on what kinds of pedagogies, learning experiences, and rubrics (Table 4.4) will best ensure content learning and intellectual development. The overall result of deliberation and practice that begins with knowledge surveys is a course with

increasingly sophisticated organization, good development of learning outcomes, and clear conveyance of a plan for learning to students.

FIGURE 4.3

**Comparison of Normalized Reported Knowledge and
Final Examination Results from an Astronomy Class**

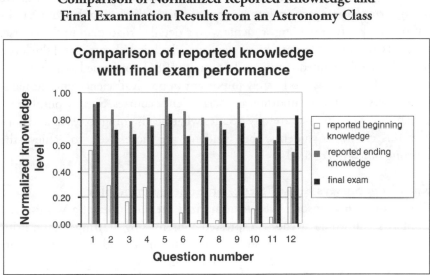

(after Knipp, 2001)

Note: Students were slightly overconfident about their knowledge on several of the
questions from the first part of the course and less confident about their knowledge
level of material toward the latter part of the course. The latter portion of the course
covered material that was conceptually and mathematically new to the students.

Knowledge Surveys Promote Preparation and Organization

Feldman (1998) used meta-analyses to tease apart the instructional practices
that produce learning as opposed to those that produce high ratings of student
satisfaction. He discovered that the most important instructional contribution to learning was the instructor's preparation and organization of the
course. However, this practice ranked only sixth in importance in gaining high
ratings of satisfaction. Satisfaction depended much more strongly on the professor's enthusiasm and stimulation of interest. The National Survey for Student Learning (Pascarella, 2001) thoroughly supports Feldman's findings
about student learning. The use of knowledge surveys as a best practice can be
justified on the basis of the dominant evidence: Nothing a teacher can do to

produce learning matters more than the efforts put into course preparation and organization.

The process of making a knowledge survey—laying out the course in its entirety—considering the concepts, the content, levels of thinking, and questions suitable for testing learning of chosen outcomes is extremely conducive to organization and preparation. Further, the act of disclosing the course in its entirety is akin to providing students with a detailed road map to the course. Students know the content, the sequence in which it will come, and the levels of challenge demanded. Erdle and Murray (1986) confirmed that students perceive disclosure as moderately important in physical science and humanities courses, and more important in social science courses. Simply put, the research shows that if one carefully decides what one is going to teach and conveys this clearly to students, then students are more likely to achieve the learning outcomes desired.

Knowledge Surveys Boost Practice of the Seven Principles

Chickering and Gamson (1987) summarized the outcomes of a Wingspread Conference in which attendees expressed consensus by drafting "Seven Principles of Good Practice" for succeeding with undergraduates. Developers know well that getting some faculty to adopt progressive pedagogical practices can be difficult. Most faculty relate better to content learning than to the practices that might better produce learning. The fact that knowledge surveys reach faculty where they are—with an obvious relationship to the content they value—makes them a good tool developers can use to introduce faculty to thinking toward improved practice. Knowledge surveys predispose a class to making use of all seven principles.

1) Good practice encourages student-faculty contact. One reason that few students ever come to a professor's office for help is because they are often unaware of what they do not know or understand. Once students confront a knowledge survey and understand its use, students can more clearly see their need to seek help. A pre-course survey can also reveal which students have the most confidence with the material and which do not (Figure 4.4). Such insights permit faculty to know something about each student and make them aware of each student's possible needs for extra assistance before the class is even underway. Knowledge surveys also indicate which individual students really have the prerequisites needed to engage the challenges forthcoming in the course.

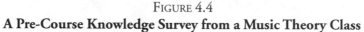

FIGURE 4.4

A Pre-Course Knowledge Survey from a Music Theory Class

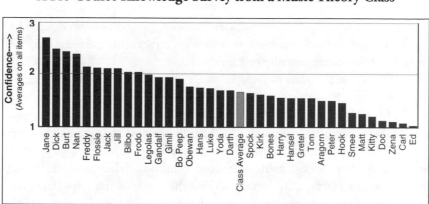

Note: Here the data is used to identify students (names have been changed) by confidence level at the start of the course. Data here are averages of responses to a 50-item survey plus a separately calculated class average (lighter bar).

2) Good practice encourages cooperation among students. Knowledge surveys help to impart several of the five basic elements of cooperative learning (Johnson, Johnson, & Smith, 1991; Millis & Cottell, 1998). Individual accountability includes the critical ability of individuals to be able to accurately assess their own level of preparedness or lack thereof. When a course has detailed disclosure, students more readily know when they have deficiencies, making them more receptive to engaging in positive interdependence, promotive interaction, and group processing to overcome deficiencies. Pre-course knowledge survey results such as the kind shown in Figure 4.4 provide the information needed to form heterogeneous cooperative groups composed of members with known, varied abilities.

3) Good practice encourages active learning. Knowledge surveys can be a powerful prompt for addressing high-level thinking. When students receive both good example items and a copy of Bloom's taxonomy, they can make up their own new test questions for a unit. Such questions will address the material and appropriately high Bloom levels. A simple assignment could be:

> You already have seven questions on this unit in your knowledge survey. Address the material in the unit, use Bloom's taxonomy, and see if you can produce seven good questions that are even more challenging.

If yours are better, I may use them on the knowledge survey for this course next term.

When students know the important concepts and outcomes desired in a unit lesson, groups can become resources, thus structuring peer teaching into a course while assuring quality outcomes.

4) Good practice gives prompt feedback. When a detailed knowledge survey is furnished, it allows students to monitor their progress through the course. One of the first signs that an instructor has produced a survey of good quality is a query from a student: "Will I really be able to learn all these new things?" Prompt feedback delivered by a survey is the students' own continuous tracking of knowledge gains as the course unfolds. When students can create their original test questions that address the material at a respectable level of thinking, they have reached what probably constitutes adequate preparation and understanding. If any student must be absent, the survey immediately discloses the material missed and reveals to an extent the work required to master it.

5) Good practice emphasizes time on task. Full disclosure at the start of a course allows timely planning and study. A review sheet given out before an exam will not reveal to students what they do not know in a timely manner, and it will promote mere cramming rather than planned learning. Faculty who plan courses well and disclose them at the detail of a knowledge survey quickly discover that the survey keeps them honest. A student who is following his or her progress will invariably say, "Excuse me, Dr. ——, but it seems like we didn't address that item #— about——." Perhaps that class launched into a discussion that carried more value than the item skipped and an expressed item of more value now replaces the original item. On the other hand, perhaps the class launched into a digression and the instructor forgot to address a particularly important point that he or she must yet address. When a class inadvertently strays off track, knowledge surveys reveal whether straying resulted in any important omissions. Surveys also require students to engage material repeatedly. Some of the earliest research on cognition deduced the benefits of time spent in repetition to learning. The use of knowledge surveys ensures at least two additional structured engagements with the entire course material.

6) Good practice communicates high expectations. Students sometimes complain that instructors teach at one level and test at a more challenging level. Knowledge surveys offer the opportunity to detail, in a timely manner, the level of challenge that students should expect. The materials needed to build a rudimentary knowledge survey already reside in most professors' computers—in the past examinations, quizzes, and review sheets they provided the last time they taught the course. The only work required is to arrange items from these in the order of course presentation. Students appreciate the focus that a knowledge survey brings to the study process, and they will rise to expectations conveyed in a survey, particularly if instructors assert that some of the higher-level items will likely appear on a final exam.

7) Good practice respects diverse talents and ways of learning. One of the best ways to address diverse learners is to be certain to present and engage materials in a variety of ways, in particular ways that make sense in terms of how the brain operates in the learning process (Leamnson, 1999). When one actually has a blueprint of content and levels of thinking that one wants to present, it quickly allows one to ask "What is the best way to present this item, then the following item?" Without such a plan, one can too easily end up lecturing through the entire course, even when the desired outcomes literally scream for alternative methods. A detailed plan of outcomes will obviate a correlative plan for reaching these (see "Pedagogies" Table 4.4).

APPLICATIONS AT THE UNIT LEVEL

It is easy to conceive of tools applied to a single course (Figures 4.1 & 4.2) as applied to a four-year curriculum, with the content outcomes and levels of thinking desired plotted on the abscissa from freshman through senior year. We authors have just begun to scratch the surface of using knowledge surveys in unit-level development, but it is exciting and we hope readers will extend this kind of thinking to units at their own institutions.

When professors have detailed blueprints of their own courses, this permits a larger unit to sit down and have the necessary conversations about what content should be taught and when, what levels of thinking should be stressed and when, and what pedagogies and experiences should occur and when. One department at the senior author's institution has now committed to post syllabi and knowledge surveys for all courses on the web. A senior comprehensive exit exam will draw its questions from the knowledge surveys of courses taken by students. A student can thus see in detail every course and will have relevant study guides to any exit examination. A college at the same institution is now using knowledge surveys to plan and assess the curricula of various departments in that college. Both authors' institutions have discovered that when adjunct faculty are recruited or an institution has high turnover of instructors, knowledge surveys convey expectations for outcomes to new or part-time professors and help maintain course continuity and standards.

Table 4.3 shows 11 learning outcomes for a university-level general education requirement. These resulted after eight science professors gathered to answer the question: Why are we requiring students to take a science course, and what outcomes justify their costs in time and tuition dollars? Together, these items constitute a model for science literacy—understanding what science is, how it works, and how it fits into a broader plan for education. The institution regularly assesses these items by knowledge survey in each required core science course.

TABLE 4.3
Global Outcomes for a Core Science Course

CORE Questions for Science Literacy
1. What specifically distinguishes science from other endeavors or areas of knowledge such as art, philosophy, or religion?
2. Provide two examples of science and two of technology and use them to explain a central concept by which one can distinguish between science and technology.
3. It is particularly important to know ideas, but also where these ideas came from. Pick a single theory from the science represented by this course (biology, chemistry, environmental science, geology, or physics) and explain its historical development.
4. Provide at least two specific examples of methods that employ hypothesis & observation to develop testable knowledge of the physical world.
5. Provide two specific examples that illustrate why it is important to the everyday life of an educated person to be able to understand science.
6. Many factors determine public policy. Use an example to explain how you would analyze one of these determining factors to ascertain if it was truly scientific.
7. Provide two examples that illustrate how quantitative reasoning is used in science.
8. Contrast "scientific theory" with "observed fact."
9. Provide two examples of testable hypotheses.
10. "Modeling" is a term often used in science. What does it mean to "model a physical system?"
11. What is "natural and physical science"?

Figure 4.5 shows a less positive outcome in a course given in a department that had not held the necessary conversations. The process shows that the course tied poorly into preceding courses. The students initially engaged new material and then spent a substantial amount of the course on material already previously covered elsewhere. By recognizing the duplication, the instructor was able to revise the course, and she achieved much better results the following year.

FIGURE 4.5

Knowledge Survey Revealing Curriculum Design Deficiency

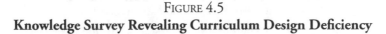
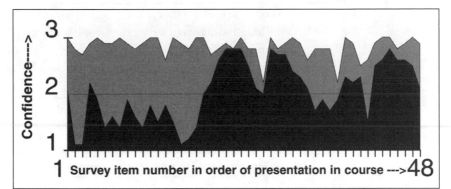

Note: This 48-item survey of a course in graphic arts revealed significant material taught to students that the students had already learned from some previous course(s). Minimal duplication occurs when a department uses knowledge surveys to inform curriculum design and prevent such unplanned duplication of content.

TABLE 4.4

**A Knowledge Survey Utilized as a Basis to Select Pedagogies,
Assign Homework, Author Rubrics, and
Design an Exercise for a Self-Assessment Journal**

CHOSEN OUTCOMES (1) Apply the definition of science to a real problem and use the framework of the methods of science to recognize the basis for evidence and the difficulty associated with arriving at a sound conclusion. (2) To understand the asbestos hazard, what the material is, and how it became identified as a hazard. (3) To be able to evaluate the true risks posed to the general populace based upon what constitutes the currently strongest scientific argument.

CONTENT LEARNING and LEVELS of THINKING (Bloom taxonomy chosen)

Item #	Bloom Level	Content topic: asbestos hazards
20	1	What is asbestos?
22	2	Explain how the characteristics of amphibole asbestos make it more conducive to producing lung damage than other fibrous minerals.
23	3	Given the formula $Mg_3Si_2O_5(OH)_4$, calculate the weight percent of magnesium in chrysotile.
24	4	Two controversies surround the asbestos hazard: (1) it's nothing more than a very expensive bureaucratic creation, or (2) it is a hazard that accounts for tens of thousands of deaths annually. What is the basis for each argument?
25	5	Develop a plan for the kind of study needed to prove that asbestos poses a danger to the general populace.
26	6	Which of the two controversies expressed in item 24 above has *the best* current scientific support?

PEDAGOGIES — Numbers correlate with content items above. (20) Lecture with illustrations, crossword, short answer drill; (22) guided discussion with formative quiz; (23) demonstration calculation, handout and in-class problems followed by homework; (24) paired (jigsaw) with directed homework on web; (25) based on data taken from "24," teams of two reflect on two scientific methods and relative strengths weakness of each in this; (26) personal evaluation of conflicting evidence submitted as short (250 word maximum) abstract.

CRITERIA FOR ASSESSMENT (Rubric) — Be able to realize the basis for distinction between types of asbestos. Understand the nature of chemical formulae that describe minerals. Clearly separate testable hypotheses from advocacy of proponents as a basis for evidence. Clearly distinguish the method of repeated experiments from the historical method in the kinds of evidence they provide. Use science as a basis to recognize evidence, and formulate and state an informed decision about the risks posed to oneself.

SELF-ASSESSMENT — What do you now know about asbestos as a hazard that you did not know before this lesson? You have investigated two competing hypotheses about the degree of hazard posed to the general populace, and you now know the scientific basis for each argument. Do you feel differently now about the asbestos hazard than you did before this lesson? Whether your answer is "yes" or "no," explain why. Describe some possible non-scientific factors that could affect the arguments presented by each sides of the argument. How do you now feel about the risks posed to yourself, and what questions do you still have?

(see Loacker, 2000)

Note: By stating the content learning outcomes in detail, clear choices emerge that engage learners in diverse experiences. The rubrics and self-assessments relate to both the course content and the global core learning outcomes (Table 4.3). Such an approach epitomizes the "instructional alignment" concept of Cohen (1987), wherein alignment of intended outcomes with instructional processes and instructional assessments produces learning outcomes about two standard deviations beyond what is possible without such organization.

CONCLUSION

Knowledge surveys offer a powerful way to achieve superb course organization and to enact instructional alignment. Surveys serve as powerful assessment tools that provide a direct, detailed assessment of content, learning, and levels of thinking. The time invested to produce a knowledge survey returns much benefit in enhanced learning that results from their use. Faculty appreciate that knowledge surveys require no in-class time to administer, that they improve planning and preparation, that they validate student learning much better than summative student ratings, and that knowledge surveys can be constructed mostly from what is already available in their office computers.

ACKNOWLEDGMENTS

The authors thank colleagues Barbara Millis (USAF Academy) and Carl Pletsch (CU-Denver) for their pre-reviews and helpful suggestions, and Mitch Handelsman (CU-Denver) for help with APA styling.

REFERENCES

Bloom, B. S. (1956). *Taxonomy of educational objectives—The classification of educational goals: Handbook I—cognitive domain.* New York, NY: David McKay.

Chickering, A. W., & Gamson, Z. (1987). Seven principles for good practice in undergraduate education. *AAHE Bulletin, 39,* 3–7.

Cohen, P. A. (1981). Student ratings of instruction and student achievement: a meta-analysis of multisection validity studies. *Review of Educational Research, 51,* 281–309.

Cohen, S. A. (1987). Instructional alignment: Searching for a magic bullet. *Educational Researcher, 16* (8), 16–20.

Derek Bok Center for Teaching and Learning, Harvard University (Producer). (1993). *Thinking Together: Collaborative Learning in Science* [Videotape]. Boston, MA: Derek Bok Center for Teaching and Learning, Harvard University.

Erdle, S., & Murray, H. G. (1986). Interfaculty differences in classroom teaching behaviors and their relationship to student instructional ratings. *Research in Higher Education, 24* (2), 115–127.

Feldman, K. A. (1998). Identifying exemplary teachers and teaching: evidence from student ratings. In K. A. Feldman & M. B. Paulsen (Eds.), *Teaching and learning in the college classroom* (2nd ed., pp. 391–414). Needham Heights, MA: Simon & Schuster.

Gardiner, L. F. (1994). *Redesigning higher education: Producing dramatic gains in student learning.* (Higher Education Report No. 7). Washington, DC: ASHE-ERIC. (ERIC Document Reproduction Service No. ED 394 442)

Johnson, D. W., Johnson, R. T., & Smith, K. A. (1991). *Active learning: Cooperation in the college classroom.* Edina, MN: Interaction Book Co.

King, P. M., & Kitchener, K. S. (1994). *Developing reflective judgment.* San Francisco, CA: Jossey-Bass.

Knipp, D. (2001, Spring). Knowledge surveys: What do students bring to and take from a class? *United States Air Force Academy Educator.* Retrieved March 18, 2002, from http://www.usafa.af.mil/dfe/educator/S01/knipp0401.htm

Leamnson, R. (1999). *Thinking about teaching and learning: Developing habits of learning with first year college and university students.* Sterling, VA: Stylus.

Loacker, G. (Ed.). (2000). *Self assessment at Alverno College.* Milwaukee, WI: Alverno College.

Millis, B. J., & Cottell, P. G. (1998). *Cooperative learning for higher education faculty.* Westport, CT: Greenwood.

Nuhfer, E. B. (1993). Bottom-line disclosure and assessment. *Teaching Professor, 7* (7), 8.

Nuhfer, E. B. (1996). The place of formative evaluations in assessment and ways to reap their benefits. *Journal of Geoscience Education, 44* (4), 385–394.

Nuhfer, E. B., & Pavelich, M. (2001). Levels of thinking and educational outcomes. *National Teaching and Learning Forum, 11* (1) 5–8.

Pascarella, E. T. (2001). Cognitive growth in college. *Change, 33* (1), 21–27.

Perry, W. G., Jr. (1999). *Forms of ethical and intellectual development in the college years.* San Francisco, CA: Jossey-Bass (a reprint of the original 1968 work with minor updating).

Tobias, S., & Raphael, J. (1997). *The hidden curriculum: Faculty-made tests in science, Part I lower-division courses.* New York, NY: Plenum.

Contact:

Edward Nuhfer
Director, Teaching Effectiveness and Faculty Development
University of Colorado, Denver
PO Box 173364, Campus Box 137
Denver, CO 80217
Voice   (303) 556-4915
Fax   (303) 556-5855
Email   Ed_Nuhfer@ceo.cudenver.edu

Delores J. Knipp (Lt Col Ret)
Professor of Physics
Suite 2A25 Fairchild Hall
USAF Academy, CO 80840
Voice   (719) 333-2560
Fax   (719) 333-3182
Email   delores.knipp@usafa.af.mil

Geology professor **Edward Nuhfer** describes himself as "an absolutely incurable teacher." In 1990, he founded the Teaching Excellence Center at University of Wisconsin, Platteville, and in 1992 was hired as the first director of the Office of Teaching Effectiveness at the University of Colorado at Denver, which was recently (2001) reviewed by the evaluation team for the North Central Association of Colleges and Schools as "an exemplary program and an outstanding resource." He directs "Boot

Camp for Professors," authors the one-page newsletter, *Nutshell Notes,* and writes occasional columns for the *National Teaching and Learning Forum.* After July 1, 2002, he will assume directorship of the Center for Teaching and Learning at Idaho State University.

Delores Knipp has been a resident physics instructor at the United States Air Force Academy since 1989. She earned her bachelor's degree in atmospheric science from the University of Missouri in 1976 and entered the Air Force as a weather officer shortly thereafter. She was a NORAD Command weather briefer before earning an MS in atmospheric science and joining the US Air Force Academy physics faculty. In 1989 she earned a PhD in Space and Atmospheric Physics at the University of California, Los Angeles. Since her return from UCLA she has been engaged in teaching introductory physics, meteorology, space physics, and astronomy and in researching the effects of solar activity on the near-earth environment. She is the recipient of both NASA and NSF grants and is currently the director of the Solar Terrestrial Interactions Group (STING) in the Physics Department. She became interested in knowledge assessment and knowledge surveys after she attended the 2000 Boot Camp for Professors at Leadville, Colorado.

5

Establishing a Teaching Academy: Cultivation of Teaching at a Research University Campus

Patricia Kalivoda
Josef Broder
William K. Jackson
University of Georgia

The University of Georgia (UGA) has worked hard over the last 22 years to increase the respect and reward for teaching through the faculty development programs of the office of instructional support and development and through the establishment of two campus-wide teaching awards. Looking for a means to extend a celebration of teaching beyond one-time recognition or one-time participation, the university established a campus-wide teaching academy. The purpose of this chapter is to chronicle the evolution of the teaching academy that was founded at the University of Georgia in 1999. The mission, goals, membership, funding, and programs and activities of the teaching academy will be described, as well as the faculty development programs and teaching awards that laid the foundation for the teaching academy.

INTRODUCTION

Over the last 40 years, faculty development programs and teaching awards have been key components in recognizing and rewarding individuals for teaching excellence on research university campuses. In the last ten to 15 years, campuses have looked for a structural model that can marshal the collective energy of individuals who have participated in faculty development programs or who have received teaching awards. For a growing number of campuses the model has been found in the form of a teaching academy. Chism, Fraser, and Arnold (1996) define a teaching academy as

> a group of faculty who are considered excellent or highly interested in teaching and who have been tapped by their institutions to engage in advocacy, service, or advising on teaching matters. The central idea of the academy is that effective teachers, working through an honorary and service-oriented collective, can have a significant impact on an institution's pursuit of teaching excellence. (p. 25)

Chism, Fraser, and Arnold (1996) go on to say that "the notion of an academy transforms the concept of singling out individuals into the concept of a community of expertise, changing one-time recognition into an opportunity for continued celebration of excellence" (p. 25). Teaching academies vary in their evolution, mission, structure, membership, goals, and activities. The purpose of this chapter is to chronicle the formation of a teaching academy at the University of Georgia

EFFORTS TO ESTABLISH A CULTURE THAT RESPECTS TEACHING

The Early Days at the University of Georgia

Prior to the mid-1960s, professors at the University of Georgia (UGA) were by and large a "traditional group of teaching faculty" (Dyer, 1985, p. 340). A shift occurred in the late-1960s and 1970s as the university struggled to become a modern university. Within this 20-year period, observers noted "enormous growth in the institution's research activities" (Dyer, 1985, p. 341). Concomitant with an increase in research activities, the institution's reward system underwent a transformation that resulted in a focus on research publications. Dyer (1985) notes that "new guidelines made promotion more difficult and gave a much heavier emphasis to assessment of quality, and some would have said quantity, of scholarly publications" (p. 353). The pendulum swung so far in the research direction that teaching was devalued.

During the late 1970s, three separate faculty committees recommended that an office dedicated to the improvement of teaching be established at the University of Georgia. In fall 1979, with final approval from the vice president for academic affairs, the office of instructional development (OID) was created. The central mission of OID was to provide campus-wide leadership on matters relating to instruction. Over its nearly 25-year history, OID (now called the Office of Instructional Support and Development [OISD]) has co-ordinated a wide variety of programs and activities. OISD serves faculty, administrators, and graduate teaching assistants (TAs) in each of the university's 14 schools and colleges.

The programs and activities of OISD include faculty and TA development programs, instructional grants, consultation services, publications, and instructional resources and media services. In addition, seminars, workshops, and conferences that address a wide range of topics are offered throughout the year. Since its inception, OISD has sought to promote vitality among faculty and administration and to foster an institutional climate that reinforces excellence in teaching and learning. Information about OISD may be found at http://www.isd.uga.edu/.

Faculty Development Programs
Two of the central programs of OISD that celebrate faculty passion for and commitment to excellence in teaching are the Lilly Teaching Fellows Program and the Senior Teaching Fellows Program.

The Lilly Teaching Fellows Program. The Lilly Teaching Fellows Program was originally established at the University of Georgia in 1984 as a result of a grant from the Lilly Endowment. In 1987, the program was continued with full support from the university. Each year, up to ten faculty members are selected to participate in this two-year program. Participants must be tenure-track faculty members in their second, third, or fourth year at UGA. The goals of the program are to:

- Provide new faculty with an opportunity to further develop basic skills associated with effective teaching and other roles required by a research university

- Provide new faculty with information concerning instructional policies, resources, and services that exist at the university

- Offer a support system for sharing of ideas with colleagues from other disciplines who may have similar interests and who face similar challenges

- Develop instructional skills through exposure to and interaction with senior faculty who are master teachers

- Provide funding for an instructional project designed to strengthen courses and teaching methods in each participant's academic department

- Help reinforce an instructional environment that honors and recognizes dedicated teaching scholars; that values a synergistic relationship between teaching, research, and service; and that promotes a learning-community spirit on a large campus

To date, over 160 faculty members have participated in the Lilly Fellows Program. Over 100 of these faculty members are still at UGA and are active in promoting excellence in teaching and learning on the campus.

The Senior Teaching Fellows Program. The Senior Teaching Fellows Program was originally established at the University of Georgia in 1987 through a three-year grant from the United States Department of Education's Fund for the Improvement of Post-Secondary Education (FIPSE). In 1990, the program was continued with full support from the university. Each year, eight faculty members are selected to participate in this one-year program. Any faculty member with the rank of associate or full professor who has been at the University of Georgia for at least five years is eligible for nomination to the program. Candidates may be self-nominated or nominated by their colleagues, department head, or dean. The goals of the program are to:

- Provide senior faculty with an opportunity to focus on undergraduate instruction

- Provide senior faculty with opportunities for the sharing of ideas with other dedicated, highly motivated, and innovative teachers from other disciplines who may have similar interests and who face similar teaching challenges

- Provide senior faculty with opportunities for professional and personal renewal

- Provide funding for an instructional project designed to strengthen courses and teaching methods in each participant's academic department

- Help reinforce an instructional environment that honors and recognizes dedicated teaching scholars; that values a synergistic relationship between teaching, research, and service; and that promotes a learning community spirit on a large campus

To date, 111 faculty members have participated in the Senior Fellows Program. Only two participants are now at other institutions (one is now dean of a law school, the other is a vice provost). Twenty-nine participants are retired. Many of these retired faculty members are actively engaged in the life of the university (13 are now members of the UGA teaching academy).

Teaching Awards

Two campus-wide teaching awards were established in the late 1980s and early 1990s that have significantly enhanced the visibility and respect for teaching at the university.

Meigs Award for Excellence in Teaching. As part of the perceived need to promote and recognize teaching excellence, the university established a campus-wide teaching award in 1982, in honor of the university's second president, Josiah Meigs. Award winners were recognized at a campus-wide award ceremony and received discretionary funds to support their teaching programs. In 1988, the vice president for academic affairs elevated the status of the awards by including a permanent salary increase of $5,000, in addition to the one time $1,000 discretionary allowance. The salary increment has since been raised to $6,000.

Today, up to five Josiah Meigs Teaching Awards are given each year to faculty members across all disciplines. Meigs Award recipients are recognized at a campus-wide teaching award banquet. Video teaching biographies of each winner are produced. The videos are premiered at the award banquet, used for public relations purposes, and are run periodically on the university's cable channel. Biographical pieces are also run in the campus newspaper. (In some past years, the awardees rode in the homecoming parade.) As of this publication, 65 faculty members have been recipients of the Meigs Award.

The Meigs Award is significant because it both recognizes and rewards teaching, while conveying to young faculty members and graduate students that the university is serious about teaching. The award is also a means for addressing salary differences between outstanding teachers and outstanding researchers. For the most part, however, award winners receive their awards and return to their private lives as teachers. Until 1999, the Meigs Award lacked a mechanism for award winners to share their teaching expertise with one another or with the larger university community.

Richard B. Russell Undergraduate Teaching Award. The Richard B. Russell Undergraduate Teaching Award at the University of Georgia is named to honor university alumnus Richard B. Russell, a United States Senator of the state of Georgia from 1932 to 1970, who had a love for new knowledge and an appreciation of our nation's youth. The award was established in 1992, and its purpose is to recognize excellence in undergraduate instruction at UGA by faculty members in their early academic careers. Three awards are made each year. Awardees receive a $5,000 cash award from the Richard B. Russell Foundation.

Eligibility for the Russell Award is limited to tenure-track faculty members engaged in undergraduate instruction, who have been at the university a minimum of three years at the time of the actual award, and who have been in a tenure-track position for a total of no more than ten years. To date, 30 faculty members have received the award.

Formation of the UGA Teaching Academy

With the hard work of many administrators and faculty members throughout the 1980s and 1990s the research-teaching pendulum has swung back toward the middle where teaching is valued—perhaps not equally to research, but much closer than it was in the 1960s and 1970s. The establishment of an office of instructional support and development with its suite of faculty development programs, and the establishment of two significant teaching awards are tangible evidence of this shift in the campus culture. By the end of the 1990s, the conditions and climate for establishing a teaching academy at UGA were ideal. A survey was administered in spring 1998, asking faculty for their thoughts on forming a teaching academy at UGA. The responses were overwhelmingly positive. An ad hoc committee was formed to suggest a framework for an academy. In October 1999, after deliberating and planning for some 15 months, the committee (later to be called the executive committee) established the University of Georgia Teaching Academy.

Mission, goals, and values. The first and most critical issue addressed by the executive committee was to establish the Academy's mission, goals, and core values. After much debate, the following was adopted:

- Mission: The mission of the academy is to promote and celebrate excellence in teaching and to foster learning through inquiry

- Goals: The Academy will promote faculty leadership to enhance teaching and learning, to advocate for effective educational environments, and to foster a community of scholars

- Core values: We believe that educating students is a fundamental responsibility of every faculty member of the University of Georgia and that teachers are catalysts for effective learning

A preamble was drafted to integrate the teaching academy's mission statement into the larger context of the university's mission (Table 5.1).

TABLE 5.1
The University of Georgia Teaching Academy Preamble

Whereas the great purpose of higher education is the strongest obligation to form the youth, the rising hope of our land, to render the like capable and dedicated to glorious and essential service.

Whereas the faculty of the University of Georgia share a special commitment to the value and practicality of higher education and an obligation to promote a culture of inquiry, a passion for learning, a community of scholars and a contempt for ignorance, apathy and indifference.

Whereas the University was founded on the vision of a land-grant institution with its roots in and commitment to serving all people of the state with the knowledge and skills that uplift the economic, cultural and spiritual well-being of the common citizen.

Whereas the public's expectations and sensibilities of the University's commitment to teaching and learning are great and prudent.

Whereas the teaching and learning mission of the University is the strength and only non-proprietary enterprise of the University.

Whereas the University's tripartite mission in teaching, research and service enhances and enriches the learning environment and whereas faculty engaged in such activities have the fortune and obligation to share the fruits of their knowledge and activities in the glorious enterprise of teaching.

Therefore we solemnly commit ourselves to establishing a University of Georgia Teaching Academy to celebrate and engage the larger University community to embrace the joy, passions and rewards of teaching and learning. The charter members of the University Teaching Academy duly enact and embrace this assembly of scholars and promote its just and necessary causes and ambitions on this twenty-seventh day of October in the year nineteen hundred ninety-nine. We declare by these signatures that this body be hereby created.

Membership. The second and equally critical issue was membership. That is, what criteria should be established for membership? In developing membership guidelines, members of the executive committee were concerned that the teaching academy play a significant service and advocacy role for teaching and learning at the university. They wanted the academy to be more than merely honorific. They recognized that there are many excellent and committed faculty members on campus, but felt it important for would-be members to express a commitment to the academy and its goals and activities.

In 2000, Meigs Teaching Award recipients and faculty members who had participated in the Senior Teaching Fellows Program were invited to join the teaching academy. Meigs recipients had been recognized for their teaching excellence and would bring a rich set of expertise and experience to the academy. Senior Teaching Fellows work together as a group for one year, have experience in developing collaborative teaching projects, and were expected to bring that collaborative spirit to the academy. As a prerequisite for membership, nominees were asked to submit reflective essays on their teaching philosophy and their personal vision for the academy. Fifty-two nominees accepted the invitation and comprised the academy's inaugural class of 2000.

In 2001, 126 faculty members were invited to join the academy. Those invited included the four 2001 Meigs Award recipients, the eight 2001–2002 Senior Teaching Fellows, all Richard B. Russell Award recipients up to 1995, and all Lilly Teaching Fellows still at UGA from the years 1984 through 1994. The purpose of expanding to the Russell Award recipients and Lilly Teaching Fellows was to ensure that views of less senior members of the faculty were included in the work of the academy. In the spirit of inclusiveness, the teaching academy now consists of 130 members who represent the university's most outstanding and dedicated teachers.

Funding. The third issue faced by the academy was one of support and funding. In its formative years, the academy partnered with the office of instructional support and development (OISD), the institute of higher education (IHE), and the office of the senior vice president for academic affairs and provost. OISD and the provost's office serve as the support units for the academy and the IHE serves as the academy's academic partner. The academy represents the faculty-initiated and faculty-driven component of this triad. To date, the academy's support needs have been shared among these units and the offices of the executive committee. As the academy grows, a more permanent support structure will be established. With respect to funding, the academy requested and received a $6,000 grant from the university president's venture fund. These funds are available for start-up projects and organizations with the potential to benefit the university community. These venture funds have served as seed monies in the academy's efforts to identify donors.

Programs and activities. The fourth issue faced by the academy was to define programs and activities. That is, what roles were these outstanding and dedicated faculty members expected to play as members of the teaching academy? The academy's programs are expected to complement and build upon faculty teaching roles. The executive committee wanted to create a forum for members to share their teaching expertise and to learn from each other.

PROGRAMS AND ACTIVITIES OF THE UNIVERSITY OF GEORGIA TEACHING ACADEMY

In its first years of operation (2000–2002), the teaching academy sponsored a number of projects and activities to promote interaction among teachers across disciplines. The working philosophy of the academy has been to encourage opportunities for participation and engagement at all sponsored events. This section describes some of the major programs and activities sponsored by the academy.

Member Workshops

Inaugural workshop: Fall 2000. At the outset, the academy wanted to convey that membership was not merely honorific but that its members were expected to contribute to and participate in the academy's activities. Hence, a workshop was held as part of the induction ceremony for the inaugural class of teaching academy members. The workshop, "Taking Teaching Seriously: An Agenda for the Georgia Teaching Academy," asked members to discuss the proper role of the academy and to develop goals and action plans to promote teaching and learning on campus. It was suggested that the teaching academy work toward:

- Making teaching "community property"
- Creating a center for undergraduate teaching opportunities
- Encouraging the establishment of chaired teaching professorships
- Engaging the teaching talents and experience of retiring faculty
- Establishing interdisciplinary teaching circles
- Establishing teacher mentoring programs
- Sponsoring workshops and seminars to promote excellence in teaching and learning

Workshop recommendations were used by the executive committee to develop an agenda of activities for the teaching academy. Clearly, some recommendations are long term in nature and require considerable funding. It is hoped that others can be implemented rather quickly and with minimal resources.

Fall 2001 workshop. The teaching academy's fall 2001 workshop, "Roles and Rewards of Teaching Faculty at Georgia: Teaching Academy Recommendations," discussed possible changes in the reward system for the role of teaching. Over 80 faculty members attended, and the workshop results have been presented to the provost.

Teaching Academy Forums

For faculty engagement to be effective and sustaining, opportunities for frequent interaction must be created. To promote interaction among its members, the academy sponsors or co-sponsors a major teaching forum each semester. These forums feature prominent speakers and include meal functions, small group sessions, a major lecture, panel discussions, and a reception. In these early years, the forums have focused on prominent speakers from outside the university who are renowned from their contributions to teaching and learning. A summary of teaching academy speakers to date is shown in Table 5.2.

TABLE 5.2
University of Georgia Teaching Academy Lectures

Semester	Speaker	Biographical Information	Lecture Title
Fall 2000	John Gardner	Senior Fellow of the National Resource Center for the First-Year Experience and Students in Transition	*The Undergraduate Bookends: The First-Year Experience and the Senior-Year Experience*
Spring 2001	James Muyskens	Chief Executive Officer and Dean of Faculty, Gwinnett University Center	*Education By All Means*
Fall 2001	Richard J. Light	Professor of Education, Kennedy School of Government and Graduate School of Education, Harvard University	*What Students, Faculty, and Administrators Can Do to Enrich the College Experience*

Attendance at teaching academy forums has exceeded expectations and the quality of interaction at the presentations has been excellent. Still, not all academy members fully participate in these forums because of scheduling problems. Hence, other opportunities for interaction were explored.

Other Activities and Special Projects

The teaching academy consists of the university's most outstanding and recognized teachers. Many of its members are involved in faculty governance at the department, college, and university levels. The expertise and citizenship of academy members are in high demand. Recognizing the demands on the members' time, the executive committee has been guarded in requests made of its members. Thus far, the academy has been reluctant to assume complete responsibility for ongoing campus teaching activities. Instead, efforts have been made to tap the expertise of the academy without asking them to commit large amounts of time. Three such requests were made of the academy this past year. First, the academy was asked to recommend books that would be assigned reading for entering freshmen. *A Civil Action* by Jonathan Harr (1995) emerged from the academy's recommendation and was assigned to students entering the university's freshmen college, summer 2001.

Second, the university recently created what we hope will be a new tradition for the institution: an opening convocation to welcome all new students and faculty members to the campus. The first two years, an alumnus delivered the main speech. In 2001, the teaching academy was asked to nominate members from its ranks to deliver a message from the faculty.

Third, the academy was asked to recommend topics and issues for the university's annual academic affairs faculty symposium. For the past ten years, the provost has sponsored a two-day symposium at an off-campus location to discuss critical issues in academic affairs. Each year, some 60 to 80 faculty members from across the university are invited to participate in these symposia. The recommendations of the teaching academy will be used to plan future symposia. Six teaching academy members will serve on the planning committee for the 2002 academic affairs symposium titled "The Challenge of Becoming Extraordinary Teachers at a Public Research University: How Do We Get There?"

Future Projects

Recognizing that faculty members are busy people, the executive committee has explored ways for teaching academy members to interact on their own schedules. After all, the academy's goals are to promote interaction among members and between members and nonmembers. That is, the energy and expertise in teaching and learning lies with the academy's members, and interaction at the member level is thought to be the most productive. With this in mind, the executive committee surveyed the membership to explore their interest in various mentoring arrangements. It is hoped that these various mentoring projects can be implemented in the coming years. A critical resource for the mentoring project is the new book, *Extraordinary Teachers,* edited by Teaching Academy member Fred Stephenson (2001). The book is a collection of 36 inspiring and thought-provoking essays by the university's outstanding teachers and Meigs Award recipients, many of which are members of the teaching academy, and represents more than 1,000 years of teaching experience.

The teaching academy now has a web site (http://teachingacademy.uga .edu), and the reader can see how the teaching academy continues to evolve over the coming years.

IMPLICATIONS FOR FACULTY DEVELOPMENT

The formation of the University of Georgia Teaching Academy represents a culmination of efforts to change the culture of this research university. The academy is an affirmation by a major research university that teaching and learning are central to the mission of the institution. Moreover, it represents a major step to extend the recognition of teaching by outstanding faculty members beyond one-time recognition.

The academy is another means by which teaching and learning can be celebrated and promoted. The academy creates a community of scholars who value and promote teaching and learning, a community that can energize and celebrate teaching and learning on a larger scale than has been possible on this campus. The academy is a logical and opportune outgrowth of the faculty development initiatives in the office of instructional support and development and the university's highest teaching awards. The academy will build upon and enhance the impact of these initiatives. One way the academy can extend faculty development efforts is by providing an ongoing forum for campus conversations on teaching and learning. That is, the academy represents an institutionalized forum for peer collaboration of teaching and learning. The academy, as a faculty organized and directed organization, democratizes the vision for teaching and learning on campus and gives faculty ownership to setting the teaching and learning agendas on campus.

CONCLUSION

The University of Georgia Teaching Academy is in its formative years. Assessing the academy's impact on the university community is premature at this point. Until an assessment is made, what outcomes would the teaching academy like to accomplish? An overriding goal has been to create a forum for interaction among teachers across disciplines. As an inclusive organization, the academy seeks to blur the distinction between teaching and research and to create a more collaborative model for teaching and learning. The academy would like to cultivate a campus climate where teaching and learning are shared responsibilities of all faculty. Finally, it is hoped that the academy can have a significant impact on the teaching and learning process at the University of Georgia.

Acknowledgments

The authors wish to acknowledge and thank their colleague and dear friend, Ronald D. Simpson, who was the first permanent director of the office of instructional development and the inspiration for so many good things related to teaching at the University of Georgia. They also thank their fellow members on the executive committee of the teaching academy: Robert Anderson, Jeanne Barsanti, Patricia Bell-Scott, Joe Crim, Ron Carlson, Sylvia Hutchinson, Jeremy Kilpatrick, Peter Shedd, Fred Stephenson, and Susette Talarico.

References

Chism, N. V. N., Fraser, J. M., & Arnold R. L. (1996). Teaching academies: Honoring and promoting teaching through a community of expertise. *New directions for teaching and learning: Honoring exemplary teaching.* San Francisco, CA: Jossey-Bass.

Dyer, T. G. (1985). *The University of Georgia: A bicentennial history 1785–1985.* Athens, GA: The University of Georgia Press.

Harr, J. (1995). *A civil action.* New York, NY: Vintage Books.

Stephenson, F. J. (2001). *Extraordinary teachers: The essence of excellent teaching.* Kansas City, MO: Andrews McMeel Publishing.

Contact:

Patricia Kalivoda
Assistant Vice President for Academic Affairs
Administration Building
University of Georgia
Athens, GA 30602
Voice   (706) 542-0415
Fax   (706) 542-2698
Email   tlk@uga.edu

Josef Broder
Assistant Dean for Academic Affairs
College of Agricultural and Environmental Sciences
University of Georgia
Athens, GA 30602
Voice   (706) 542-1611
Fax   (706) 542-2130
Email   jbroder@arches.uga.edu

William K. Jackson, Director
Office of Instructional Support and Development
University of Georgia
Athens, GA 30602
Voice   (706) 542-1355
Fax   (706) 542-6587
Email   bjackson@arches.uga.edu

Patricia Kalivoda is Assistant Vice President for Academic Affairs at the University of Georgia and Coordinator of Faculty Development for the university's Office of Instructional Support and Development. She also holds an adjunct faculty position in the university's Institute of Higher Education. Dr. Kalivoda is a charter member and serves on the Executive Committee of the University of Georgia Teaching Academy.

Josef Broder is Assistant Dean for Academic Affairs in the College of Agricultural and Environmental Sciences and D. W. Brooks Distinguished Professor of Agricultural and Applied Economics at the University of Georgia. He is a charter member and serves as executive committee chair of the University of Georgia Teaching Academy. Dr. Broder is best known for his numerous publications on teaching and undergraduate student affairs. He has developed and used case studies for classroom instruction and professional development.

William K. Jackson is Director of the Office of Instructional Support and Development at the University of Georgia. In this role he is responsible for a comprehensive array of faculty, teaching assistant, and instructional development programs. He is also a charter member of the University of Georgia Teaching Academy and serves on the academy's executive committee. Jackson holds graduate degrees in physics and educational administration (higher education) from the University of South Carolina and has 34 years of experience in faculty and administrative positions.

6

Using Cooperative Games for Faculty Development

Barbara J. Millis
United States Air Force Academy

Learning through games has been going on for centuries. Faculty developers, however, are only now realizing the impact of well-structured and well-planned games. They not only "educate" engaged faculty members, but they can also motivate them. This chapter discusses the educational value of games, reveals their key underlying principles, and offers two examples of successful faculty development games (scavenger hunt and Bingo) that can be replicated on any campus.

INTRODUCTION

Games probably go back to the times when early homo-sapiens needed to relax after a strenuous mammoth hunt. Costello (1991) states that the earliest known game board, measuring only seven by three inches, probably can be dated between 4000–3500 BC. Found in a predynastic cemetery in El-Mehasna, Egypt, it seems to be an early version of Senet, a backgammon-type game known through tomb paintings to be popular in ancient Egypt. Games have been found wherever humans gather and appear to have been adapted from culture to culture. For example, variations of the popular African strategy game, Mancala, have been found in East and West Africa, southern India, and Sri Lanka. Because of their competitive nature, games can have more sinister consequences, as in the Mayan and Aztec ball courts, but, for the most part, games typically appeal to the human love of play.

In fact, faculty developers who downplay individual competition and emphasize cooperation can capitalize on the team-building camaraderie of games as well as their potential to enhance learning. This chapter will explore some of the theory behind creative games and conclude with two specific games easily adapted for a number of faculty development opportunities.

THE SOLID EDUCATIONAL BASIS OF GAMES

El-Shamy (in press) defines a game as a "competitive activity played according to rules within a given context, where players meet a challenge in their attempt to accomplish a goal and win" (p. 21). She distinguishes a game from a simulation in that the latter often deliberately sets up an uneven playing field where players begin unequally or receive unequal treatment as the simulation progresses. Furthermore, unlike the fantasy worlds prevalent in some games, simulations often mirror real-life situations and encourage players to gain insights and/or to build their professional skills by making informed decisions.

Both games and simulations prove to be effective learning tools for several reasons. They reinforce many theories of educational development. Adult learning theory, for example, emphasizes self-directed, goal-oriented learning. When adult faculty members are invested in the subject matter and the game itself, they willingly support one another and master critical material such as the laws governing harassment in the workplace or university guidelines regarding diversity issues. Games also appeal to a variety of senses, particularly the visual, auditory, and kinesthetic, making them attractive to different types of learners. New developments in cognitive psychology emphasize the role of emotions in learning: Games create a positive association and also allow for the repetition and deeper processing that strengthens neural pathways. Further, they offer multiple opportunities for feedback on learning. Bransford, Brown, and Cocking (2000) emphasize that "students need feedback about the degree to which they know when, where, and how to use the knowledge they are learning" (p. 59). Many games offer opportunities for application with immediate feedback. As Thiagarajan (1999) reminds us, "Learners cannot master skills without repeated practice and feedback" (p. vii).

When cooperative elements are introduced, games can become even more effective. Having participants work in teams or pairs offers tremendous advantages over individuals competing against other individuals. The research base for this conclusion comes from a variety of disciplines, including cognitive psychology, as suggested above. Social interdependence theory, for example, postulates that individuals focused on a common goal (winning!) develop positive links. Kurt Lewin (1948) states that groups develop their interdependent identity through their common goals. Additionally, the anxiety level lessens when faculty members are able to pool their knowledge and resources. The social context heightens team motivation. Furthermore, the dialogue and discussion that occurs within the teams as they respond to questions encourages higher-order thinking such as analysis and evaluation. Feedback is enhanced by the immediate response of peer faculty members, leading to reflection and reinforcement.

PRINCIPLES UNDERLYING EFFECTIVE GAME USE WITH FACULTY

In the classroom, instructors will assign students specific material to master prior to the game and then use the in-class game activity as a means of processing the information and providing feedback on whether or not it has been mastered. Occasionally, a game will precede formal instruction. Popular in corporations and training settings, games and simulations can also play an important role in developing positive interrelationships. Depending on the context and goal, when using games—usually in a workshop setting—faculty developers probably place equal weight on the social elements and the knowledge acquisition aspects. As with students, they are cognizant of key principles to optimize faculty learning and collegiality.

First, faculty participants must understand the relevance of any games to the workshop/university goals. Adult learners typically find games a waste of time if they perceive them to be frivolous. Faculty members in particular want a practical pay off: How can I use what I have experienced to further my own professional goals? Where, down the road, is the payoff, particularly in the classroom? Thus, any game activity must be preceded by clear explanations, including a careful rationale linked to overall goals.

Second, to ensure the educational value of games, faculty developers must match the level of challenge to faculty members' skills. A key credo here is "know thy faculty." During an orientation, for example, adjunct faculty new to the institution but with considerable experience will bring a variety of teaching/learning skills that can be tapped during an interactive game. Faculty totally new to teaching, on the other hand, can provide insights gleaned as learners but may not be able to augment them with teaching applications. Thus, games used during faculty development activities should offer challenges to all faculty participants, but the material should not be so complex that anyone feels overwhelmed—and thus gives up—or so simple that more knowledgeable faculty members lose interest in participating. In the latter case, sometimes faculty may relish the opportunity to help less experienced colleagues, but unless an event has been publicized with that goal, it is unlikely they will return to a second event out of pure altruism.

Third, to ensure continuing interest, games should be designed so that they are predicated on a combination of knowledge and luck. This premise is extremely important because otherwise one or two dominant faculty teams will discourage other teams from contributing their best efforts. If only knowledge is involved, then the same teams will repeatedly win, a disincentive for other teams to master the material prior to play (if applicable) or to continue trying to score if they fall behind. If the game is predicated only on luck, then obviously faculty members have no incentive to review the material prior to play. Because the luck of the draw determines the placement of markers, Bingo illustrates well this combination of knowledge and luck.

Fourth, to maximize learning, as mentioned earlier, games should be structured cooperatively. There can be competition between teams, but optimum learning will take place during the independent learning accomplished prior to the game (if this is possible with a faculty workshop) and the peer coaching that occurs as the team players agree on a response. Peer consultations reinforce learning or provide instantaneous feedback that learning was nonexistent, incomplete, or misguided. Plus, in a faculty development setting, these interactions cement team bonds and promote faculty interactions beyond the workshop itself (for a complete look at cooperative principles, see Millis & Cottell, 1998).

Fifth, games must emphasize the targeted learning goals. Both faculty development facilitators and faculty participants must recognize that the greatest learning occurs during "processing" periods either as the game unfolds or at the end. A post-game instructor "debrief" helps faculty members learn what they have mastered or should have mastered. Too often, faculty development facilitators may gloss over these critical teachable moments in the spirit of fun or in an understandable desire to avoid preaching to the choir. This is a serious mistake—however unconscious—because the game then loses its relevance. As Sugar (1998) admonishes, "Know what you want your audience to learn or demonstrate during and after the game" (p. 8). Keen, dean of the faculty at Antioch College, states that the research on whether games promote learning is still mixed:

> It depends on whether you're savvy about why you are doing it and if you take the time to work up to it and to debrief. The rule is to spend at least as much time debriefing as you spend playing the game; otherwise, what did you do it for? (qtd. in Rhem, 1996, p. 3)

Finally, any game—but particularly those used with faculty who look for role modeling and positive teaching examples—must be well organized and well structured so that the workshop does not founder on vague instructions and confusion. Obviously, the game playing period must be appropriate for the length of time available, and the physical environment must allow faculty teams to work together. There should be an intriguing blend of novelty and familiarity. That is why well-known formats—modified to maximize learning and collegiality—such as a scavenger hunt and Bingo are particularly effective.

TWO GAMES TO PROMOTE FACULTY LEARNING AND COLLEGIALITY

The Faculty Scavenger Hunt

Like Bingo, a faculty scavenger hunt is highly versatile. It can be used for any number of faculty development activities, including graduate student workshops or new faculty orientations. The questions on the sheets given to participants are tailored to the appropriate content. Sometimes they can even reflect faculty input so that faculty developers are certain that experts in the room will be available. Prior to a faculty orientation, for example, the proposed form (Appendix 6.1) can be mailed to new faculty, asking them to indicate their confidence in responding to the given items. More important, new faculty should be asked what additional areas of expertise should be added.

To begin the play, each faculty member receives a form and listens to the instructions, which are also printed on the top of the form. Unlike traditional scavenger hunts where participants rush from person to person, frantically seeking signatures to complete their form, this faculty game emphasizes deep conversations and collegiality. Within the allotted time frame, usually 20 minutes or so, faculty are encouraged to engage in meaningful conversations with three colleagues who can exchange with them valuable insights about teaching. The faculty developer emphasizes, however, that there is no need to terminate valuable conversations because of an arbitrary time line. If two faculty members end up deeply engaged in an insightful give and take for the entire session, then that is perfectly fine. The parties involved share contact information—usually email addresses—which they each retain on their scavenger hunt forms.

As faculty mingle, the conversations are animated, intense, and totally collegial. Everyone has something to share. In fact, a problem for the faculty developer is getting everyone's attention for the concluding "awards ceremony."

The session concludes with a noncompetitive drawing that emphasizes collegiality. Faculty tear off the bottom portion of their form, which indicates their name, and place it in a designated container (they will have to be reminded to do this). The faculty developer then draws a slip and calls out the name of the lucky person. Up to three slips can be drawn in sequence (it adds a nice touch to have the "winner" draw the next slip). As their name is called, the designated faculty members then consult their signed scavenger hunt sheets and introduce in turn the colleagues they discovered as resource persons. These colleagues, who stand to be recognized, then—briefly—share their insights. Each cluster becomes, virtually instantaneously, a celebrated team. Teaching ideas abound, with many faculty (12 or more) receiving recognition from a roomful of peers. The "prizes" can be merely the recognition itself or they can be token awards (candy bars, Post-it Notes, Kleenex packets, etc.) which are claimed by each "team."

Faculty developers may wish to emphasize the classroom applications of a scavenger hunt. It can be used, for example, as a first- or second-day-of-class icebreaker. The scavenger hunt form can contain questions based on information previously collected from students (find someone who was born in Maryland/likes country-and-western music/skis) or on class-related topics (find someone who has read *The Red Badge of Courage*/invests in the stock market/considers themselves a Democrat). It can also be used as a way to identify "study buddies" prior to an exam (find someone who can explain clearly the principle of momentum/the symbolism in *Moby-Dick* the laws of supply and demand).

A faculty scavenger hunt is relatively easy to set up and conduct. More demanding are faculty development games such as Bingo.

Bingo

Bingo offers a game format easy to adapt to many faculty development needs. Bingo sheets can be created using the "Table" option on most word processing packages. Alternatively, Sugar (1998) of the Game Group has developed a set of reusable materials for a variation of Bingo called QUIZO. Bingo, often classified as a "frame game" or a "matrix game," is easily adapted to virtually any faculty development scenario where there is sufficient time for meaningful execution. If this game is used as a faculty development activity, then it is essential to also emphasize its classroom applications, such as its use for a viable, engaging review for a midterm or final examination.

Bingo becomes valuable for faculty development particularly when there is a core body of knowledge to both learn and apply. The game works best when participants come prepared to display and to share their knowledge. When a handbook is involved, for example, faculty not only study it, but they become even more involved by submitting creative Bingo questions prior to play. Thus, suitable topics might include sexual harassment laws, procedures, and case studies. A Bingo game could also be predicated on topics such as accommodations and modifications for individuals with disabilities. Perhaps one of the most effective uses of Bingo would be during a new faculty orientation where questions came from the faculty handbook. Too often new faculty have little time to read—let alone absorb—the esoteric, but often critically important "bureaucratese" in the handbooks. Thus, in a typical college/university orientation, a series of well-meaning, earnest administrators typically lecture on far-from-stimulating topics such as parking regulations, book orders, or student services. Bingo offers a refreshing alternative that virtually ensures greater retention. When new faculty receive their invitation to attend the orientation, they also receive important material such as the faculty handbook. However, their invitation also includes an instruction sheet clearly announcing the Bingo game and charging them to submit via email two (or more) well-crafted questions (Appendix 6.2). The instructions must clearly model the type of question requested, including examples, and also provide the format for submission. Faculty must submit one factual question, not a "nitpicky," irrelevant fact, but something important for all new faculty to know. For example, they might ask the location of the student counseling center, the three steps needed to obtain a parking sticker, or the name of the college/university president. The second question must involve multiple possible responses and promote higher-order thinking. Faculty, in fact, could be encouraged to write one-paragraph case studies. Typical examples might be "You are teaching an adult education class in the evening and during the break a student approaches you and confesses that he is dyslexic. He wonders if he might have some special considerations, particularly during the exam periods. How do you respond?" or "You are in your third week of teaching for IU, and you notice that students tend to be disrespectful. They eat during your class, read newspapers, accept cell phone calls, etc. What can you do to turn this situation around?"

Ironically, some faculty members need to be coached on question writing. But, this coaching also gives them a powerful incentive to strengthen their own student-directed questions in the classroom or for distance learners. Faculty tend to make their questions too rigid for the Bingo format. They need to allow for some "wiggle room" (e.g., not, "Give verbatim the university's policy on sexual harassment," but, "Paraphrase the university's policy on sexual harassment"). They also need to learn to realistically quantify answers (e.g., not "List the seven steps in a student grade appeal," but, "List three of the seven steps in a student grade appeal"). A typical entry would look like this:

Factual Question

Define plagiarism
Name: Teacher Doe

Answer: To steal or pass off the words or ideas of another as one's own, without crediting the source.

Source: *Faculty Handbook*, p. 77.

Learning to pose viable, cogent questions is a valuable skill in and of itself. For example, a Nobel prize–winning physicist, Isidor Rabi, credits his mother with prompting him to value the questions he asked above the answers he gave. When he returned from school, she would never ask him what he learned that day. Instead, she would ask, "What good questions did you ask today?" (Barell as qtd. in Costa & O'Leary, 1992, p. 59).

Faculty developers play a critical role in evaluating and categorizing the faculty-submitted questions. They eliminate any weak or inaccurate ones. They also add any significant questions that will help faculty members learn critical material. Faculty developers rank order the questions within the two categories (factual and open-ended) so that the most valuable questions will occur early in the play. They cut and paste the questions to a document that will later to be given to faculty members—or posted to a convenient web site—as a useful information sheet.

To use the questions during play, faculty developers enlarge the fonts to prepare transparencies. At the top of the transparency appears the question and the person submitting it. Space between the faculty member's name and the answer that follows it allows the answer to be easily covered when the question is posed.

Instructors purchase needed supplies: Skittles or M&Ms for the markers (seasonal markers can be candy corn or Valentine hearts), and candy bars—large and snack sizes—for the prizes (healthier prize alternatives can be bags of pretzels, cocoa packets, ballpoint pens, etc.).

To play the game, the faculty developer pairs the participants (if there is an uneven number of participants, triads can be formed). Although most faculty members know the object of Bingo (five markers in a row in any direction) and the rules of play, it is important to explain the procedures so that anyone unfamiliar with Bingo will not feel compromised or inept. Each pair receives markers and two colored work sheets (as an example, green for the factual; gold for the higher level, open-ended questions) where they record their answers and if they were right or wrong. They can also note the space where the marker is to go. An abbreviated work sheet looks like this:

Factual Questions		
Faculty Pair or Trio:		
Answer	Rt or Wrong?	Space
1. Writing Center	Rt	B2
2.		

The faculty developer then poses the questions in sequence within each category, giving sufficient time based on their complexity. To make the game faculty-centered and to allow faculty members to receive feedback on the viability and fairness of their questions, the faculty member who submitted the question is the expert/arbitrator who decides what alternative answers are acceptable. The most important questions, of course, are the open-ended ones, particularly if they involve mini-case studies that will prompt meaningful discussions. Thus, it is important to allow sufficient time for ideas to unfold.

Pairs with correct answers place a marker on the designated square (e.g., B3 or G1). The square is determined by having the pairs in turn draw a Scrabble tile or a homemade variation (B,I,N,G,O) and roll a die (they roll again if a six emerges or faculty developers can purchase ten-sided die with only five numbers at novelty shops).

Pacing is very important. The factual questions speed up play and the higher-order thinking questions, as indicated earlier, lead to valuable discussions. Thus, always mindful of the clock, a savvy Bingo facilitator will offer frequent open-ended questions for their learning value but speed up play with factual questions. This process is facilitated by having the transparences, sorted in order of their significance, on either side of an overhead projector. Faculty developers comfortable with computer projections can toggle between the two types of questions.

The first pair (often there will be ties) to cover five contiguous squares in any direction declares "Bingo." After the two (or sometimes three) faculty members select a prize, they then clear their board and continue playing until the time period ends. In a one-hour session, it is theoretically possible for every pair to become "winners."

There are many reasons to use a Bingo game format, particularly for new faculty orientations. Because faculty submit in advance questions for which they are responsible, they are far more likely to read and reflect on the desired material. Furthermore, the very process of framing questions and later receiving feedback on their value, efficacy, and fairness encourages faculty members to concentrate on a useful teaching skill. Bingo also has assessment value on a different level after the orientation session concludes. The worksheets completed by faculty pairs during play should not be discarded. Reviewed collectively, without trying to single out individuals, they offer the faculty developer —and other administrators—valuable insights into what faculty members know and do not know. They also uncover important misconceptions that might be addressed on other occasions.

Bingo games keep faculty members actively engaged with the material, thus increasing the likelihood of their remembering it. Enthusiastic and energetic, like students, they often "high-five" each other when they get a correct answer. They listen attentively to the answers and suddenly care about the material, even arcane but critically important details, such as how to prepare a proposal for the institutional review board committee.

The Bingo format used during faculty development activities models positive teaching approaches. It emphasizes what faculty should be attempting to do in their own classes and provides a concrete take-away that can be easily adapted for classroom use, particularly when used as a review for a midterm or final.

Best of all, Bingo games build faculty collegiality. The pairs who work together develop personal bonds and the whole-group discussions over the open-ended questions allow faculty to engage in meaningful conversations that would likely not occur in less structured settings.

CONCLUSION

The word "game" carries with it a certain amount of "baggage" for many educators who may echo Ms. Trunchbull's credo in the movie *Matilda:* "If you are having fun, you are not learning." Other instructors, on the contrary, have found that students become engaged in learning through carefully structured, highly interactive game formats such as Jeopardy. Similarly, faculty expecting passive lectures during faculty development events usually welcome the interactive collegiality prompted by well-organized games. Realistically, there will be the occasional curmudgeon, but by and large, if the game is introduced well—with an emphasis on its learning potential—most faculty members become eager participants. Making the games cooperative enhances both faculty involvement and their learning. Besides promoting both learning and collegiality, games can be wonderfully satisfying for faculty developers who welcome opportunities to exercise their creativity.

REFERENCES

Bransford, J. D., Brown, A. L., & Cocking, R. R. (Eds.). (2000). *How people learn: Brain, mind, experience, and school.* Commission on Behavioral and Social Sciences and Education National Research Council. Washington, DC: National Academy Press.

Costa, A. L., & O'Leary, P. W. (1992). Co-cognition: The cooperative development of the intellect. In N. Davidson & T. Worsham (Eds.), *Enhancing thinking through cooperative learning.* New York, NY: Teachers College Press.

Costello, M. J. (1991). *The greatest games of all times.* New York, NY: John Wiley and Sons.

El-Shamy, S. (in press). *Training games: Everything you need to know about using games to reinforce learning.* Sterling, VA: Stylus Press.

Lewin, K. (1948). *Resolving social conflicts.* New York, NY: Harper Press.

Millis, B., & Cottell, P. (1998). *Cooperative learning for higher education faculty.* Phoenix, AZ: Oryx Press.

Rhem, J. (1996). Urgings and cautions in student-centered teaching. *The National Teaching & Learning Forum, 5* (4), 1–5.

Sugar, S. (1998). *Games that teach: Experiential activities for reinforcing learning.* San Francisco, CA: Jossey-Bass.

Thiagarajan, S. (1999). *Teamwork and teamplay: Games and activities for building and training teams.* San Francisco, CA: Jossey-Bass.

Contact:

Barbara J. Millis
Director, Faculty Development Center for Educational Excellence
United States Air Force Academy
2354 Fairchild Dr.
Suite 4K25
USAF Academy, CO 80840
Voice   (719) 333-2549
Fax   (719) 333-4255
Email   Barbara.millis@usafa.af.mil

Barbara J. Millis received her PhD in English literature from Florida State University. The former Assistant Dean of Faculty Development at the University of Maryland, University College, she frequently offers workshops at professional conferences (AAHE, Lilly Teaching Conference, etc.) and for various colleges and universities. She publishes articles on topics such as cooperative learning; classroom observations (she was a FIPSE Project Director on this topic); the teaching portfolio; microteaching; syllabus construction; program, course, and classroom assessment/research; peer review; focus groups; and academic games. She co-authored *Cooperative Learning for Higher Education Faculty* with Philip Cottell (Oryx Press, 1998). In 2002, she co-authored *Using Simulations to Promote Learning in Higher Education* with John Hertel (Stylus Press). In 1998, she received the United States Air Force Academy's prestigious McDermott Award for Research Excellence in the Humanities and Social Sciences and the Outstanding Educator Award. After the Association of American Colleges and Universities (AAC&U) selected the Air Force Academy as a Leadership Institution, she began serving in 2001 as a liaison to the AAC&U's Greater Expectations Consortium on Quality Education.

APPENDIX 6.1

FACULTY SCAVENGER HUNT

A Dozen plus One Potential Conversations/Connections about Teaching

- This game enables you to get acquainted with at least three resource people in this room, sharing with them a meaningful conversation about teaching.

- After you have talked with three people and obtained their signatures and email addresses, please drop the bottom portion of the sheet in the designated container.

- Continue talking with people and obtaining more signatures until time is called.

- Keep the top portion of this sheet for future reference.

Find someone who...	Get his/her signature and email address
1. Is working on or has completed a teaching or professional portfolio:	
2. Can share an active learning technique they feel is particularly effective:	
3. Uses one or more games in their teaching and can explain why they do so:	
4. Finds that case studies are effective learning tools:	
5. Can tell you about a classroom challenge they overcame:	
6. Uses permanent or semi-permanent groups or teams in a class:	
7. Has published an article in a teaching journal:	
8. Has something unusual in their syllabus:	
9. Has won a teaching award and can explain why they thought the judges awarded it:	

10. Has ever designed a poor exam or a poor
    exam question:

    _____

11. Considers themselves effective at motivating
    students to learn:

    _____

12. Can share an approach for learning
    student names rapidly:

    _____

13. Uses technology in a creative, effective way:

    _____

- Detach Here -

Your Name:

APPENDIX 6.2

Dear Joe/Josephine New-Faculty-Member:

Welcome to Innovative University! We encourage/require you to attend the Orientation meeting scheduled...

Because our college/university believes in active learning and student involvement, we intend at Orientation to "practice what we teach." Thus, rather than lecture to our captive audience, we prefer that you come prepared to share what you know about the institution, about higher education regulations and required practices, and about effective teaching. You will find enclosed materials [Listed] that will help you to become more knowledgeable.

To reinforce this knowledge and to add an element of fun and collegiality, we will use the final hour of the orientation session to play in pairs "Innovative University Bingo." Prizes are involved! You will literally be a key player not only during the game, but beforehand as well. Thus, we need you to submit by August XX two well-crafted questions to our Dean of Faculty, Dr. Ima Believer, preferably at her email address, ImaB@IU.edu, or alternatively, at her office address in the enclosed *IU Faculty Handbook.*

The questions should be of two types: 1) factual, with one right answer, and, 2) open-ended with alternative solutions. For the latter, you might want to write a one-paragraph mini-case, based on information/guidance in the faculty handbook. These questions should lead to productive paired discussions as options are weighed and then informative whole-group discussions as the possible solutions are evaluated by the person who submitted the question. [Note: Knowledgeable orientation staff will also share information when appropriate.]

These questions need to be suitable for a Bingo game format. Thus, they should not require rote memorization of overly complex material. They should, however, promote both learning and discussion about complex issues. They should also be questions predicated on what new faculty genuinely need to know. Please don't include anything obscure or irrelevant such as the name of the assistant librarian for technological frustrations. Be certain that you understand both your questions and the appropriate answers because you will be the expert/arbitrator called upon to approve/disapprove alternative answers, particularly with the open-ended questions.

Because we will be enlarging the font size to prepare transparencies for the game and also using your questions to prepare a useful information sheet for all attendees, we ask that you follow a set format. Please indicate the following: The question, followed by your name underneath, and then the answer, preferably with a direct reference to the source (e.g., *IU Faculty Handbook*, p. 16). Sample questions from last year's orientation are below.

We look forward to seeing you soon!

Sincerely,

Dr. I. Love Orientation

7

Proven Faculty Development Tools That Foster the Scholarship of Teaching in Faculty Learning Communities

Milton D. Cox
Miami University

Faculty learning communities have played a key role in the development of the scholarship of teaching and learning at Miami University for over 20 years. This chapter describes a sequence of developmental steps, evidence of success, and supporting documents and artifacts that can guide faculty developers in a community approach to the development of this scholarship.

INTRODUCTION

Two of the most interesting and challenging initiatives at the forefront of faculty development involve the scholarship of teaching and learning (SoTL) and faculty learning communities (Cox, in press). These two items are relatively new to faculty development; for example, neither is mentioned in the Wright and O'Neil (1994) international survey of teaching improvement practices. This chapter outlines the faculty development tools that have been developed over the last 23 years to aid the successful connection and implementation of these two initiatives in the Faculty Learning Community Program at Miami University.

Development, institutionalization, and national recognition of SoTL is now of keen interest. For example, in 1998 the Carnegie Academy for the

Scholarship of Teaching and Learning (CASTL) began three interrelated approaches (Cambridge, 2001; Hutchings, 2000): 1) the PEW National Fellowship Program for Carnegie Scholars, which brings together nationally selected scholars to carry out SoTL projects in their disciplines, 2) the Teaching Academy Campus Program, in which faculty at an institution come together to determine what SoTL should be on their campus and ways to build a culture that will foster SoTL, and 3) work with professional disciplinary societies to foster SoTL. Miami University's Faculty Learning Communities Program provides a long-term picture of how the first two approaches can evolve successfully at an institution over a 20-year period.

In the following sections, faculty learning communities will be briefly reviewed, SoTL issues in relation to Miami University's Faculty Learning Communities Program will be discussed, and the faculty development process and enabling artifacts will be provided.

FACULTY LEARNING COMMUNITIES AND SoTL ISSUES

Faculty Learning Communities

Faculty learning communities—their goals, activities, format, examples, outcomes, compensation and rewards, application process and selection criteria, role as change agents, evidence of success, and recommendations for initiation, etc.—are discussed by Cox (2001a). Briefly, each faculty learning community is a cross-disciplinary community of eight to ten faculty engaged in an active, collaborative, year-long curriculum focused on enhancing and assessing student learning, with frequent activities that promote learning, development, the scholarship of teaching and learning, and community. A faculty participant in any faculty learning community selects a focus course in which to try out innovations, assess resulting student learning, and prepare a course mini-portfolio to report the results. Each participant develops a teaching project, engages in retreats and biweekly seminars, works with student associates, and presents project results to the campus and at national conferences. Evidence shows that faculty learning communities provide effective deep learning that encourages and supports faculty to investigate, attempt, assess, and adopt new (to them) methods. In 2001–2002 there were six faculty learning communities running at Miami University. Four are topic-based (issue-focused): problem-based learning, technology, United States cultures course development, and ethics across the honors curriculum. The other two faculty learning communities are cohort-based: one for junior faculty, in place for 23 years (Cox, 1995, 1997), and one for senior faculty, in place for 11 years (Cox & Blaisdell, 1995).

The Definition and Meaning of SoTL

The definition and meaning of SoTL is a matter of debate (Hutchings & Shulman, 1999; Kreber, 2001a; Kreber & Cranton, 2000; Richlin 2001a). Boyer (1990) and Rice (1990) identified and named the concept of the scholarship of teaching (and learning) and associated it with scholarly teaching rather than the type of scholarship they defined for the scholarships of discovery, integration, and application. Miami University's Faculty Learning Communities Program interprets scholarly teaching and SoTL as articulated by Richlin (2001a):

> [S]cholarly teaching and the scholarship of teaching are closely inter-related. However, they differ in both their intent and product.... [T]he purpose of scholarly teaching is to impact the activity of teaching and the resulting learning, whereas the scholarship of teaching results in a formal, peer-reviewed communication in the appropriate media or venue, which then becomes part of the knowledge base of teaching and learning in higher education. (p. 58)

In Miami's Faculty Learning Communities Program, this has always been the interpretation of SoTL. For example, a Miami junior faculty learning community participant in English wrote the following in her 1980–1981 final report (Miami University, 1981):

> My project for the year—to revise and improve my American Literature survey classes—has proved most interesting. At the moment I am still compiling the materials and examining the results of the class that I revised and taught in the Spring. Preliminary indications suggest that the class was one of my most successful thus far at Miami— the students' writing apprehension decreased at a significance rate below the .01 level of confidence, their interest in reading and interpreting literature increased, and their overall abilities to write about literature improved. I have submitted a proposal to present material from my class at a national conference next year, and I am working on an article on combining literature and writing instruction in the classroom. (pp. 7–8)

This faculty learning community participant's scholarly approach resulted in SoTL. In 1985, the above project was incorporated into a book, *Literature: Options for Reading and Writing* (Daiker, Fuller, & Wallace, 1989), now in its second edition, which the faculty learning community participant coauthored with her faculty learning community mentor and a colleague.

Developmental Stages of Individuals

There are several models that attempt to describe an individual's progress toward practicing SoTL. Smith (2001) adapts two models of expertise: Kennedy's (1987) views of expertise and Dreyfus and Dreyfus's (1986) stages of expertise from novice to expert.

Weston and McAlpine's (2001) developmental three-phase continuum of growth describes a professor's journey toward SoTL. In each phase, processes are listed vertically in the order of less complex to more complex. Vertical (within a phase) and lateral (across phases) movement is possible. In Phase 1, growth in one's own teaching, a professor develops a personal knowledge of his or her teaching and students' learning. In Phase 2, dialogues with colleagues about teaching and learning, faculty start with conversations in their discipline and move to multidisciplinary engagement, for "It is necessary to get a sense of community before moving into scholarship" (Weston & McAlpine, 2001, p. 91). This model confirms the effectiveness of faculty learning communities in the development of SoTL. Phase 3, growth in SoTL, covers the same vertical ground as shown in Table 7.1 and is explained in the next section. Cox (in press) modifies and refines this model in light of faculty learning community evidence over the years.

Ronkowski (1993) describes the development of TAs as scholarly teachers in three categories using three stages. The three categories are from Boyer (1990) and Rice (1990): synoptic capacity, pedagogical content knowledge, and knowledge about student meaning making. For example, in the third category, Stage 1 involves the understanding of student backgrounds, concerns, expectations, and abilities similar to those that TAs themselves have experienced. Stage 2 involves developing and using general teaching strategies and skills to address course content. Stage 3 concerns student learning and experiences with various learning styles and cognitive development. Cox (in press) provides a model adapted from Baxter-Magolda (1992); Belenky, Clinchy, Goldberger, and Tarule (1986); and Perry (1970). For example, in Stage 1, faculty are in silence, having developed no voice in SoTL, or they are dualistic in that they believe there is only one right way to teach, or that the teaching experts have the answers.

Other SoTL Issues

Additional SoTL issues that have appeared in the recent literature also have links to faculty learning communities. Although these take us away from the focus of this chapter, they are worth noting. They include ways to do SoTL (Cross, 1998; Cross & Steadman, 1996; Hutchings, 2000), the connection of SoTL to practice (Menges & Weimer, 1996; Weimer, 2001), the publication of SoTL (Richlin, 2001b; Weimer, 1993), the assessment of SoTL (Glassick, Huber, & Maeroff, 1997; Theall & Centra, 2001), and the relationship of SoTL and teaching portfolios (Hutchings, 1998; Kreber, 2001b).

THE SoTL: FACULTY LEARNING COMMUNITY CONNECTION

Miami University's first faculty learning community was for junior faculty and was initiated in 1979 as a result of a grant from the Lilly Endowment. As part of the endowment's Teaching Fellows Program during 1979–1980 through 1981–1982, the Miami faculty learning community incorporated all five of the Lilly components: regular group meetings, release time, senior faculty mentors, individual projects, and retreats and conferences (Austin, 1990, 1992; Cox, 1995). Each of these components played a role in the development of SoTL in faculty learning communities at Miami. Viewed in the current construct, the five components had the potential of providing community and, thus, support for and peer review of projects (the group meetings), scholarly teaching, time to investigate and implement a project (release time), experience and advice for scholarly investigations and peer review (senior faculty mentors), potential for SoTL (the teaching projects), and a venue for making public the SoTL (the retreats and conferences).

Fostering SoTL in a faculty learning community involves a sequence of developmental steps. Developed over the years, these faculty learning community steps and their SoTL results are indicated in Table 7.1. These steps also illustrate the ongoing cycle of scholarly teaching and SoTL (Richlin, 2001a).

TABLE 7.1
The Scholarship of Teaching and Learning (SoTL):
Faculty Learning Community (FLC) Connection—
A Sequence of Ten Developmental FLC Steps and SoTL Results

Step 1: Application for FLC Membership

- Applicants prepare a response to a question asking for preliminary ideas about an individual teaching and learning project

Results

Addressing an observation—perhaps in an uninformed or indirect way—about a problem or opportunity in the teaching><learning ^{TM} connection

Step 2: Early Planning for the FLC

- FLC coordinator selects a community focus book that includes extensive references connected to the FLC topic. For a listing of books by community, see Cox (2001c)

Results

Connecting the FLC to the knowledge base of SoTL

Step 3: The Opening/Closing Retreat Before the Start of the Year

- Coordinator, new, and graduating members discuss meaning and examples of scholarly teaching, SoTL, and the ongoing cycle of scholarly teaching and SoTL (see Table 7.2)

- FLC coordinator distributes and discusses the focus book, multidisciplinary book list for optional readings, (for listing, see Cox, 2001b) and information about "hot" topics in SoTL as evidenced by Lilly Conference theme tracks (Table 7.3)

- Coordinator, new, and graduating members discuss the "Miami University Guidelines for the Design and Description of a Teaching and Learning Project" (Table 7.4) (Richlin, 2001a, pp. 66–67)

- Graduating members present their projects to the new members and then consult in breakout groups

- The new community plans the first-term activities and seminar and retreat topics

Results

Making public through peer authority the ongoing cycle, scholarly teaching, and SoTL; guiding SoTL research; connecting to a more extensive literature

Step 4: Participants Prepare for and Start the Year

- Each community member selects one course he or she is teaching in the upcoming term to be a focus course

- Each participant searches for and reads articles to inform his or her teaching and learning in the focus course and project

- Each individual designs and writes a description of his or her teaching and learning project

- Each individual prepares an initial learning plan, placing his or her teaching and learning project in context with other FLC components and activities

Results
Connecting SoTL to teaching practice; consulting the literature; choosing an intervention

Step 5: Seminars and Retreat

- Coordinator prepares and distributes and members read a booklet containing initial learning plans, focus course syllabi, and teaching and learning projects

- An external consultant familiar with the difference between scholarly teaching and SoTL reads the members' teaching and learning projects and meets with each individual to sharpen research design

- Each community member makes a short presentation to the FLC about his or her project, and the group discusses each project, making suggestions

Results
Making public SoTL for peer review

Step 6: Working on the Project During the Year

- Participants investigate other pedagogical areas, looking for connections to project

- Individuals carry out their teaching and learning projects

- Student associates and mentors (for junior faculty) consult

- Participants assess student learning and other project outcomes

- Coordinator, participants, and community consult about project outcomes

Results

Progressing along the ongoing cycle; moving from scholarly teaching toward SoTL; "conducting systematic observation, documenting observations, analyzing results, obtaining peer evaluation, identifying key issues, synthesizing results" (Richlin, 2001a, p. 59)

Step 7: Presentations During the Second Term

- Individuals, teams, and perhaps the entire community present their work at a campus-wide teaching effectiveness retreat

- Presenters incorporate feedback from peers in the audience at the campus sessions

- Individuals, teams, and perhaps the entire community present at a national conference

- Presenters incorporate feedback from the audience at the national conference

Results

Presenting SoTL; peer evaluation

Step 8: The Opening/Closing Retreat at the End of the Year

- Graduating members present their projects to and consult with the new incoming community members

Results

Teaching, mentoring, and making public SoTL

Step 9: Continuation of the Project During the Summer or the Upcoming Year

- Each individual on his or her own may apply for and use a Miami small grant or summer fellowship to continue his or her project

Results

Engaging in another round of the ongoing cycle

Step 10: Publication

- Each participant, team, or community may prepare a manuscript about the project for publication in a refereed multidisciplinary or disciplinary journal

Results
Adding to the knowledge base of SoTL

The following narrative illuminates the steps in Table 7.1 and provides documents and examples that enable the intended faculty development.

In Step 1 of the sequence, the application for membership in a faculty learning community, one question asks the applicant to indicate his or her initial ideas for an individual teaching and learning project. While this is not a crucial part of the application, it provides an opportunity for the applicant to shape an early vision of his or her project. An individual's project may change once the program is underway and the participant becomes acquainted with SoTL.

Each new participant receives a focus book selected by the faculty learning community coordinator after careful review of the literature (Step 2). The focus book provides an introduction to the faculty learning community topic and its scholarship (references) and helps generate seminar topics for the start of the upcoming term. Information about recent focus books selected by faculty learning community coordinators, who are exemplary and talented faculty graduates of faculty learning communities, are in Cox (2001c). The new members also receive a list of key multidisciplinary books that have been helpful in developing the recent teaching projects of former participants (Cox, 2001b).

In Step 3, a discussion about SoTL and its difference from but relation to scholarly teaching takes place at the faculty learning community's opening/closing retreat. Key questions direct the SoTL discussion (Table 7.2) (Cox, 1999a). Richlin's (1993, 2001a) diagram of the ongoing cycle of scholarly teaching and SoTL is helpful in explaining and understanding this relationship and difference.

TABLE 7.2

**Faculty Learning Communities: Questions to Ask
About the Scholarship of Teaching and Learning**

1. What is the scholarship of teaching?
   What is scholarly teaching?
   What is excellent teaching?

2. How do I get started?

3. What are the resources at my institution?
   Examples at Miami University:
   • Committee for the Enhancement of Learning and Teaching: Small
     Grants (submit anytime) and Summer Fellowships (due October
     16)
   • Teaching Effectiveness Library: 102 Roudebush Hall
   • *Journal on Excellence in College Teaching*
     Online: http://ject.lib.muohio.edu/

4. Will the publication or presentation be valued for promotion and
   tenure? Do I put it under teaching or scholarship?

5. What topics are "hot"?

6. Where do I present it and publish it?

The faculty learning community retreat participants then focus on their
individual teaching and learning projects. Graduating members report on
their projects and consult with the new members. For new members searching
for feasible and timely topics, the theme tracks of the most recent Lilly Conference on College Teaching can provide insight and direction (Table 7.3). An
important document distributed and discussed at the retreat is the "Guidelines for the Design and Description of Your Teaching Project" (Table 7.4). Although faculty may enter a faculty learning community as excellent scholars in
their disciplines, they often are at a loss to design a publishable teaching project. The guidelines have been developed over the years to meet this need
(Richlin, 2001a). A cost/benefit approach to selecting projects is offered by
Angelo (2000), whose questions to the project designer include: How
costly/difficult is the innovation? How beneficial/valuable is the innovation?

TABLE 7.3
What SoTL Areas Are Hot: 2001 Lilly Conference Theme Tracks
(at least five sessions on each topic)

1. Assessment
2. Cognitive Development
3. Community in Teaching and Learning
4. Creativity
5. Critical Thinking
6. Diversity/Multiculturalism
7. Early-Career Faculty
8. Ethical/Moral Issues
9. Group Learning
10. Learning Styles
11. Motivation
12. Portfolios
13. Problem-Based Learning
14. Reading
15. Research and Teaching
16. The Scholarship of Teaching and Learning
17. Science/Science Teaching
18. Service-Learning
19. Student-Centered Learning
20. Teams/Teamwork
21. Technology (Electronic)
22. Web-Based Opportunities
23. Writing

New community members depart the opening retreat more prepared to work through and write up the items in Step 4 of Table 7.1. They are also ready to attempt placing their project in the context of their teaching and other components of their faculty learning community. This document is their initial learning plan. The guidelines for and an example of an initial learning plan are in Appendixes 7.1 and 7.2, respectively. An example of a teaching project description at this pre-consultation stage is in Appendix 7.3.

Step 5 of the sequence, which occurs early in the first term, provides the first opportunity for the community to share their initial drafts of teaching projects. Another key element at this point is the consultation with an outside reviewer and consultant who is experienced with scholarly teaching and SoTL

TABLE 7.4

**Faculty Learning Communities: Guidelines for the
Design and Description of Your Teaching Project**

---

1. The Problem or Question

What is the problem (or opportunity) you wish to address with your project?

Describe what you see in your students' behavior that you wish to change, for example, aspects of content (e.g., test scores), process (e.g., ability to work in a group), or climate (e.g., morale). Be as specific as possible about what you have seen.

List the learning objectives that students will be able to achieve better after you implement your project. Put them in active statements, such as, "After completing this course, you will be able to define (analyze, identify, etc.) . . .

2. Context

What have others done (at Miami or elsewhere) to address this problem? Early in the program you may not have much of an answer here; in fact, investigating the literature may be part of your project. What topics will you investigate on databases such as ERIC?

3. Proposed Solution

How do you plan to solve the problem or answer the question? Describe what you will do to change/improve the behavior you described in question 1 above.

Are you doing anything differently than others have attempted? Why or why not? Why do you propose that your approach will succeed better than prior attempts or will work better with your students or course?

4. Evaluation

How will you determine the success and effectiveness of your solution and the impact of your project? Do you plan to determine pre- and post-results? How will you know that the behavior of your students has changed/improved? Note: You may not be able to obtain your results by the end of your year. However, you should have a plan in place to evaluate your project and report on the results. Remember, "You cannot save by analysis what you bungled by design" (Richard Light, in *By Design*).

5. Timeline

What are the dates of project initiation and completion for each step of your design, implementation, and evaluation?

(and the difference between them). In just a 20-minute individual consultation, an expert can provide valuable insights for a new and budding scholar in the SoTL field. At this point, participants are ready to move through Step 6, working on their project during the academic year.

In Step 7, the faculty learning community participants make public their teaching scholarship. They are often concerned about presenting SoTL, a "discipline" in which they are novices. After all, it took them years of graduate work to become experts in their disciplines. Appendix 7.4 on suggestions for engaging in SoTL addresses these concerns and provides guidelines for the initial presentations. This document has been most helpful in encouraging the "making public" part of SoTL. Presentations are peer reviewed, and feedback is incorporated into the next phases of the project. A list of recent presentation titles from the various communities is in Cox (2001c), and titles of SoTL publications from Miami faculty learning community participants from various disciplines are in Cox (in press).

The ongoing cycle of SoTL development for the faculty learning community project may continue once the faculty learning community participant has graduated from his or her faculty learning community. As Step 9 in the sequence indicates, internal teaching grant support is available to members for doing further investigation (Cox, 2001b).

EVIDENCE OF SUCCESS

In addition to producing their SoTL products, faculty learning community participants rate the SoTL part of the faculty learning community experience highly in their reports and evaluations of their faculty learning community experience. For example, results from the question, "Estimate the impact of the community on you with respect to each of the following components," where 1 indicates a very weak impact and 10 a very strong impact, yield an impact rating of 8.1 for the teaching project. The table of ratings for the eight common faculty learning community components across all communities up through 1999–2000 is in Cox (2001a). More recent results are in Cox (2001c). A similar analysis of 11 faculty learning community faculty development outcomes indicates that three of them, "your view of teaching as an intellectual pursuit," "your understanding of and interest in the scholarship of teaching," and "your perspective of teaching, learning, and other aspects of higher education beyond the perspective of your discipline," rank second, third, and fifth on the list with respect to the impact that members' faculty learning community had on developing that outcome. This table is in Cox (2001a); the ranking has not changed through the 2000–2001 faculty learning communities.

Another measure of the program's success is seen in the results of a year 2000 survey of faculty learning community participants to determine how their faculty learning community participation influenced student learning in their classes. One question asked the participants to "Circle the number in front of each item that indicates the degree of change in student learning due to a change in your attitude as a result of your faculty learning community participation." Table 7.5 indicates how the eight items were ranked, with the mean response and percentage of those respondents selecting the item. SoTL ranks an impressive second and was selected by 92% of the 50 respondents.

TABLE 7.5

Degree of Change in Student Learning Due to a Change in Attitude as a Result of Faculty Learning Community Participation

0	1	2	3	4
Students learned less.	No change in students' learning.	Students learned more to a small degree.	Students learned more to a medium degree.	Students learned more to a great degree.

%	$\bar{x}$	Item
98	3.3	Your general enthusiasm about teaching and learning
92	3.2	Your appreciation of teaching and learning as an intellectual pursuit: scholarly teaching and the scholarship of teaching
94	3.2	More reflective
88	2.9	More comfortable
90	2.8	More confidence
90	2.7	Revitalization
92	2.9	Inspiration
86	2.7	Courage to teach
2	4	Other: More connections to other faculty
2	4	Other: Write my own PBL problems
2	4	Other: Dynamic class participation
2	4	Other: Respect of regional campus teaching by Oxford faculty
2	4	Other: Introspection
2	3	Other: Capacity to reuse and to research on topic of instruction
2	4	Other: Examples from industry
2	4	Other: Ability to help more non-white students

Other affirmations of the program's success come from the awarding of grants to support dissemination of Miami University's Faculty Learning Communities Program to other campuses. A grant from the Ohio Board of Regents has supported the initiation of faculty learning communities for early career faculty at seven institutions to date. A three-year grant from the Fund for the Improvement of Post-Secondary Education (FIPSE) is supporting the development of 12 faculty learning communities at each of five institutions, a project just underway in 2001–2002.

IMPLICATIONS FOR FACULTY DEVELOPMENT

It is clear that faculty learning communities support the effective development of SoTL. Community is a necessary phase in the Weston and Alpine (2001) model of individual development. Although at Miami University the development of SoTL is embedded in the Faculty Learning Communities Program, at other institutions—for example, at Indiana University (Thompson & Nelson, 2000)— it is the reverse: Community comes as a result of a SoTL initiative.

Faculty learning communities and a community approach to SoTL are not generally recognized by most faculty developers, however. Instead, individual consultations and campus-wide workshops are the usual approach (Cox, 1999b). Kreber (2001c) recommends five approaches to faculty development and SoTL:

1) introduce department-wide collaborative action research in the discipline with assistance from faculty developers

2) allow faculty to negotiate contracts to focus on SoTL for a number of years, including leaves to support their SoTL investigations

3) base workshops and seminars on pedagogical research

4) establish departmental reading circles on SoTL in the discipline and encourage team teaching

5) base courses on college teaching and learning on a SoTL model

Healy (2000) also argues for a disciplinary approach. While there is potential for developing community in some of these departmental approaches, it is not the main theme or focus of the initiatives.

Kreber's (2001c) approaches also engage the question about taking departmental and/or campus-wide approaches to faculty development. Both are important. The Carnegie Academy for the Scholarship of Teaching and Learning (CASTL) initiative tends to involve both, in addition to an approach involving professional disciplinary societies. Table 7.6 indicates the advantages, challenges, and disadvantages that developers face when considering these three options for developing SoTL at their institutions.

TABLE 7.6

Developing SoTL: Three Approaches for Developers

	Campus-Wide Multidisciplinary Approach	Campus-Wide Department Approach	Approach Involving Specific National Disciplinary Organizations
The Faculty Developer's Approach/ Role	Traditional role: Coordinating campus-wide workshops, communities, consultations, and TA development—the traditional role.	Working individually with departments: department chairs, committees, etc.	"Connecting" departments to national SoTL disciplinary initiatives (awareness; helping initiate such activities locally).
Advantages	Developing future faculty leaders who may return to their departments to ferment, then lead, change and perhaps become department chairs. Providing safe support and campus community for faculty who are isolated in their departments.	Cutting right to departments, the location where there must be success in the long run, where the key rewards and prestige are located—the fastest way to initiate SoTL in cooperating departments.	Focusing the "pressure" from national disciplinary organizations to motivate departmental change.
Challenges	Getting faculty to go back and promote initiatives in their departments. Making faculty aware of risks. Moderating faculty loyalty to their disciplines and departments and increasing commitment to interdisciplinarity and campus-wide programs.	Developing committed department chairs and faculty. Finding faculty qualified, motivated, and rewarded to lead SoTL departmental efforts. Overcoming total focus on the scholarship of discovery. Encouraging department rewards for publishing SoTL.	Becoming familiar with national SoTL initiatives in all disciplines, then getting departments to consider and join them.
Disadvantages	Taking time to trickle down to departments. Perhaps putting faculty at risk when they return to their departments (e.g., SoTL publications not valued).	Working with some uninterested or hostile departments and department chairs. Results fragmented, uneven across departments.	Having no direct connections with SoTL leaders in national disciplinary organizations.
Relationships with Administrators	Needed and often found: Support and praise from provosts and presidents who favor SoTL.	Concern: Opposition from department chairs and deans who do not favor broadening the concept of scholarship and who find value only in traditional discovery scholarship in the discipline.	Needed: Connection with a SoTL liaison in each national disciplinary organization.

CONCLUSION

No matter which mixture of approaches are selected for the development of SoTL, community must play an important role, and the SoTL faculty learning community connection has a record of success.

REFERENCES

Angelo, T. A. (2000, November). *Twenty years of teaching and learning: Tracing trends, teasing out lessons, and looking ahead.* Paper presented as Part II of the closing plenary at the 20th annual Lilly Conference on College Teaching, Oxford, OH.

Austin, A. E. (1990). *To leave an indelible mark: Encouraging good teaching in research universities through faculty development. A study of the Lilly Endowment's teaching fellows program 1974–1988.* Nashville, TN: Vanderbilt University, Peabody College.

Austin, A. E. (1992). Supporting junior faculty through a teaching fellows program. In M. D. Sorcinelli & A. E. Austin (Eds.), *Developing new and junior faculty* (pp. 73–86). New Directions for Teaching and Learning, No. 50. San Francisco, CA: Jossey-Bass.

Baxter-Magolda, M. B. (1992). *Knowing and reasoning in college: Gender-related patterns in students' intellectual development.* San Francisco, CA: Jossey-Bass.

Belenky, M. B., Clinchy, B. M., Goldberger, N. R., & Tarule, J. M. (1986). *Women's ways of knowing: The development of self, voice, and mind.* New York, NY: Basic Books.

Boyer, E. L. (1990). *Scholarship reconsidered: Priorities of the professoriate.* Princeton, NJ: The Carnegie Foundation for the Advancement of Teaching.

Cambridge, B. L. (2001). Fostering the scholarship of teaching and learning: Communities of practice. In D. Lieberman & C. Wehlburg (Eds.), *To improve the academy: Vol. 19. Resources for faculty, instructional, and organizational development* (pp. 3–16). Bolton, MA: Anker.

Cox, M. D. (1995). The development of new and junior faculty. In W. A. Wright & Associates (Eds.), *Teaching improvement practices: Successful strategies for higher education* (pp. 283–310). Bolton, MA: Anker.

Cox, M. D. (1997). Long-term patterns in a mentoring program for junior faculty: Recommendations for practice. In D. DeZure & M. Kaplan (Eds.), *To improve the academy: Vol. 16. Resources for faculty, instructional, and organizational development* (pp. 225–268). Stillwater, OK: New Forums Press.

Cox, M. D. (1999a, November). *The teacher as scholar of teaching: What, how, why?* Paper presented at the Faculty Development Seminar for the College of Nursing at the University of Cincinnati, Cincinnati, OH.

Cox, M. D. (1999b). Peer consultation and faculty learning communities. In C. Knapper & S. Piccinin (Eds.), *Using consultants to improve teaching* (pp. 39–49). New Directions for Teaching and Learning, No. 79. San Francisco, CA: Jossey-Bass.

Cox, M. D. (2001a). Faculty learning communities: Change agents for transforming institutions into learning organizations. In D. Lieberman & C. Wehlburg (Eds.), *To improve the academy: Vol. 19. Resources for faculty, instructional, and organizational development* (pp. 69–96). Bolton, MA: Anker.

Cox, M. D. (Ed.). (2001b). *Teaching communities, grants, resources, and events: 2001–2002.* Oxford, OH: Miami University.

Cox, M. D. (2001c). *Sourcebook 2001: Designing, implementing, and leading faculty learning communities.* Oxford, OH: Miami University.

Cox, M. D. (in press). Fostering the scholarship of teaching and learning through faculty learning communities. *Journal on Excellence in College Teaching.*

Cox, M. D., & Blaisdell, M. (1995, October). *Teaching development for senior faculty: Searching for fresh solutions in a salty sea.* Paper presented at the 20th annual Conference of the Professional and Organizational Development Network in Higher Education, North Falmouth, MA.

Cross, K. P. (1998). Classroom research: Implementing the scholarship of teaching. In T. Angelo (Ed.), *Classroom assessment and research: An update on uses, approaches and research findings* (pp. 5–12). New Directions for Teaching and Learning, No. 75. San Francisco, CA: Jossey-Bass.

Cross, K. P., & Steadman, M. H. (1996). *Classroom research: Implementing the scholarship of teaching.* San Francisco, CA: Jossey-Bass.

Daiker, D., Fuller, M., & Wallace, J. (Eds.). (1989). *Literature: Options for reading and writing* (2nd ed.). New York: Harper & Row.

Dreyfus, H. L., & Dreyfus, S. E. (1986). *Mind over machine: The power of human intuition and expertise in the era of the computer.* New York, NY: Free Press.

Glassick, C. E., Huber, M. T., & Maeroff, G. I. (1997). *Scholarship assessed: Evaluation of the professoriate.* San Francisco, CA: Jossey-Bass.

Healey, M. (2000). Developing the scholarship of teaching in higher education: A discipline-based approach. *Higher Education Research & Development, 19* (2), 169–189.

Hutchings, P. (Ed.). (1998). *The course portfolio: How faculty can examine their teaching to advance practice and improve student learning.* Washington, DC: American Association for Higher Education.

Hutchings, P. (Ed.). (2000). *Opening lines: Approaches to the scholarship of teaching and learning.* Menlo Park, CA: The Carnegie Foundation for the Advancement of Teaching.

Hutchings, P., & Shulman, L. S. (1999). The scholarship of teaching: New elaborations, new developments. *Change, 31* (5), 11–15.

Kennedy, M. (1987). Inexact sciences: Professional education and the development of expertise. *Review of Research in Education, 14,* 133–167.

Kreber, C. (Ed.). (2001a). Scholarship revisited: Perspectives on the scholarship of teaching. *New Directions for Teaching and Learning, No. 86.* San Francisco, CA: Jossey-Bass.

Kreber, C. (2001b). Designing teaching portfolios based on a formal model of the scholarship of teaching. In D. Lieberman & C. Wehlburg (Eds.*), To improve the academy: Vol. 19. Resources for faculty, instructional, and organizational development* (pp. 285–305). Bolton, MA: Anker.

Kreber, C. (2001c). The scholarship of teaching and its implementation in faculty development and graduate education. In C. Kreber (Ed.), *Scholarship revisited: Perspectives on the scholarship of teaching* (pp. 79–88). New Directions for Teaching and Learning, No. 86. San Francisco, CA: Jossey-Bass.

Kreber, C., & Cranton, P. A. (2000). Exploring the scholarship of teaching. *The Journal of Higher Education, 71* (4), 476–495.

Menges, R. J., Weimer, M., & Associates. (Eds.). (1996). *Teaching on solid ground: Using scholarship to improve practice* (pp. xi–xxii). San Francisco, CA: Jossey-Bass.

Miami University. (1981). *Lilly post-doctoral teaching awards program end-of-the-year report, January 1–May 8, 1981.* Oxford, OH: Author.

Perry, W. G. (1970). *Forms of intellectual and ethical development in the college years.* New York, NY: Holt Reinhart.

Rice, E. (1990). Rethinking what it means to be a scholar. In L. Ekroth (Ed.), *Teaching excellence: Toward the best in the academy.* Stillwater, OK: POD Network.

Richlin, L. (1993, November). *The ongoing cycle of scholarly teaching and the scholarship of teaching.* Paper presented at the 13th annual Lilly Conference on College Teaching, Oxford, OH.

Richlin, L. (2001a). Scholarly teaching and the scholarship of teaching. In C. Kreber (Ed.), *Scholarship revisited: Perspectives on the scholarship of teaching* (pp. 57–68). New Directions for Teaching and Learning, No. 86. San Francisco, CA: Jossey-Bass.

Richlin, L. (2001b, November). *Making public the scholarship of teaching. Part 1: Designing publishable projects. Part 2: Presenting and publishing the scholarship of teaching.* Paper presented at the 21st annual Lilly Conference on College Teaching, Oxford, OH.

Ronkowski, S. A. (1993). Scholarly teaching: Developmental stages of pedagogical scholarship. In L. Richlin (Ed.), *Preparing faculty for new conceptions of scholarship* (pp. 79–90). New Directions for Teaching and Learning, No. 54. San Francisco, CA: Jossey-Bass.

Smith, R. (2001). Expertise and the scholarship of teaching. In C. Kreber (Ed.), *Scholarship revisited: Perspectives on the scholarship of teaching* (pp. 69–78). New Directions for Teaching and Learning, No. 86. San Francisco, CA: Jossey-Bass.

Theall, M., & Centra, J. A. (2001). Assessing the scholarship of teaching: Valid decisions from valid evidence. In C. Kreber (Ed.), *Scholarship revisited: Perspectives on the scholarship of teaching* (pp. 31–43). New Directions for Teaching and Learning, No. 86. San Francisco, CA: Jossey-Bass.

Thompson, S., & Nelson, C. (2000, November). *Scholarship of teaching and learning (SOTL): Programs, progress, problems, and prospects.* Paper presented at the 20th annual Lilly Conference on College Teaching, Oxford, OH.

Weimer, M. (1993, November/December). The disciplinary journals of pedagogy. *Change, 25* (6), 45–51.

Weimer, M. (2001). Learning more from the wisdom of practice. In C. Kreber (Ed.), *Scholarship revisited: Perspectives on the scholarship of teaching* (pp. 45–56). New Directions for Teaching and Learning, No. 86. San Francisco, CA: Jossey-Bass.

Weston, C. B., & McAlpine, L. (2001). Making explicit the development toward the scholarship of teaching. In C. Kreber (Ed.), *Scholarship revisited: Perspectives on the scholarship of teaching* (pp. 89–97). New Directions for Teaching and Learning, No. 86. San Francisco, CA: Jossey-Bass.

Wright, W. A., & O'Neil, M. C. (1994). Teaching improvement practices: New perspectives. In E. C. Wadsworth (Ed.), *To improve the academy: Vol. 13. Resources for faculty, instructional, and organizational development* (pp. 5–38). Stillwater, OK: New Forums Press.

Contact:

Milton D. Cox
University Director for Teaching Effectiveness Programs
Miami University
109 Bonham House
Oxford, OH 45056
Voice   (513) 529-6648
Fax   (513) 529-3762
Email   coxmd@muohio.edu

Milton D. Cox is University Director for Teaching Effectiveness Programs at Miami University. He currently oversees eight faculty learning communities at Miami University and directs a FIPSE grant to extend the faculty learning community concept to other campuses. He also co-directs the Ohio Teaching Enhancement Program for early career faculty, a statewide program to provide teaching support and community for new faculty in Ohio. He is director of the Lilly Conference on College Teaching and Editor-in-Chief of the *Journal on Excellence in College Teaching*.

APPENDIX 7.1

MIAMI UNIVERSITY ALUMNI TEACHING SCHOLARS COMMUNITY ALUMNI TEACHING SCHOLAR INITIAL LEARNING PLAN

Format and Hints

Your initial learning plan provides an opportunity for you to reflect on and plan your strategies and activities for the year. Your plan should be three to four pages in length. It is an initial plan and, hence, not set in stone; you may change it later. Before you proceed, you may wish to review your Alumni Teaching Scholar (ATS) application form. You should discuss your plan with your mentor and department chair and/or coordinator. The initial learning plans will be assembled in a booklet that will be shared with program participants at the Berea Retreat. Please submit your plan to Milt Cox by September 5. This early date is necessary to prepare and distribute the booklet before the Berea retreat. Thank you.

1. List your ATS **goals** and **objectives** for the year.

   As you ponder and write about items 2–8 below, indicate how they may help you meet your goals and objectives.

2. List the courses you are teaching this semester and how you plan to teach them; identify a **focus course** and include its **syllabus** as a separate document.

   Select one course each semester to focus on with respect to the ATS Program. You may wish to try out strategies or techniques discussed in ATS seminars. Perhaps this course will be part of your teaching project. For this course, schedule a midterm SGID with Gail Johnson, Applied Technologies. Please send your syllabus for this course to Milt by September 7. We will collect these in a booklet to share with the group. At the end of the first semester, you can revise this syllabus, indicating changes made, successes and failures, etc. This may help you start a course teaching portfolio.

3. Indicate how you plan to interact with your **mentor**.

   A structured approach with scheduled meetings is best for most mentoring pairs. Robert Boice (1992), in his chapter on "Lessons Learned About Mentoring," indicates three outcomes of his research on mentoring pairs: 1) frequent nudges to meet regularly helped ensure pair bonds;

2) left to themselves, most mentoring pairs displayed disappointingly narrow styles; and 3) mentors assumed the role of interventionist with reluctance.

Thus, it's up to you and me to provide the nudges and expand the discussion. The semester can slip away unless you plan your mentoring interaction carefully. Possible activities include visits or audits of each other's classes; attending seminars together; exchanging and discussing videotapes or Small Group Instructional Diagnosis (SGID) visits; partnerships in the style of the New Jersey "Partners in Learning" Program; luncheon or informal meetings to discuss teaching, contraries raised in seminars, university politics, the profession, etc. Plan to attend some Lilly Conference sessions with your mentor. To avoid narrow styles, try a broad variety of activities.

Please use the "mentor log/journal" that is enclosed. This will help you structure and plan meetings, reflect on your mentoring experiences, and provide a record for your interim and final reports.

4. Describe your plans for interacting with your **student associate(s)**.

See the enclosed "Information About Student Associates," that describes opportunities for working with your student(s). Use the student log/journal.

5. Describe your **teaching project(s)**.

Prepare this section of your initial learning plan as a separate document. Use the format described in the enclosed "Guidelines for the Design and Description of Your Teaching Project."

Choose something you can complete by the end of the year, and keep it simple. On the other hand, select a teaching challenge of interest to you and your discipline or in general; plan for a result that would be appropriate to share with colleagues in a department seminar, at Miami's Teaching Effectiveness Retreat, or at a Lilly Conference. Your participation in the ATS Program gives you a license to experiment. Identify the problem you wish to solve and your objectives, your proposed solution, and the assessment you will use to determine the extent to which you have solved the problem and met your objectives. Prepare and stick to your time line. You may wish to use your $125 in program funds here. If you have additional expenses, apply for a CELT Small Grant of up to

$300. Consider a CELT Summer Fellowship for completion of an extended project; applications for next summer are due October 31.

6. Describe your plans to involve the **scholarship of teaching.**

   For one aspect of your participation in the program, consider teaching innovations and experiments to improve the learning of your students (again, the Program gives you a license to do this). Plan to evaluate innovations—their impact on your students' learning. Your method for evaluation may be simple but should be thought out carefully ahead of time; a good reference is the book *By Design* (Light, Singer, & Willett, 1990). If you are interested in classroom assessment techniques, Angelo and Cross's (1993) book, *Classroom Assessment Techniques,* is a good source of ideas. You could present these ideas at February's Teaching Effectiveness Retreat, at Lilly-West, and perhaps publish your results.

7. Describe your **use of funds** ($125).

   Indicate your ideas with "ballpark" costs here.

8. Indicate your **time line.**

   Write it out and stick to it—time passes quickly—especially the opportunity to meet with mentors, student associates, and to complete teaching project tasks. In your time line, include stages of project completion, mentoring activities, etc. Share this timeline with your mentor and student.

Appendix References

Angelo, T. A., & Cross, K. P. (1993). *Classroom assessment techniques: A handbook for college teachers* (2nd ed.). San Francisco, CA: Jossey-Bass.

Boice, R. (1992). Lessons learned about mentoring. In M. D. Sorcinelli & A. E. Austin (Eds.), *Developing new and junior faculty* (pp. 51–61). New Directions for Teaching and Learning, No. 50. San Francisco, CA: Jossey-Bass.

Light, R. J., Singer, J. D., & Willett, J. B. (1990). *By design: Planning research on higher education.* Cambridge, MA: Harvard University Press.

Appendix 7.2

Alumni Teaching Scholars Learning Plan

Glenn Stone, Family Studies and Social Work

1. ATS Goals and Objectives for the Year

- To learn new ways to engage students in class

- To learn more about cooperative learning theory

- To be able to apply cooperative learning techniques in my classes

- To find ways to use cooperative learning techniques to help students learn how to use technology in social work practice

- To meet faculty from other areas and discuss teaching

2. Courses Taught this Semester

I am only teaching FSW 162: Men in Families this semester. My focus course during Spring 2001 is FSW 395: Research and Evaluation in Social Work and Family Studies.

3. Mentor

I plan to meet with my mentor, William Berg (PHS), throughout the semester to discuss my course handouts, web site, lecture topics, and experiential exercises. I will be asking for his critical feedback on the quality of these materials. I will also invite him to attend a class period to observe and evaluate my teaching style. It is also my plan to share the results of my SGID with him as well as the feedback I receive from my student associate.

4. Student Associate

My student associate, Heather Morton, will make at least one visit to my class to observe my teaching techniques. She is also reviewing my course handouts and the course web-based materials available through the course home page. We are also meeting outside of class to discuss her observations. Heather has had me in two courses as a student, and she plans to use this experience to provide me with constructive feedback.

5. Teaching Project

See attached document

6. Scholarship of Teaching

I plan to read materials on cooperative learning theory and strategies. I hope to develop ways to better evaluate student reaction to cooperative learning techniques. I'm particularly interested in how cooperative learning may help students overcome their attitudes related to advanced computer technology and its use in social work practice.

7. Funds

I plan on using my funds to purchase books and a notebook computer to assist in technology instruction within class.

8. Timeline

September:
- Meet with faculty mentor to discuss our meeting schedule, to give him copies of course materials and web-based information, and to set up objectives for our meetings
- Meet with student associate to discuss our meeting schedule, to give her copies of course materials and web-based information, and to set up objectives for our meetings
- Develop course home page
- Begin working on teaching project
- Videotape class
- Review relevant books, articles, etc., on cooperative learning theory and strategies
- Begin planning cooperative learning strategies and technology-based assignments for FSW 395

October
- Continue working on my teaching project and continue reviewing information on cooperative learning
- Schedule SGID for FSW 162
- Discuss the results of the SGID with my faculty mentor
- Discuss the results of the SGID with my student associate
- Have student associate visit my class
- Have faculty mentor visit my class

- Continue course home page development
- Continue developing cooperative learning strategies within computer lab assignments for FSW 395

November

- Continue working on teaching project
- Continue meeting with my faculty mentor
- Continue meeting with my student associate
- Redesign syllabus for FSW 395 to incorporate new strategies

December

- Assess benefits of cooperative learning strategies, particularly related to use of technology
- Student associate completes focus groups within my class
- Continue meeting with faculty mentor and student associate—discuss results of assessment with them

January to May 2000

- Implement strategies in FSW 395
- Implement evaluation strategies for FSW 395
- Continue meeting with mentor and student associate

Appendix 7.3

Miami University Alumni Teaching Scholars Community Teaching Project

Processes and Outcomes of Teaching for Reflective Practice Using Service-Learning Pedagogy Joan Fopma-Loy, Nursing

Design and Description of Teaching Project

1. The Problem or Question

Those faculty teaching students in applied fields, such as nursing, social work, and teaching, are called upon to assist students in applying understanding and judgment to problems that are increasingly complex and highly situational (Peterson, 1995). Effective practice in this reality of the "swampy lowland" (Schon, 1983, p. 42) of situations of deep societal concern requires the formulation and continual reshaping of a critical rationale for practice. As Brookfield (1995) asserts, this rationale is not only a professional necessity, but is essential psychologically and politically as well. Yet, traditionally, education has not focused on enhancing the abilities essential to reflective practice. Students are often unable to articulate those factors affecting practice decisions and their cognitive processes in making clinical judgments. Students must be guided through processes of examining assumptions, identifying societal and professional contexts underlying assumptions and behaviors, discussing implications of unexamined assumptions and behavior, and creating new ways of being and doing. What pedagogies best facilitate the development of these abilities and processes underlying the development of these abilities so that professional growth continues? After completing the course, students will be able to:

1. Comprehend the meaning and value of critical reflection to professional expertise and citizenship

2. Identify personal levels of reflection and methods of enhancing levels of reflection

3. Analyze structures and processes that facilitate development of their ability to reflect critically on experience

2. Context

Theoretically, this project builds on the work of scholars such as Baxter-Magolda and King and Kitchener (1994), who have furthered my understanding of the cognitive development of undergraduates and factors that may foster or impede this development. The literature on service learning as pedagogy also provides as foundation for my teaching and this project. In reading much of this literature prior to this year and during the past summer, several questions warranting further investigation were noted. Bradley (1995), who developed criteria for assessing levels of reflective judgment based on the work of King and Kitchener (1994), stated that his model needed to be tested by instructors in different types of courses. Bradley (1995) also noted "measurements of change in students' reflective levels over the development of their personal learning summary, in which they are reflecting critically on their learning throughout the semester." Students will also be completing weekly reflections in which they are drawing connections between their experiences and central course concepts. With written student permission, I may also use selected excerpts to address project questions.

3. Participants
Participants in this project will be all students enrolled in NSG 311: Health Promotion Across the Lifespan, fall semester 1997 and spring semester 1998, and all students enrolled in NSG 44: Aging: Current Perspectives and Issues. This will enable me to compare processes and outcomes in a course of nursing majors (NSG 311) and a thematic sequence course in which students come from a variety of majors (NSG 441). While the journal questions and final reflection paper will differ somewhat, the fundamental issues addressed (reflection on service-learning and on self as a learner) will be the same across courses. I anticipate that the combined enrollment in these three classes will be approximately 100 students.

I am using or adapting methods to develop critical reflection described in the service-learning literature. My project may be different in the degree to which processes and outcomes are being evaluated.

4. Evaluation
See above. Evaluation is a major component of the project.

5. Timeline

June–August
- Review literature
- Redesign NSG 311, embedding critical reflection assessment/evaluation strategies and teaching strategies
- Submit study to University Research Comm./Protection of Human Subjects for approval
- Get NCR forms made

September
- NSG 311 begins. Students complete initial assessment
- Rough analysis of results to modify teaching strategies as needed
- Weekly analysis of Classroom Critical Incident Forms
- Journaling of any impressions from student weekly reflections
- Begin redesign of NSG 441 for Spring semester
- Apply for CELT Small Grant?

October
- Weekly analysis of Classroom Critical Incident Forms
- Journaling of any impressions from student weekly reflections
- Continue redesign of NSG 441 for Spring semester
- Apply for CELT Summer Fellowship Grant?

November
- Weekly analysis of Classroom Critical Incident Forms
- Journaling of any impressions from student weekly reflections
- Continue redesign of NSG 441 for Spring semester
- Initial analysis of Student Process Analysis of Critical Reflection

December
- Analysis of student final assessment
- Weekly analysis of Classroom Critical Incident Forms
- Journaling of any impressions from student weekly reflections
- Complete redesign of NSG 441 for Spring semester

January
- Students complete initial analysis (NSG 311 and NSG 441)
- Rough analysis of results to modify teaching strategies as needed
- Weekly analysis of Classroom Critical Incident Forms

        • Journaling of any impressions from student weekly
         reflections

February   • Weekly analysis of Classroom Critical Incident Forms
         • Journaling of any impressions from student weekly
         reflections

March   • Weekly analysis of Classroom Critical Incident Forms
        • Journaling of any impressions from student weekly
         reflections
        • Initial analysis of student final assessment

April   • Weekly analysis of Classroom Critical Incident
         Forms
        • Journaling of any impressions from student weekly reflec-
         tions

May   • Initial analysis of student final assessment
        • Weekly analysis of Classroom Critical Incident Forms
        • Journaling of any impressions from student weekly reflec-
         tions

Appendix 7.4

Miami University Faculty Learning Communities

**Suggestions About Presentations at Teaching and Learning Conferences:
Engaging in the Scholarship of Teaching**

Background
Individual or small-group presentations at the Teaching Effectiveness Retreat, First Tuesday Seminars, and Lilly Conferences are 40 to 45 minutes in length, and 75-minute time intervals are also available at Lilly-West. Your audience will include people from a variety of disciplines.

You, an Expert?
You may have concerns about presenting about teaching and learning on campus and at a national teaching conference. After all, it takes years to become qualified in your discipline. However, the topic of teaching and learning in higher education is a new discipline where there are relatively few experts. All instructors are welcome to share innovations that add to the growing, but small, knowledge base of teaching and learning in higher education. (The discipline of K–12 education is much more established, so don't confuse the two.)

The culture at these retreats and conferences is supportive, not competitive. They are not the same as disciplinary conferences where often one's role becomes critical and competitive. You will find that your audience will be helpful and positive in offering suggestions and references for your further investigation. They will welcome you to a community that is developing the scholarship of teaching.

Topic Selection
Teaching project
Consider a progress report that includes your initial problem or opportunity, your proposed solution, and what you have done so far. If you have learning outcomes from the first semester, that is a bonus. If the results are disappointing, they are still worth reporting so that others may modify a try at the same thing. Those in your audience may have suggestions, and that "helpful, contributing feeling" is a positive one for an audience member.

Seminar topic

If there is a teaching and learning topic from a seminar or experience that has interested you, do some background reading and present on it, for example, decentering your classroom, student intellectual development, writing, using group work, etc. This might be particularly interesting as a team presentation in which more than one discipline is involved.

Joint Presentations

With colleague, mentor, and/or student associate

Consider the possibility of presenting with one of your learning community colleagues, your mentor, and/or your student associate. In this case, we might be able to fund your team member's journey to a Lilly Conference.

Presentations by the entire faculty learning community

The whole group may wish to do a presentation about the community or your group experience as, for example, a junior faculty member, a senior faculty member, learning about a topic such as problem-based learning across several disciplines, etc.

Presentation Strategies

Handouts

Be sure to have handouts that include any overheads or PowerPoint. To make your presentation scholarly, include references to articles or books you have cited or read in order to learn what others have done or what has helped form your solutions to a teaching problem or opportunity.

Time for questions and discussion

Be sure to allow 25% of your time for this. Audience members want to share their experiences with you and the group. Sometimes people say that this is the most important part of your session. Take a deep breath and sacrifice content for dialogue.

Model your topic

If your topic is learning in groups, include a small-group activity in your session; if it is about classroom assessment techniques, include one in your session.

Include student work

If your session is about writing, include some student writing; if it is about student intellectual development, include some student work illustrating movement on some scale; if it is about using the web, include some student reports.

Assessment

Your session will be evaluated by the participants. Use this feedback to improve your presentation for the next time.

Publication

Consult your learning community coordinator as to the suitability of writing up your session as a manuscript for a refereed journal or an article in a teaching magazine. Milt Cox, Editor-in-Chief, and Gregg Wentzell, Managing Editor, the *Journal of Excellence in College Teaching*, are good consultants here.

8

Assessing and Reinvigorating a Teaching Assistant Support Program: The Intersections of Institutional, Regional, and National Needs for Preparing Future Faculty

Kathleen S. Smith
University of Georgia

This chapter discusses an assessment of an 11-year old teaching assistant (TA) support program at a Research I institution. The TA support program was developed on the premise that professional preparation of teachers includes fundamental teaching competencies or skills that can be identified, developed, and evaluated (Simpson & Smith, 1993; Smith & Simpson, 1995). The purpose of this longitudinal study was to identify and enhance the institutional enabling factors that help graduate teaching and laboratory assistants in performing their duties and in using their graduate experience to prepare for careers at a variety of academic institutions.

INTRODUCTION

Institutions of higher education invest heavily in the undergraduate teaching environment, in graduate education, and in the identification of faculty who will further the institutional mission. These factors make it imperative to support the successful development of graduate students as instructors in the undergraduate classroom and as future faculty. In addition, graduate students are a tremendous source of intellectual inspiration for undergraduates and constitute a renewable resource for the future of higher education. The teaching assistant (TA) support program at this Research I institution was developed based on the concept that professional preparation of teachers includes fundamental teaching competencies which can be identified, agreed upon, and evaluated (Simpson & Smith, 1993; Smith & Simpson, 1995). Effective graduate preparation should include many opportunities to develop these teaching competencies as these are the skills new faculty will have to demonstrate to be successful teacher-scholars. This chapter describes a longitudinal study of a cohort of outstanding graduate students and their graduate teaching experiences as they prepared for and moved into faculty roles. Pivotal events related to the development of teaching competencies shape graduate students' professional development and allow them to be knowledgeable and successful participants in the academic culture of their institution. The researcher identified those pivotal events that contributed to or detracted from the successful preparation of the participants in this study for their faculty teaching responsibilities. The rationale for this ongoing longitudinal study is to identify and support the institutional enabling factors that contribute positive experiences while reducing the events that seem to detract from the development of a professional approach to the scholarship of teaching.

BACKGROUND

In the early 1990s, the investigator in this study sought the expert opinion of academic staff who were involved in faculty and teaching assistant support at Carnegie I or II institutions to identify and validate teaching competencies for graduate teaching assistants and faculty (Simpson & Smith, 1993; Smith & Simpson, 1995). National leaders involved in the professional preparation of teaching assistants and faculty were able to validate competencies or skills as they applied to teaching roles. These competencies were then considered in the context of professional preparation for graduate teaching assistants at a Research I institution. Each of the competencies was assigned to six fundamental skill areas including scholastic, planning, management, presentation/communication, evaluation/feedback, and interpersonal skills. The development of these competencies or skills became the foundation of professional preparation for graduate teaching assistants at this Research I institution (Figure 8.1). Graduate students who have achieved a certain level of teaching skill or competency are nominated by their departments each year for several teaching awards given by the institution. All teaching award recipients who are preparing for faculty careers are invited to apply for the TA mentor program, a preparing future faculty program. Each year, ten to 15 TA mentors representing disciplines from across campus are selected for the TA mentor program. These future faculty work with the teaching support office in preparing for their faculty careers and in increasing departmental opportunities for all TAs (Smith, 1993). The investigator has documented the professional development and career path of TA mentors since 1990 as well as the impact of departmental and institutional support. Currently, there are over 100 present and former TA mentors included in the database. The rationale for following the professional preparation of these outstanding graduate students and future faculty was to document their successful use of resources and strategies in becoming competent instructors, in obtaining faculty positions, and in becoming knowledgeable participants of the culture of their academic institutions, and then to use this information to provide better support for all TAs at this institution. TA mentors participate in a year-long mentoring experience that includes group discussions on teaching, individual mentoring by faculty members, and mentoring by and for TA peers. In addition, past and present TA mentors are able to participate in a private listserv discussion on teaching (Smith, 1993). This network of teaching support from TA mentors who have moved to other institutions is a unique strength of this TA support effort. These past TA mentors continue to mentor new TAs at this institution on the reality of faculty positions at a variety of institutions. They also continue to give a cross-discipline perspective on the teaching and learning enterprise and reflect on how their graduate teaching experience is currently affecting their career. As new faculty members, they also frequently mentor TAs at their new institution, often by sharing the TA mentor list discussions.

METHODOLOGY

This is a qualitative, multicase study (Merriam, 1988). The pattern of behavior we were interested in documenting is how graduate teaching assistants successfully use their graduate experience to prepare for academic careers. Our goal was to generate theory that accounts for a pattern of behavior that is relevant and problematic for those involved (Strauss, 1987) and to identify the events that contributed or detracted from successful teaching preparation. With the constant comparative method to develop grounded theory as outlined by Glaser and Strauss (1967), we continually asked our respondents to clarify or enlarge upon our interpretation of the data. Over a ten-year period, we analyzed the intersections of institutional, regional, and national needs for well-prepared instructors and our respondents' use of the resources and support services on our campus. The assessment of how graduate students became outstanding teachers and knowledgeable faculty members helped to expand and reinvigorate our TA support structure.

DATA ANALYSIS AND INTERPRETATION TECHNIQUES

At this point in the study, data collection and analysis has occurred simultaneously over a ten-year period and includes 96 former TA participants at 55 institutions of higher education in the United States. Phase I of the study occurs each year as the new TA mentor group participates in qualitative interviews (Spradley, 1979) and observations (Spradley, 1980) related to their teaching. The researcher transcribes and enters data from interviews, observations, group discussions on teaching, and from the listserv (TAMENTOR) into a computerized database manager. In addition, graduate experiences that seem to contribute or detract from their development as teacher-scholars are noted. We also track their job search to identify the factors which enabled them to successfully secure their first faculty position. These data are coded and categorized to identify patterns and roles that contribute to the TA experience and a smooth transition into faculty positions (Smith, in press).

The focus of the Phase II data collection is to determine what aspects of the graduate experience help participants, from a variety of backgrounds, successfully move into academic careers. Phase II of the study began in 1994 as members of the first cohort of the TA mentor study moved into their first faculty positions and began to use their graduate experience as the basis for a career. Data from Phase II participants comes from TAMENTOR listserv discussions, mailed questionnaires, and individual interviews. Participants on the TAMENTOR listserv discussion are able to compare perceptions and strategies and to verify our understanding of the data. Integrative diagrams are used from the early stages of the data collection to visualize and conceptualize data. We identified background, intervening, enabling, and outcome variables that affected the transition process in moving from a graduate teaching role to a faculty role (Smith & Kalivoda, 1998).

In 1999, Phase III of the study began as the early TA Mentor cohorts completed the third-year review process or were put up for promotion. A questionnaire was mailed to 96 former TA mentors at 55 institutions of higher education in the United States and abroad. Of these 96, 52 are female, 44 are male, and 11 are minority or international participants. In this phase of the study, the participants identified the events in their graduate program that contributed to their professional development as teacher-scholars as well as the events that negatively influenced their professional growth. Response to the mailed survey totaled 42. We followed up with those not responding to the initial survey with questions via the TAMENTOR listserv discussion. We coded and analyzed the insights of the 42 responding to the survey as well as the comments and responses from the 72 former TA mentors currently active on the TAMENTOR listserv discussion (Smith, in press). This chapter details three representative cases to illustrate the process of successful graduate teacher preparation for a career in higher education.

CASE STUDY TYPES

This is a multicase study that seeks to build abstractions across cases to understand the process of successful graduate teaching development leading to an academic career. The following individual cases provide a compelling interpretation of how graduate students use the assistantship to become competent instructors and to navigate academic cultures eventually leading to an academic career.

Case 1: Kurt Rose

When Kurt Rose was several years into his doctoral program he already knew he preferred to become a faculty member at a four-year college with a master's program. He had a strong interest in teaching but also valued meaningful research. During his doctoral program, he was teacher of record for eight sections of three different 500 level classes with an enrollment of about 50 students each. His department had no formal support for TAs to develop their teaching, although a number of outstanding teaching faculty mentors were available to answer questions.

Kurt took the required teaching support seminar offered by the faculty development office where the teaching competencies and skills were addressed. In the seminar, he also became familiar with technology opportunities and support available to faculty and TAs. He sought teaching support from his departmental faculty and the central teaching support program and developed his teaching to the point that he won an outstanding teaching award from the university. As an award-winning TA, Kurt was selected for the TA mentor program. Kurt's teaching goal was to expand his use of technology and encourage more interactive learning.

As a TA mentor, Kurt interacted with other award-winning TAs and faculty from other disciplines in using technology and discussing the scholarship of teaching in preparing for faculty roles. During the TA mentor year, he learned how to document his graduate experience and how to interview and identify a good institutional match for his professional goals. He entered a very tough job market with more than 300 hundred applicants vying for 50 positions in the United States and abroad. Based on his strong teaching credentials, he landed a one-year international teaching position. During the year, he expanded his teaching and research to include an international perspective and had time to focus on various aspects of his professional scholarship. During his time abroad, he was an active participant on the TAMENTOR listserv with past and present TA mentors.

The next year he accepted a job offer at a four-year state university in the United States with a strong emphasis on teaching. While maintaining his teaching excellence, he also concentrated on research publications in this second faculty position. As a result of his enhanced professional experiences he was offered a position at a prestigious private university and a state university. He accepted the offer at the state university knowing it had a major research focus. However, within a year, he made a decision to return to his second position at the four-year university because its teaching focus meshed better with his professional and personal goals. He was welcomed back by that institution.

Case 2: Ann Green

Ann Green aspired to become a faculty member at a small teaching college as she began her doctoral program. Her goal was to develop alternate teaching strategies that emphasized student thinking. However, she felt her first teaching experience was less than she had hoped for in terms of student investment in the material and in her own ability to assess student learning. Her department had a structured teaching support program consisting of a resource room established by a former TA mentor and a semester-long teaching support seminar conducted by an award-winning TA under the supervision of the department head.

Ann worked diligently for several years on becoming a more effective teacher. Eventually, she developed her teaching to the point she won a teaching award from the institution. As an award-winning TA, she was selected for the TA mentor program where she interacted with award-winning TAs and faculty from other disciplines in discussing the scholarship of teaching and in preparing for faculty roles. As a TA mentor, she was encouraged to present at teaching conferences and to develop her teaching scholarship. The year following the TA mentor program, Ann was awarded a teaching assistantship to lead the departmental teaching support seminar for her department.

In this mentoring leadership position, she worked with new TAs in the department as they developed and documented their graduate teaching experiences. Ann won a national teaching excellence award based on the teaching portfolio she had developed in the TA mentor program. She received funding to travel to the meeting from the institution where she met leaders in her field in both teaching and research. Upon graduation, she was sought after by a variety of institutions. She decided to accept a teaching postdoctoral position at a university where she would teach two classes a semester and have time to further develop her teaching and research. During that time she attended teaching conferences and worked with undergraduates in the research setting. She also participated in a listserv discussion on teaching issues with over 100 former TA mentors across the United States and abroad. After a very successful two years in this position, she wrote a grant that enabled her to accept a prestigious three-year research post-doctoral position. Ann's professional goals have developed to include a broad spectrum of academic roles including teaching and research opportunities. She feels her discipline job market makes these post-doctoral positions crucial in securing the kind of position she now feels she would like to pursue.

Case 3: Pam Cane

Pam Cane's long-range career plans were to work at a research institution upon receiving her doctorate. She was in a professional school that had no formal support for teaching. However, she had a very supportive major professor and a strong graduate student cohort. Institutional policy required her to take the central teaching support seminar offered by the faculty development office. She was also very proactive in seeking out teaching support from departmental faculty and the faculty development office, including funding to improve courses. In addition, she offered to help with the revision of the TA handbook that made her more aware of good pedagogy and the teaching resources on campus.

During her graduate preparation she taught discussion sessions, independent classes in the evening classes division of her department, large lecture survey classes of over 200 students, and senior-level seminars. Her teaching evaluation averages consistently ranked above departmental and college averages. Eventually, she was awarded the outstanding teaching assistant award from the department and institution. As an award-winning TA she was selected for the TA mentor program where she interacted with other outstanding TAs, faculty, and teaching support staff.

During the year she was a TA mentor, she developed a teaching portfolio, increased peer mentoring efforts in her department, and discussed the scholarship of teaching related to the reality of the job market at diverse institutions. She went on to win the excellence in teaching award given to only five individuals per year. Following the TA mentor year, she entered the job market and was successful in getting numerous interviews and offers from a variety of institutions. She accepted a tenure-track position at a very prestigious Research I institution.

Pam continued to discuss the scholarship of teaching and the politics of academic life on the TAMENTOR listserv. She also shared many of these discussions with graduate students at her new institution. In her new faculty position, she received the senior class favorite faculty award and several course enhancement grants from the teaching support office. She was also an active researcher and published numerous articles and several book chapters as well as presented at discipline-related conferences both on her research and teaching. Within six years, Pam was promoted with tenure.

DISCUSSION

The three cases exemplify the complexity of preparing graduate students from diverse disciplines for a variety of teaching assignments, career goals, and academic job markets. Nevertheless, there were pivotal events in their graduate preparation that contributed positively to their development as teacher-scholars. The most important event was that the institution required support for teaching. Neither Kurt nor Pam had formal support in their departments, but there was an institutional requirement that all TAs receive some support. They were asked to take the teaching support seminar offered by the central faculty development office which introduced them to a wide dimension of developmental opportunities.

Our data clearly indicated that some TAs were not getting any teaching support except in the required orientation and classes. Many new graduate students do not even know the questions to ask or the process to follow to improve teaching so required teaching support makes the process easier. All three of these TAs also had many opportunities to teach and gradually accepted more and more responsibility for teaching until they were teacher of record with full responsibility. The institution also provided a mechanism for them to be recognized and rewarded for their successful teaching. This was identified as an extremely important pivotal event because it was public recognition and permission for them to be identified for their teaching efforts. This recognition also led to many other opportunities including the TA mentor program, assistantships associated with departmental teaching support efforts, and national awards and opportunities to attend teaching conferences.

Each of these TAs became leaders in their departments in mentoring new TAs and in discussing the scholarship of teaching. They have continued this mentoring leadership on the TAMENTOR listserv and in their new departments. In the TA mentor year, they developed a clear sense of themselves as teacher-scholars; they learned how to document their graduate experiences and to identify their professional goals and values. They were also introduced to the concept of career stages when it may be necessary to focus for a while on one area and then switch gears to focus on other areas. In addition, they learned to realistically assess the job market in their field and set goals that would eventually get them the kind of academic position that meshed with their talents and interests.

We chose to track the graduate preparation and career path of this particular group of graduate students because they had been outstanding graduate students in terms of successful teaching, the completion of meaningful research and doctoral programs, and had successfully navigated a variety of academic job markets to secure academic positions that fit their particular goals and talents. It was our belief that if we could understand the process by which these students appeared to benefit from their graduate preparation for an academic career, we could strengthen our support structure for all graduate students at this institution. Our ten-year survey of the TA mentors confirmed the importance of the teaching skills and competencies upon which we had built our teaching support program. It also revealed that there was a set of pivotal events which contributed to graduate teaching preparation for a career in higher education as well as persistent events in some departments which seemed to hinder a graduate student's ability to develop the scholarship of teaching (Figure 8.1).

FIGURE 8.1
Pivotal Events in Graduate Teacher Preparation for a Faculty Career

Scholastic Skills
- Recognize and accept teaching as a fundamental and challenging dimension of scholarship.
- Demonstrate mastery of subject matter.
- Advise students of career opportunities in the discipline or profession.
- Demonstrate relationships between the course and the broader liberal education curriculum.
- Enhance motivation of students by demonstrating relevance to future needs and goals of students.

Positive Events Contribute to Success
- Introduced to teaching as scholarship

- Teaching opportunities in department—developmental and variety of classes
- Opportunity to attend teaching conferences and publish in teaching journals
- Taking the initiative to improve teaching
- Official recognition—opportunity for teaching awards
- Cross campus perspective of teaching from teaching support class, TA mentors
- Sense of community—being accepted as a peer by colleagues

Negative Events Detract from Success
- Little support of teaching expressed in department
- Little interest in the developmental needs of undergraduates
- Reluctance of department to recognize outstanding teaching by nominating TAs for teaching awards
- Lack of community related to the scholarship of teaching

Planning Skills
- Select course material suited to the background, ability level, and interests of students.
- Match varying teaching methods with specific instructional objectives.
- Present material that is sequenced and paced appropriately for learners.
- Promote individual involvement of students through learner-centered teaching methods.
- Encourage cooperation and collaboration among students.
- Enhance motivation of students by demonstrating relevance to future needs and goals of students.

Positive Events Contribute to Success
- Feedback on teaching—departmental, student, peer
- Opportunity to revise and develop new courses
- Exposure to learning styles and student developmental needs
- Exposure to multidisciplinary approaches to teaching
- Institutional or departmental support structure—credit classes, resource room, individual consultation, mentoring

Negative Events Detract from Success
- No opportunity to develop teaching—laboratory teachers or same class year after year with focus directed by department

- Negative message on undergraduate abilities
- Lack of faculty understanding of undergraduate cognitive needs

Management Skills

- Communicate important departmental policies that relate to the goals of the course.
- Manage administrative responsibilities such as ordering books, handling withdrawals, and complying with other departmental requirements.
- Communicate and manage appropriate expectations for achievement in the course.
- Communicate and implement important safety measures in the classroom.
- Deal appropriately with matters of discipline, academic honesty, and legal information.
- Manage the learning environment so that optimum learning will result.

Positive Events Contribute to Success

- Strong departmental teaching support structure
- Opportunity and encouragement for improving a course
- Well-publicized institutional guidelines for teaching
- Development of priorities—clear goals in professional and personal life
- Learning time-management skills
- Leadership in mentoring other TAs

Negative Events Detract from Success

- Lack of departmental communication about teaching and teaching resources
- Negative departmental message on undergraduate abilities
- Personal responsibilities—balance of professional and personal life
- TAing for poorly organized courses

Presentation and Communication Skills

- Communicate effectively in both written and oral formats in English.
- Lead class discussions that stimulate learning and enhance the goals of the course.
- Use technology to enhance learning.
- Promote individual involvement of students through learner-centered teaching methods.
- Encourage cooperation and collaboration among students.
- Enhance motivation of students by demonstrating relevance to future needs and goals of students.

Positive Events Contribute to Success

- Developmental support for presentations and writing
- Technology support to improve pedagogy and learning
- Introduction to other possibilities for teaching
- Modeling from professors and peers and from teaching support seminar and TA mentor program

Negative Events Detract from Success

- No departmental feedback on teaching
- No access to technology in department
- Overzealous use of technology
- Classes too large to promote interaction among students

Evaluation and Feedback Skills

- Construct valid and reliable tests and administer fairly other evaluation measures.
- Provide helpful feedback to students in a variety of ways.
- Develop a reflective approach to teaching through collecting feedback and continually modifying instructional approaches.

Positive Events Contribute to Success

- Opportunity for student evaluations
- Learning classroom assessment strategies
- Learning how to reflect on teaching and document successes
- Guidance in kinds of feedback students find useful
- Culture of respect for students and for the TA role

Negative Events Detract from Success

- Having to respond to someone else's exam procedure with little TA input
- Little training in constructing good exams
- No mechanism for TA feedback
- Message from faculty to ignore student evaluations

Interpersonal Skills

- Enhance motivation of students through personal enthusiasm for the subject.
- Exhibit respect and understanding for all students.
- Demonstrate a general belief that all students are capable of learning.
- Deal appropriately with issues that relate to various aspects of diversity.
- Enhance motivation of students by demonstrating relevance to future needs and goals of students.

Positive Events Contribute to Success

- Finding pleasure in a student's understanding of a difficult concept
- Knowing that, long term, efforts in teaching would outdistance efforts in research in terms of people impact
- Understanding that students learn in different ways
- Acknowledging multicultural issues
- Multidisciplinary interactions with TA mentors

Negative Events Detract from Success

- Departmental weed out course mentality
- Little departmental understanding of how students learn and how to provide learning support
- Lack of leadership opportunities in teaching

Smith, K. S. (2001, Fall). *The Journal of Graduate Teaching Assistant Development,* Vol. 8, No. 3, Stillwater, OK: New Forums Press

The pattern of behavior we were interested in documenting is how graduate teaching assistants successfully use their graduate experience to prepare for academic careers. It is evident that many of our respondents have made the transition into their academic roles because of the confidence they developed as graduate students in their teaching ability. Data from the longitudinal study identified the developmental aspect of the TA support program as the key factor in their successful preparation for an academic position. Although many also went on to be outstanding researchers, they acknowledged that having their teaching well in hand made it possible to concentrate on meaningful research. Those who had prepared for the third-year review process and tenure did so with ease because of the practice they had as graduate students in documenting their teaching and in creating a teaching or professional portfolio.

A significant finding of this study was the level of contentment among those who were not in tenure-track positions. Some are in rewarding postdoctoral positions that are further preparing them for the kind of faculty position they would eventually like to secure. Others have chosen nontenure-track positions, while several have moved from tenured positions to nontenured positions because these positions meshed better with their professional goals. They credit their graduate school teaching experiences with helping to make these important decisions and with easing this transition. With years of teaching experience documented in a professional portfolio, they came into their new positions recognized as teacher-scholars. Being knowledgeable teacher-scholars helped them to quickly ascertain the expectations of their new institution, at least in the teaching arena. Those who had extensive practice in developing courses and in teaching a variety of courses could more easily step into a new course while balancing other institutional expectations. Having also developed a reflective approach to teaching improvement, they actively sought peer feedback on their new roles and in some cases established strong mentoring relationships. Even without formal feedback mechanisms, these new faculty were able to seek out feedback on how they were doing as they moved through the first several years of academic positions.

A significant characteristic of the participants in this study was the entrepreneurial approach they took to managing their careers. They sought out and took advantage of teaching support as graduate students and continued to do so as new faculty.

CONCLUSION

The intersections of institutional teaching needs and regional and national needs for preparing future faculty seemed to mesh well for the cohort of graduate students in our study. They credited many of their successes to institutional policy that mandates teaching support that they were able to take advantage of or seek out on their own initiative. However, in assessing these pivotal events and the impact on graduate preparation for faculty positions, the data indicated that our TA support programming needed to reach a wider graduate student population. In some cases, TA mentors felt their graduate preparation was not shared by departmental peers. By expanding the TA mentor peer support effort in the departments and by expanding the teaching support seminar initiatives, we have begun to provide better support for all teaching and laboratory assistants. In 2000, we had 15 TA mentors setting up departmental seminars on everything from creating a teaching portfolio to using WebCT. In addition, we had over 300 graduate students enrolled in the semester-long departmental sections of our teaching support seminar. We accomplished this by providing partial assistantships to award winning TAs such as the TA mentors to help the faculty teacher of record develop a departmental teaching support seminar.

The departmental teaching seminar uses a graduate school course name, eliminating the need to have a new course approved. These efforts reduce the impression that teaching is not valued in a department. Departmental faculty are increasingly involved in very productive teaching discussions with their graduate students. These discussions influence departmental cultures and change the way individuals approach teaching and learning in the department. In addition, many departments are working to provide more teaching opportunities for their graduate students by allowing them to guest lecture and teach a variety of classes. The teaching support that is established by these seminars continues beyond the semester course because peers are readily available in the department to discuss teaching issues. In addition, we have added a very strong professional development component to these departmental efforts to address methods of professional documentation, the realities of the job market, and academic positions at nonresearch-oriented institutions.

This study has helped to reinvigorate our TA support program because it confirmed the skill and competency-based efforts we had in place were effective to meet institutional teaching needs. It also helped to identify areas of expansion and to garner the needed administrative support to provide stronger TA support structures in academic departments. We confirmed that teaching must be recognized and validated by the institution to optimize graduate student development as teacher-scholars. A teaching emphasis also reflects the reality of the job market (Menges, 1996; Western Interstate Commission for Higher Education, 1992). Graduate students continue to take the initiative to improve and refine their teaching as new faculty members if they have developed confidence and pride in their abilities to teach. Being knowledgeable participants in academic cultures made the transition into a faculty position smoother and provided a framework for successfully managing multiple dimensions of academic life.

REFERENCES

Glaser, B., & Strauss, A. L. (1967). *The discovery of grounded theory: Strategies for qualitative research.* Chicago, IL: Aldine.

Menges, R. J. (1996). Experiences of newly hired faculty. In L. Richlin (Ed.), *To improve the academy: Vol. 15. Resources for faculty, instructional, and organizational °development* (pp. 169–182), Stillwater, OK: New Forums Press.

Merriam, S. B. (1988). *Case study research in education: A qualitative approach.* San Francisco, CA: Jossey-Bass.

Simpson, R. D., & Smith, K. S. (1993, Winter). Validating teaching competencies for graduate teaching assistants: A national study using the Delphi method. *Innovative Higher Education, 18* (2), 133–146.

Smith, K. S. (1993, Spring). Investment in teaching: Mentoring for teaching assistants. *The Journal of Graduate Teaching Assistant Development, 1* (1), 43–48.

Smith K. S. (in press). Pivotal events in graduate teacher preparation for a faculty career. *The Journal of Graduate Teaching Assistant Development.*

Smith K. S., & Simpson R. D. (1995, Spring). Validating teaching competencies for faculty members in higher education: A national study using the Delphi method. *Innovative Higher Education, 19* (3), 223–233.

Smith, K. S., & Kalivoda, P. L. (1998). Academic morphing: Teaching assistant to faculty member. In M. Kaplan & D. Lieberman (Eds.), *To Improve the Academy: Vol. 17. Resources for faculty, instructional, and organizational development* (pp. 85–102). Stillwater, OK: New Forums Press.

Spradley, J. P. (1979). *The ethnographic interview.* Chicago, IL: Holt, Rinehart and Winston.

Spradley, J. P. (1980). *Participant observation.* Chicago, IL: Holt, Rinehart and Winston.

Strauss, A. L. (1987). *Qualitative analysis for social scientists.* New York, NY: Cambridge University Press.

Western Interstate Commission for Higher Education. (1992). *Bringing into focus the factors affecting faculty supply and demand: A primer for higher education and state policy makers.* Boulder, CO: Author.

Contact:

Kathleen S. Smith
Office of Instructional Support and Development
University of Georgia
Instructional Plaza
Athens, GA 30602
Voice   (706) 542-1355
Fax   (706) 542-6587
Email   ktsmith@arches.uga.edu

Kathleen S. Smith is a Senior Academic Professional at the University of Georgia and has directed the TA Program for the Office of Instructional Support and Development since 1990. Dr. Smith's research and professional interests include the professional development of international TAs in the North American classroom, the institutional mechanisms to encourage globalization of the teaching and learning environment, and the professional development of future faculty.

9

Transforming Instructional Development: Online Workshops for Faculty

Laurie Bellows
University of Nebraska, Lincoln

Joseph R. Danos
Delgado Community College

Two vastly different institutions, the University of Nebraska, Lincoln and Delgado Community College, cooperated in the delivery of online faculty development workshops in syllabus construction. This chapter describes the experiences of a flagship university and an urban community college in employing electronic delivery of the same workshop content to their respective faculty members. It shares successful and unsuccessful strategies, nuts and bolts, and the discovery of an unexpected, pleasant irony: The technology that can separate and isolate us has the potential to bring us together, as though we were on electronic legs in a virtual Athenian agora.

Introduction

Technology is transforming higher education. For the most part, it has made our work easier; it has changed how we communicate and interact with our colleagues and our students, and in some cases, it is changing what we do in the classroom (Baldwin, 1998). Recent research indicates that instructors are increasingly using web-based resources in some form to supplement their teaching (Bonk, 2001). Likewise, there are increased online opportunities available to help faculty improve their instruction (Gillespie, 1998; Shea,

Sherer, & Kristensen, 2002). Shea, Sherer, and Kristensen (2002) note that the proliferation of technology use in the classroom—both on the ground and online—presents new challenges and opportunities for those of us in faculty development: expansion of services, continuous delivery of programs through asynchronous communication, easier access to information, and opportunities for collaboration across departments, divisions, and campuses. The most important opportunity, perhaps, is that technology creates "new avenues for faculty to learn together" (Shea, Sherer, & Kristensen, 2002, p. 170).

This chapter describes how we took advantage of the many opportunities technology provides to plan, design, develop, and deliver an online workshop in syllabus construction for faculty. It explains how two highly diverse institutions, the University of Nebraska, Lincoln (UNL) and Delgado Community College in New Orleans, collaborated to deliver the workshop to their faculties. We begin with a brief overview of the learner-centered syllabus and provide a rationale for developing an online instructional development workshop for faculty in syllabus construction. Next, we describe the workshop: illustrating the process with activities, materials used in the workshop, and the assessment tool used to evaluate the workshop's effectiveness and usefulness. We will share our individual campus experiences in offering and delivering the workshop, as well as the lessons learned. Finally, we examine the benefits and drawbacks in facilitating online workshops for faculty members.

THE LEARNER-CENTERED SYLLABUS

In their 1995 article describing a new paradigm for undergraduate education, Robert Barr and John Tagg distinguished between the traditional instruction paradigm and a new learning paradigm. In the instruction paradigm, teachers are subject matter experts who transmit information to students primarily through lectures. In the learning paradigm, students are more actively responsible for their learning, often learning through cooperative groups and collaborative activities. What makes the learning paradigm so powerful is the shift of responsibility from teacher to student. This shift allows teachers to be designers of the learning environment instead of transmitters of information. An important strategy for promoting student learning is the learner-centered syllabus.

The learner-centered syllabus is one of the many outcomes of the learning paradigm. A learner-centered syllabus shifts the focus away from what we teach to what students learn (Grunert, 1997). Just as the instruction paradigm emphasized subject-matter expertise, the traditional syllabus was designed for the content-centered classroom. It was, however, ineffective in helping students understand their roles and responsibilities as active learners.

The learner-centered syllabus focuses on student learning by providing more comprehensive information about the course and instructor expectations for student learning. At the very least, it includes clearly stated course objectives, a course outline identifying specific assignments and activities with corresponding due dates, and statements about class policies and procedures. In effect, it places students at the very center of the question: What do students need to know to get the most out of this learning experience?

According to Diamond (1998), a learner-centered syllabus should accomplish the following goals:

- Define students' responsibilities as learners

- Define your roles and responsibilities to students

- Provide a clear statement of course goals and student outcomes

- Establish standards and procedures for evaluation

- Familiarize students with course logistics

- Establish a pattern of communication between instructor and students

- Include difficult to obtain materials such as readings, complex charts, and graphs

Although these ideas are not revolutionary, many teachers may never have taken the time to redesign a course syllabus that includes such comprehensive information. Thus, one objective of the workshop was to provide participants an initial opportunity to develop learner-centered syllabi.

Rationale

Our rationale for developing an online workshop in syllabus construction was threefold. First, recent campus needs assessment and focus group discussions indicate that time is the primary barrier that keeps most faculty members from participating in traditional face-to-face instructional development activities like workshops, seminars, and discussion groups. However, cutting-edge technology now makes it possible for faculty to participate in such activities at their convenience. Constructed as an online class using the Blackboard courseware management system, this workshop creates an asynchronous environment for faculty participation, allowing enrolled individuals to select both the time and place for their attendance at the workshop, while still encouraging discussion, feedback, and interactivity.

Second, both the University of Nebraska, Lincoln and Delgado Community College use Blackboard as their campus-wide online delivery system. We wanted to provide faculty an opportunity to learn how to use Blackboard and thereby create an incentive for them to utilize Blackboard in their own teaching. To reach more faculty members through the elimination of the time and place barrier, we decided to use the medium to teach the medium while delivering the desired content.

Finally, although training for the use of Blackboard is available on both campuses, it emphasizes the technology, not the pedagogy. The workshop topic, syllabus construction, arose because of its universal application, non-threatening content, and widespread need of improvement. Since many instructors may be unfamiliar with the components of a learner-centered syllabus, we viewed this workshop as an opportunity for faculty to develop or revise their own course syllabi. As a side product, we hoped participants would use the workshop to reflect on and engage in scholarly conversations about their teaching with their peers.

AN ASYNCHRONOUS, ONLINE WORKSHOP: CONSTRUCTING A LEARNER-CENTERED SYLLABUS

Workshop Structure

Following basic principles of course design, we began by asking what we want workshop participants to be able to do at the end of the online workshop. Our primary goal was to help faculty develop a learner-centered syllabus that connected their course objectives, activities, assignments, and assessment. In this context, our objectives for the workshop were to help participants:

- Develop a course rationale that could be shared with students

- Write measurable course objectives

- Identify assignments and tests that support course objectives

- Construct a course outline

- Compose a learner-centered syllabus for the next semester

Online delivery of the workshop provided additional benefits, including the opportunity for participants to 1) meet and work with colleagues in an online environment, 2) learn how to use Blackboard, and 3) experience on-line learning from a students' perspective.

The workshop was based on Judith Grunert's book, *The Course Syllabus* (1997), and was conceptualized as an asynchronous, interactive learning experience spanning a three-week period. Using our objectives as a guide, we organized the workshop around eight modules (Figure 9.1). The workshop was designed to take participants through the process of syllabus development, from start to finish, with the goal of creating or revising one for the following semester. Each module begins with a lesson to focus participants' thinking, and is followed by supplementary reading materials (i.e., brief essays) and related activities or learning tasks.

FIGURE 9.1
Learning Modules

Module 1: Overview: The Learning Centered Syllabus

Module 2: Developing a Course Rationale

Module 3: Setting the Stage: What Are Your Instructional Objectives?

Module 4: Assignments and Assessments

Module 5: Constructing a Course Outline

Module 6: Instructional Approaches and Strategies for Active Learning

Module 7: Composing the Syllabus

Module 8: Summary and Evaluation

Workshop Content

Blackboard offers a number of features that helped us organize the workshop. In the syllabus component we provided an overview of the workshop, posted the workshop goals and objectives, and included some tips on how to succeed in the process. We also provided participants a series of "how to..." instruction sheets for how to use email, the digital drop box, engage in small group discussion, and download PDF files in Blackboard. The course documents section included the eight learning modules with corresponding lessons, handouts, and activities.

The discussion board area allowed participants a place to meet socially in the Coffee Bean. In this area, we invited participants to "grab a cup of coffee, sit back, and talk to us!" Participants were encouraged to use this space to socialize, tell jokes, update each other on their family vacations, and just have fun. We also used the discussion board as a place for participants to share their course rationale statements with other workshop participants, post their lists of activities and assignments, and reflect on the teaching and learning process.

FIGURE 9.2
The Discussion Board

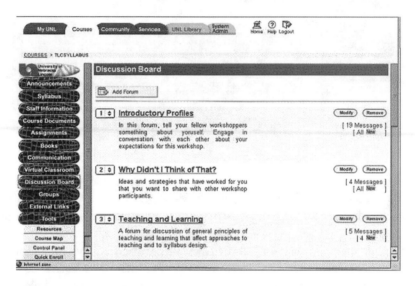

The external links feature provided participants additional resources on teaching and learning, including links to teaching and learning center sites in the United States and Canada.

Each module included three subfolders: focus your thinking, handouts, and your tasks (Figure 9.3). Module lessons contained brief overviews of the topic and questions to prompt reflections. For example, in Module 3, the importance of writing measurable and observable instructional objectives was explained, and participants were encouraged to think about 1) the kinds of skills and levels of knowledge they expected of students, 2) the level of performance they might expect from students, 3) the ways students would be "different" when they finished the course, and 4) what students should be able to do with the knowledge and skills gained in the course.

FIGURE 9.3
Example of "Focus Your Thinking"

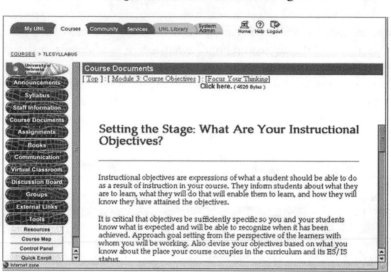

For each module, we identified various materials that would help supplement the lesson. We included essays, excerpts from our faculty instructional guide, and other text-based handouts used in previous face-to-face workshops.

In lieu of assignments, we chose to encourage participants to complete a series of short tasks that would lead to the development of a learner-centered syllabus. Each task was designed to help faculty critically examine the core assumptions about why they do what they do. In Module 2, for instance, we challenged participants to develop a course rationale that clearly communicates to their students their assumptions and expectations regarding their course. Faculty participants were asked to write a short memo describing the purpose of their course, explaining how it fits into their students' degree program and discussing how students will benefit from the course. The purpose of this task was to get participants engaged in scholarly reflection about their teaching. Once the rationale was drafted, participants were instructed to share the memo with their email buddies, and based on their feedback, rewrite the memo as a course rationale to include in their syllabus. We also created a forum for participants to share their course rationale with the entire workshop community.

In the final module, putting it all together, faculty were expected to pull together each component of their syllabus and post the final product to the discussion forum for feedback and suggestions.

Workshop Process

A three-week online workshop was piloted at the University of Nebraska, Lincoln during June 2000. In fall 2000 and then again in summer 2001, the workshop was repeated within a five-week timeframe. The workshop also was offered at Delgado Community College in New Orleans in spring 2001. In the four versions of the workshop, "Constructing a Learner-Centered Syllabus," a total of 103 faculty members (78 from UNL and 25 from Delgado) participated.

University of Nebraska, Lincoln experience. During summer 2000, all faculty members and graduate teaching assistants were invited to participate via a flier in the three-week online workshop. Twenty-five registrations were received by email. Once participants were registered, they received a confirmation of their enrollment and a login ID, a password, and other tips for participating in an online workshop. In addition, each participant was assigned an email buddy to establish a sense of online community and to help answer questions or solve problems with the technology.

The three-week workshop began in mid-June. Participants were asked to post an introductory profile identifying themselves, their departments, the course for which they would be creating a syllabus, why they were drawn to the workshop, and their learning goals for the workshop. The remaining six modules were introduced about every third day, giving participants time to complete an assigned task, share their product with their email partners, revise their work, and then post it to the discussion forum for feedback. As new modules were posted, participants received an email reminding them that the module was ready for viewing. Announcements also were posted on the course page.

The workshop was offered again during the fall 2000 semester but based on post-workshop feedback from participants, we expanded it to a five-week format. Twenty-eight faculty members registered for the fall workshop. A third workshop was offered during a five-week session in summer 2001. Prior to the summer 2001 workshop, however, we offered a face-to-face orientation and included a hands-on introduction to Blackboard. Again, 25 faculty members registered for the third workshop.

Although the actual workshop was offered within a specific timeframe, only about one-third of all participants completed the workshop within the three- or five-week schedule, while approximately one-third of the participants completed the workshop on their own as a self-paced learning experience. The remaining one-third dropped out of the workshop and did not complete it.

Delgado Community College experience. In a spirit of collegiality, the University of Nebraska, Lincoln's Teaching and Learning Center agreed to share the content of its online workshop with Delgado Community College. The workshop was announced at the convocation that began Delgado's spring 2001 semester. Fifty-two of the 350 full-time faculty members filled out registration sheets indicating their desire to participate. However, the workshop was delayed until March 1 while we awaited the arrival of a new server to house it. By that time, 27 faculty members were no longer able to participate and the workshop began with 25 participants. Nine completed the entire workshop, posted syllabi to the discussion board, and received a $200 stipend.

In recognition of the high demand placed on faculty time (the customary community college load of five courses and ten office hours per week produce a required 25-hour weekly presence on campus), we spaced the workshop over a ten-week period (March through mid-May). It began with a two-hour, hands-on introduction to Blackboard and new modules were posted every ten days. To encourage greater participation, four small groups were established, each with its own private discussion board area and virtual chat room (i.e., threaded discussion and synchronous chat). We also made use of the workshop's general discussion board area and the virtual classroom.

Workshop Assessment and Outcomes

Using the Blackboard assessment feature, we created an online survey to evaluate the workshop. Both multiple choice and short-answer items were included. Additionally, several participants provided unsolicited feedback via email.

Although only about one-third of the total number of participants completed the workshop, we considered it a success on both campuses. Faculty feedback (see Table 9.1) indicated that both workshop goals were met. When asked if they had produced a syllabus as a result of their participation in this workshop, the majority of those completing the workshop evaluation indicated "yes" or "still working on it."

TABLE 9.1
Workshop Assessment

n=32 (all four sessions)	SA	A	D	SD
The workshop provided new and useful information for my teaching.	20	12		
The workshop adequately addressed my questions about syllabus development.	12	14	1	1
I achieved the goals I set for myself in this workshop.	8	16	4	
I would participate in another online instructional development workshop.	12	16	1	
I plan to use Blackboard for teaching future courses.	12	12	4	

SA=Strongly Agree; A=Agree; D=Disagree; SD=Strongly Disagree

The majority of those responding to the workshop evaluation indicated that the workshop had helped them think about their teaching and student learning. One participant wrote, "The workshop helped me review my syllabus with a critical eye and also provided some valuable information with which to refine the work in progress." Writing a course rationale, "creating course objectives that go beyond factual knowledge and stating them clearly," and learning "how to use Blackboard from a student's perspective" were considered the most important skills gained from the workshop.

We had also hoped that faculty participants would form an online community of learners and use the workshop as an opportunity to talk about their teaching with others. We purposely designed opportunities for them to share their materials and give feedback and suggestions to their peers. And initially they did. However, as the workshop progressed, discussion seemed to wane and there was very little conversation about teaching or syllabus construction. Yet, from the very beginning, participants expressed their pleasure as they explored the potential of this novel technological tool. It may be that discussing new technology is nonthreatening because everyone is a neophyte.

Based on the feedback, we concluded that the workshop fulfilled its primary objectives of helping faculty develop a learner-centered syllabus and stimulating faculty members to become acquainted with Blackboard.

LESSONS LEARNED

Through participant feedback and our own observations, we have learned some important lessons about what worked, what did not (and why), and what we would do to improve the process.

What Worked

The workshop content was effective at an individual level. In general, participants found the workshop materials useful but, as noted above, the majority of the online discussion focused on how to use Blackboard. Through communications with individuals and the production and posting of syllabi, it was apparent that the participants were doing their homework by completing the assigned reading and tasks. However, they did not take the next step of engaging in meaningful discussion about their teaching. At several junctures in the workshop, participants were encouraged to provide feedback to their peers on the course rationale or to share the content of their course objectives, but they were hesitant to suggest changes. This hesitation probably arises from several factors, some of which include the novelty or unknown quality of the online environment, an unwillingness to be vulnerable with their peers, and a lack of trust of unknown peers (different campuses, different disciplines, etc.). The novelty factor will disappear as the participants become more comfortable using Blackboard. This factor is controllable by means of new online workshops, i.e., training, and the inception of user groups. The refusal to display professional vulnerability in a public medium will require a change in our institutional culture. We hope that the quasi-anonymity of the online environment will catalyze this change.

The method of delivery suited the content. At UNL, we originally offered this workshop in syllabus construction using the traditional face-to-face format. We scheduled two, two-hour sessions, weeks apart. During the first session we covered the background information on a learner-centered syllabus. The second session was scheduled in a computer lab so that participants could actually construct a syllabus in real time. However, the majority of faculty members who had participated in the first session did not return for the second session, citing lack of time as the major obstacle. In contrast, the online environment allowed us to present a contiguous learning experience while offering participants an opportunity to learn anytime, anywhere. Most important, the online environment allowed participants to construct the syllabus as they worked through the content of the workshop.

The online environment promotes networking. As an unexpected outcome of the workshop, we discovered that several faculty members from different campuses or disciplines met each other for the first time and formed potentially lasting relationships. Several participants suggested that we should have a face-to-face "wrap-up" meeting to end the workshop (a suggestion that we will incorporate into our next iteration). Although this may occur in any traditional campus-wide workshop, the probability of its occurrence is increased in an online workshop because more faculty members can participate in an asynchronous electronic workshop and the medium provides the opportunity for more individual and group communication (even if it is initially on a superficial, mundane, "gee-whiz" level).

Collaborating with another institution. The considerable amount of time required to develop an online workshop ensures that collaboration across institutions will increase both from the allocation of scarce resources and the wheel's-been-invented standpoints. Along with the serendipitous sharing model described herein, opportunities for inter-institution collaboration abound: between different campuses of the same institution, different institutions in the same state, four-year (flagship) universities and community colleges in the same state, and institutions with no common geographical connection. Given the customary distribution of faculty development resources (i.e., more at flagship institutions, less at other four-year institutions, and almost none at community colleges), the most fertile field for collaboration exists between flagship institutions and community colleges. Of course, co-equal institutions will also benefit from pooling their resources to produce and deliver online faculty development materials. We might expect, as well, that university administrators and state legislators will look with approval on this efficient expenditure of tax dollars.

If the two institutions use compatible online course delivery software, the workshop content is easily downloaded from one institution to the other. Since both Nebraska and Delgado utilize Blackboard, the transfer was uneventful in our case. Although Nebraska could have hosted the Delgado workshop from Lincoln, we decided to house the content on a Delgado server and to have a local facilitator. This arrangement was beneficial because it:

- Set a local tone that increased participation (increased comfort level with the known)

- Allowed faster response time for any technical problems

- Decreased the facilitation burden for Nebraska

- Decreased the technical support demands on Nebraska

Following this model, a receiving institution could then host subsequent online workshops for sister institutions that have even fewer resources. For example, Delgado could now host online workshops (with acknowledgement of the source of the content) for the other community and technical colleges in Louisiana that are incapable of offering their own. We believe that this model and subsequent variations offer excellent potential for achieving an intellectual multiplier effect (for those of you with an economic bent) within a system and producing a concomitant reputation multiplier effect for the source institution—in this case, Nebraska. Nebraska's metaphorical bumblebee has pollinated magnolias on the bayou.

What Did Not Work (and Why)

The workshop pace. Whether it was offered as a three-week, a five-week, or a ten-week event, many participants found it difficult to complete the workshop within the scheduled timeframe. Some found that if they got behind, it was difficult to catch up, while others admitted to a lack of motivation, even with a stipend as an incentive to complete the workshop.

An invisible facilitator. Experts in online course delivery suggest that facilitators should be more of the guide on the side, so in keeping with good online practice, the instructional developers took a back seat in the workshop. For the most part, we were not visible in the workshop process. Participant feedback indicated that, perhaps, we should have taken a more facilitative role in the workshop such as posing discussion questions, providing feedback on completed tasks, and challenging participants to reflect on and discuss their teaching.

Buddy systems and small groups. Although the online learning literature suggests that assigning email buddies or dividing participants into small groups are good strategies for motivating and connecting online learners, we found that, overall, neither strategy produced greater participation in the workshop. At UNL, the small groups just never materialized. At Delgado, we found that every group had one or two more active participants who experienced more responses to their postings to the general workshop-wide discussion board than to those that they sent to their group's discussion area. Lack of participation in the small groups and posting to the discussion board in lieu of the small group discussion area may have been a function of each individual's time constraints. The end result was that the general discussion board contained the lion's share of the threaded discussions. If everyone had participated fully, the division of the workshop's participants into small groups should have worked.

Improving the Process

Increase the facilitator's role. Online facilitators need to model and encourage a sense of community, at least at the beginning of the workshop. Their presence keeps the workshop participants focused and can serve as a motivator.

Provide incentives to complete the workshop. We believe it is important to reward faculty for their teaching improvement efforts. Participants suggested that, in lieu of a monetary award, a certificate of completion might be useful for their promotion and tenure files. We also learned that it would be helpful to establish deadlines for completion of individual tasks. As one participant noted, facilitators may need to be an "online nag" to keep folks engaged in the process.

Pace the workshop activities so that participants are not easily overwhelmed. We considered whether the workshop should be offered as a self-study activity. Though it is possible, such a format would emphasize the value of convenience over that of group involvement, communication, and peer-to-peer instruction and sharing. It would preclude any institution-wide community building. We truly have no solution to this problem of workshop pace other than to note that instructional developers must realistically assess the amount of content that can be effectively delivered online in a given timeframe. In addition, participants should be encouraged to recognize that while learning online may be more convenient, it can also be more time-consuming than participating in a face-to-face workshop.

BENEFITS AND DRAWBACKS OF ONLINE INSTRUCTIONAL DEVELOPMENT WORKSHOPS

There are a both benefits and drawbacks for instructional developers and faculty in delivering online instructional development workshops. From a faculty development perspective, the benefits include 1) providing a support system to help ease faculty transition into the use of technology, 2) helping faculty view the use of technology and the learning process from the students' vantage point, and 3) providing a vehicle for faculty to reflect on and discuss their teaching in a nonthreatening environment while encouraging interaction with their colleagues.

The benefits for faculty participants include 1) the asynchronous nature of online learning (any time, any place) makes it more convenient to engage in instructional development activities, and 2) the Blackboard discussion board area encourages conversation and dialogue that otherwise might not take place across disciplines, campuses, and possibly even institutions.

Of course, with every benefit there is a drawback. For instructional developers, the major drawbacks of online instructional development include the up-front work involved in developing the workshop (i.e., many workshop materials may need to be redesigned because there is not necessarily a straight translation from face-to-face to online materials), the increased amount of FTE time focused on one event (i.e., up to one hour a day for three, five, or ten weeks versus a one-time, two-hour workshop), and the ability to respond to problems inherent in the use of technology (i.e., access to instructional technologists who can solve computer problems). The drawbacks for faculty participants are similar to students who engage in any form of online learning: staying motivated, keeping pace with the workshop, and feeling connected to your fellow learners you cannot see.

CONCLUSION

As the sense of technological novelty wanes and the cultural metamorphosis occurs, online instructional development workshops will help promote deeper intellectual exchange and discussion of pedagogical topics of broad import. The cross-campus, interdisciplinary relationships developed in this environment will strengthen the institutions. A pleasant irony is that the technology that can separate and isolate us has the potential to bring us together, as though we were on electronic legs in a virtual Athenian agora. Would it display too great hubris to say that we have the opportunity to play Socrates in transforming instructional development?

REFERENCES

Baldwin, R. G. (1998). Technology's impact on faculty life and work. In K. Herr Gillespie (Ed.), *The impact of technology on faculty development, life and work* (pp. 7–21). New Directions for Teaching and Learning, No. 76. San Francisco, CA: Jossey-Bass.

Barr, R. B., & Tagg, J. (1995). From learning to teaching: A new paradigm for undergraduate education. *Change, 27* (6), 13–25.

Bonk, C. J. (2001). *Online teaching in an online world.* Bloomington, IN: CourseSHare.com.

Diamond, R. M. (1998). *Designing and assessing courses and curricula: A practical guide.* San Francisco, CA: Jossey-Bass.

Gillespie, F. (1998). Instructional design for the new technologies. In K. Herr Gillespie (Ed.), *The impact of technology on faculty development, life and work* (pp. 39–52). New Directions for Teaching and Learning, No. 76. San Francisco, CA: Jossey-Bass.

Grunert, J. (1997). *The course syllabus: A learner-centered approach.* Bolton, MA: Anker.

Shea, T. P., Sherer, P. D., & Kristensen, E. W. (2002). Harnessing the potential of online faculty development: Challenges and opportunities. In D. Lieberman & C. Wehlburg (Eds.), *To improve the academy: Vol. 20. Resources for faculty, instructional, and organizational development* (pp. 162–178). Bolton, MA: Anker.

Contact:

Laurie Bellows
Faculty and TA Consultant
University of Nebraska
201 Benton Hall
Lincoln, NE 68588
Voice   (402) 472-9764
Fax   (402) 472-4932
Email   lbellows1@unl.edu

Joseph R. Danos
Delgado Community College
2600 General Meyer Ave.
New Orleans, LA 70114
Voice   (504) 361-6157
Email   jdanos@dcc.edu

Laurie Bellows is with the Office of Graduate Studies at the University of Nebraska, Lincoln where she coordinates all centralized instructional support for graduate teaching assistants and collaborates with departments in discipline-specific TA training and development. She facilitates online workshops for faculty and teaches an online graduate course in college teaching and an undergraduate course in Educational Psychology.

Joseph R. Danos is an Associate Professor of Accounting at Delgado Community College. In his former position of Associate Dean of Business Studies, he introduced Blackboard to Delgado and oversaw the development and offering of 17 online courses for his division in three years. He has facilitated two online faculty development workshops at the college.

Section III

Student-Centered Faculty Development

10

Accommodating Students with Disabilities: Professional Development Needs of Faculty

Sheryl Burgstahler
University of Washington

Faculty members play an important role in making academic programs accessible to postsecondary students with disabilities. However, instructors do not always possess the knowledge, experiences, and attitudes that result in the most inclusive environment for these students. A literature review was conducted to explore what faculty members need to know about accommodating students with disabilities in their courses and how they can best gain this knowledge. These results were used to develop a comprehensive set of training options that can be used with postsecondary instructors nationwide. The content of these options focuses on legal issues, accommodation strategies, and resources. Modes of instruction include on-site training, printed materials, distance learning, web-based self-paced instruction, and video presentations.

INTRODUCTION

Federal legislation has resulted in higher expectations and greater participation of students with disabilities in standards-based pre-college curriculum. As a result, more young people with disabilities are encouraged to pursue further learning, more are prepared to pursue postsecondary studies, and greater numbers of students with disabilities are attending postsecondary academic institutions (Gajar, 1998; Henderson, 2001; Horn & Berktold, 1999; National Council on Disability, 2000).The largest and fastest growing subgroup of freshmen who report disabilities have learning disabilities—40.4% in 2000 as compared to 16.1% in 1988 (Henderson, 2001). Percentages of students with disabilities who report other types of disabilities are 16.1% blindness or partial sight, 15.4% health-related impairments, 8.6% hearing impairments, 7.1% orthopedic impairments, 2.9% speech impairments, and 16.9% other impairments (Henderson, 2001).

Students with disabilities who participate in postsecondary education are more likely to enroll in two-year community and technical colleges than are students without disabilities (Horn & Berktold, 1999; National Council on Disability, 2000). Students with disabilities are less likely than their counterparts without disabilities to stay enrolled or to earn a postsecondary degree or credential. After five years, 53% of students with disabilities and 64% of those without disabilities have attained a degree or certificate or are still enrolled. Of these students, only 16% of those with disabilities, compared to 27% of those without disabilities, have attained a bachelor's degree (Horn & Berktold, 1999). Clearly, postsecondary educational outcomes are not as positive for students with disabilities as for those without disabilities.

Individuals with disabilities also find it difficult to secure and maintain employment (McNeil, 2000; National Council on Disability, 2000; Phelps & Hanley-Maxwell, 1997). However, for people with disabilities, a postsecondary education is highly positively correlated with employment options and higher incomes. For individuals with disabilities there is actually a stronger positive correlation between level of education and rate of employment than for people without disabilities (Stodden, 1998). The employment rate is 16% for people with disabilities who have less than a high school diploma, 30% for those who have graduated from high school, 45% for those who have attended a college, and 50% for those who have at least four years of college (Yelin & Katz, 1994).

The low employment rates for people with disabilities coupled with the positive impact of postsecondary education makes increasing the college success of this group an important goal. The cost of failure to provide accessible postsecondary education for people with disabilities, both to these individuals as well as to society, is significant (Blackorby & Wagner, 1996; Gajar, 1998; National Council on Disability, 2000; Phelps & Hanley-Maxwell, 1997; Reskin & Roos, 1990; Stodden & Dowrick, 2001; Wagner & Blackorby, 1996).

LEGAL ISSUES

Section 504 of the Rehabilitation Act of 1973 prohibits discrimination against individuals with disabilities in programs and services that receive federal funds, which includes the vast majority of postsecondary institutions. The Americans with Disabilities Act (ADA) of 1990 reinforces and extends the requirements of Section 504 to public programs and services, regardless of whether they receive federal funds. For qualified students who disclose their disabilities and present appropriate documentation, postsecondary institutions must provide reasonable accommodations to assure equal access to program offerings (Frank & Wade, 1993; McCusker, 1995; West, Kregel, Getzel, Zhu, Ipsen, & Martin, 1993). These requirements apply to programs and services offered on the Internet as well (Patrick, 1996; Waddell, 1999). Court cases and complaints to the United States Department of Education Office of Civil Rights regarding the rights of postsecondary students with disabilities have continued to increase since the passage of the Rehabilitation Act. Students have challenged postsecondary decisions regarding requests for modifications to academic programs, changes in graduation requirements, and accommodations in specific courses (Dona & Edmister, 2001). Dealing with the complaints and litigation that result when postsecondary institutions fail to provide reasonable accommodations to students with disabilities can be costly.

PROFESSIONAL DEVELOPMENT NEEDS OF FACULTY

In order for students with disabilities to succeed in postsecondary education and for postsecondary institutions to meet their legal and ethical obligations, qualified people with disabilities must have equal access to educational programs, including those offered in classrooms, on field trips, in science labs, in computing facilities, and on the Internet. The success of these students depends upon their own efforts as well as those of campus support services and instructors (Frank & Wade, 1993; National Center for the Study of Postsecondary Educational Supports, 2000a, 2000b; National Council on Disability, 2000). In particular, the willingness and ability of instructors to make reasonable accommodations in their courses can impact student achievement (Fonosch & Schwab, 1981; Moore, Newlon, & Nye, 1986).

Research suggests that many faculty members are generally willing to provide disability-related accommodations in their courses (Aksamit, Morris, & Leuenberger, 1987; Hill, 1996; Houck, Asselin, Troutman, & Arrington, 1992; Leyser, 1989; Leyser, Vogel, Wyland, & Brulle, 1998; Nelson, Dodd, & Smith, 1990). However, as a group, faculty have little or no training or experience in teaching students with disabilities and are often not fully aware of their legal obligations to provide access, of best practices for teaching students with disabilities, of computer and other technologies that increase academic and career options for people with disabilities, or of campus resources (Dodd, Fischer, Hermanson, & Nelson, 1990; Dona & Edmister, 2001; Leyser, 1989; Leyser et al., 1998; National Center for the Study of Postsecondary Educational

Supports, 2000a, 2000b; Thompson, Bethea, & Turner, 1997). Some faculty are concerned about maintaining academic integrity and confused about their roles and responsibilities in providing accommodations.

Some instructors have mistaken beliefs about the abilities of individuals with disabilities to succeed in academic studies and careers. Faulty assumptions are due, at least in part, to lack of knowledge about disabilities and of technological innovations that can contribute to their success in academics and careers, and to stereotypical negative images of people with disabilities in the media (Alexander & Strain, 1978; Anderson-Inman, Knox-Quinn, & Szymanski, 1999; Blackhurst, Lahm, Harrision, & Chandler, 1999; Hannah & Pliner, 1983; Jamieson, 1984; Yuker, 1994). Faculty attitudes influence behavior toward students that, in turn, affects both student self-image and academic performance (Alexander & Strain, 1978). Prejudicial treatment creates obstacles for students with disabilities in higher education that can be more disabling than their physical or cognitive impairments.

Faculty attitudes about students with disabilities have been found to be related to academic discipline. For example, education, social science, and business faculty have been found to be among those more willing to accommodate students with disabilities, while science faculty are among those who are less willing (Fonosch & Schwab, 1981; Nelson, Dodd, & Smith, 1990). Some instructors feel that students with certain types of disabilities do not belong in their fields of study.

Many instructors support the integration of students with sensory and physical disabilities in higher education but are less supportive of integrating students with learning disabilities and social/psychological/emotional disabilities (Burgstahler, Duclos, & Turcotte, 1999; Hannah & Pliner, 1983; Leyser, 1989; Matthews, Anderson, & Skolnick, 1987; Minner & Prater, 1984). There is ongoing debate about how to honor both the rights of students with disabilities to receive "reasonable" accommodations and the rights of academic programs to maintain academic standards. Faculty members are more willing to implement accommodations that are easy to provide, require little extra time, and facilitate the integration of students into the planned course activities. They are less willing to provide accommodations that they perceive will lower course standards or give unfair advantage to some students, such as overlooking misspellings, allowing substitutions for courses, providing alternative assignments, and providing copies of lecture notes (Leyser, 1989; Leyser et al., 1998; Nelson, Dodd, & Smith 1990).

Some instructors feel uncomfortable talking to students with disabilities. Faculty members with more experience with and knowledge about students with disabilities, however, are more comfortable working with these students than those with less experience and knowledge (Aksamit, Leuenberger, & Morris, 1987; Fichten, Amsel, Bourdon, & Creti, 1988; Fonosch & Schwab, 1981).

Reports of negative experiences with faculty members by students with disabilities are not widespread. However, some students report that faculty members project negative attitudes and lack of knowledge about accommodations. Others report having difficulty acquiring needed academic accommodations, especially for learning and other disabilities that are not obvious, and maintaining confidentiality of disability-related information (Burgstahler, Duclos, & Turcotte, 1999; Hill, 1996; National Center for the Study of Postsecondary Educational Supports, 2000b). Students with disabilities are sometimes reluctant to ask for accommodations because of their concerns that instructors might have negative attitudes about them and may not respect their privacy (Burgstahler, Duclos, & Turcotte, 1999; Moore, Newlon, & Nye, 1986; National Center on the Study of Postsecondary Educational Supports, 2000b).

Both faculty and students express the need for faculty members to increase their knowledge and understanding of legal obligations to provide academic accommodations, typical accommodation strategies, and available resources (Burgstahler, Duclos, & Turcotte, 1999; Leyser et al., 1998; National Center on the Study of Postsecondary Educational Supports, 2000b). The role that assistive technology can play in accommodating students with disabilities as well as steps instructors can take to make their information resources (e.g., web pages) accessible has also been suggested as relevant content (Fichten, Barile, & Asuncion, 1999). In addition, faculty members could use guidance on how to more effectively communicate with students who have disabilities about the impact of their disabilities and accommodation issues.

Overall, faculty members and administrators are receptive to receiving training in these areas (Nelson, Dodd, & Smith, 1990; Leyser et al., 1998). They report a desire for multiple presentation delivery methods, including short printed publications, Internet-based resources, and in-person short presentations (Burgstahler et al., 1999; Leyser et al., 1998).

RESEARCH INTO PRACTICE

Legal mandates, poor postsecondary employment outcomes for people with disabilities, and a positive correlation between college participation and career success combine to make it critically important that postsecondary programs are accessible to students with disabilities. Since faculty members play a central role in the learning of all students, yet have limited knowledge and experience in accommodating students with disabilities, professional development for this group has the potential to improve the postsecondary academic and career outcomes for students with disabilities (Caffarella & Zinn, 1999). Training at two-year colleges is especially important because of the greater numbers of students with disabilities who attend these schools when compared to the numbers who attend four-year institutions (Horn & Berktold, 1999; National Council on Disability, 2000).

On many campuses, staff from disabled student services programs are in the best position to take the lead in delivering programs to help faculty and administrators more fully include students with disabilities in their courses. Trainers who cultivate a rich, interactive dialogue as well as develop an ongoing relationship with faculty can go a long way toward creating positive attitudes about accommodating these students. To develop the most appropriate training options, staff from the disabled student services office can collaborate with faculty from specific academic departments, as well as staff with specialized expertise from computing centers and other campus support services. Learning about the experiences of students with disabilities on campus in general and within specific departments can also help to assure that training content is relevant.

Proven practices in teaching the adult learner can provide general guidance as professional development options for faculty are being developed. This field of study suggests that trainers develop content that is relevant and useful to members of the audience; involve participants in both the development and the learning process; understand the adult need for self-directed learning; respect participant expertise in their fields; provide opportunities for participants to share insights, experiences, and information; and recognize the group's wide range in knowledge, experiences, and learning styles (Addison, 1978; Brookfield, 1993; Claxton & Ralston, 1978; Conti, 1998; Grasha, 1984; Knowles, 1980; Pierce, 1998; Thomas, 1991; Tight, 1981; Wooldridge, 1995; Yuker, 1994).

Specifically, on-site instruction about working with students who have disabilities should include opportunities for faculty participants to be engaged in learning, to share experiences and concerns in working with students who have disabilities, to learn from their peers, and to address specific questions. Faculty participants should be allowed to openly discuss fears, issues, and concerns. Strategies and materials used should address the diversity of learning needs represented in the audience. Some instructors are eager to learn about disability-related issues; others may define their interest as the minimum amount of information they need to perform their jobs; all participants have time constraints. Trainers should model an attitude of respect for the rights and responsibilities of the institution, students with disabilities, and faculty members.

Faculty development options can address the need expressed by faculty for information about disability-related accommodations, legal issues, and resources. It is also important to provide guidance about how to best communicate with students who have disabilities and how to preserve the confidentiality of disability-related information. Faculty training on disability issues can serve to dismiss incorrect perceptions regarding legal responsibilities and capabilities of people with disabilities. Carefully designed materials and strategies can offer faculty members practical strategies and meaningful discussion about disability issues. Trainers should emphasize that academic accommodations do not need to be elaborate; creativity and common sense can lead to practical measures that assure access. Special training opportunities regarding accommodating students with learning disabilities should be made available since the largest group of students with disabilities is composed of those with learning disabilities. Disabilities of this type are especially challenging for faculty members to understand and accommodate (Houck, Asselin, Troutman, & Arrington, 1992; Vogel, Leyser, Wyland, & Brulle, 1999).

Faculty development opportunities can help make instructors more comfortable with their role in providing a learning environment which, for all students, provides full access to the content and activities they offer, yet does not give unfair advantage to one group. Helping instructors make a paradigm shift from a sole focus on special accommodations for students with disabilities to employment of universal design principles as they develop instructional strategies in their courses may make them more responsive to the needs of learners with a wide range of characteristics. In contrast to considering only the average or typical student when course materials and strategies are developed, this approach requires that instructors consider the wide variety of characteristics of students who might enroll in their courses, including those with disabilities, for the purpose of creating more inclusive on-site and electronic learning environments (Bowe, 2000; Burgstahler, 2000).

Professional development tailored to specific academic units can include examples of accommodations typical in those fields of study. Specifically, training for faculty members in academic areas where advancing technology increases opportunities for the participation of students with disabilities can correct faulty assumptions about what students with disabilities can accomplish and clarify the availability of campus resources. For example, disabled students service staff might co-present with staff from the campus computing services organization to offer professional development to faculty members in information technology fields. Participants could be made aware of assistive technology that allows individuals with a wide range of disabilities to access computers and other electronic devices, as long as web pages and other electronic resources are designed in accessible formats. Instruction on how to purchase and create electronic products that are accessible to individuals with disabilities could also be included in the presentation.

Key information needed by faculty members and administrators should be provided in a variety of formats and venues in order to address differences in faculty learning styles and preferences, time constraints, schedules, knowledge and experiences, and desire for information. Besides on-site presentations, printed, web-based, and videotaped options should be explored. Assuring that follow-up, case-specific support is readily available as needs arise can serve to lower the level of concern of faculty members and reduce the time needed to provide effective accommodations.

THE DO-IT MODEL DEMONSTRATION PROJECT

DO-IT (Disabilities, Opportunities, Internetworking, and Technology), at the University of Washington, developed a set of professional development options for postsecondary faculty to increase their knowledge and skills in supporting students with disabilities. The curriculum was developed and delivered through a team of instructors and administrators from 23 postsecondary institutions nationwide. Each team member adopted a partner school with demographics different than their own, resulting in a group of 23 two-year and technical colleges and 23 four-year schools overall. A survey of the literature and the collective experiences of team members informed the development of all project products and strategies.

The *DO-IT Prof* project team created a short publication that can be modified for use on any campus (www.washington.edu/doit/Brochures/Academics/teachers.html). It summarizes the content of most interest to faculty members and administrators—legal issues, accommodation strategies, and campus resources. It also includes a sample statement that can be put on a syllabus to encourage students with disabilities to make an appointment to discuss disability-related accommodations with the instructor. Responding to the diverse content and scheduling needs and delivery options reported by faculty and administrators, the *DO-IT Prof* project created six models of professional development. All delivery options focus on typical academic accommodations for students with disabilities, legal issues, and campus resources. They also deal with ways to communicate with students with disabilities as well as assure confidentiality of disability-related information. Professional development options are adaptable and can be tailored to the individual needs of faculty members, as part of regular departmental meetings or as separate presentations.

The six models of professional development, along with evaluative data from participants, are described below (DO-IT, 2001a). Models 1, 2, and 3 are on-site presentations.

Model 1. This 20- to 30-minute presentation is designed to be delivered to faculty and administrators at regular departmental meetings to introduce participants to basic legal issues, accommodation strategies, and campus resources. The cooperative relationship between students and instructors is emphasized. An eight-minute videotape, *Working Together: Faculty and Students with Disabilities,* (DO-IT, 2001b) may be incorporated into this short presentation.

Model 2. One- to two-hour presentations focus on accommodation strategies for students with disabilities, legal issues, and campus resources. The cooperative relationship between the student, the instructor, and the campus office that supports students with disabilities is emphasized in the videotape *Building the Team: Faculty, Staff and Students Working Together* (DO-IT, 2001c).

Model 3. A series of tailored presentations were developed by the *DO-IT Prof* project. Topics were chosen in response to professional development needs expressed by faculty members and administrators. For example, one training topic deals with accommodating students who have learning disabilities, the largest group of students with disabilities on postsecondary campuses and the one for which faculty members report the most confusion and concern. One tailored training module shows educators how to make their web pages accessible to students with disabilities and another teaches them how to develop accessible distance learning courses.

In total, *DO-IT Prof* Models 1, 2, and 3 have been presented to more than 5,000 faculty members and administrators in postsecondary institutions nationwide. Short printed materials have been distributed at most of the presentations. The results from a sample of 878 surveys completed by participants suggest that faculty members and administrators who participate in these training options have a greater understanding of their legal obligations, feel better prepared to accommodate students with disabilities in their classes, and are more aware of campus resources. Respondents indicated what they learned by rating their level of agreement with statements made about the content of presentations on a scale of 1 to 5 where 1 = strongly disagree and 5 = strongly agree. Overall, participants agreed that as a result of the presentations, they were better able to find resources on their campuses to accommodate students with disabilities (mean = 4.46), and that they gained knowledge about legal obligations (mean = 4.72), specific accommodations (mean = 4.76), and technology available (mean = 4.46) to support students with disabilities (DO-IT, 2001). Personal reactions to the on-site training were also very positive. They include:

- "[I learned] tape recorders are available to students with disabilities as an accommodation in the classroom." (faculty)

- "The accommodations in the classroom were useful because [they] helped me to understand the procedure and how to accommodate the student." (faculty)

- "[I learned] specific parameters of college/university obligations to provide accommodations." (faculty)

- "This was the tip of the iceberg. I'd like more in-depth seminars to follow." (teaching assistant)

Model 4. The *DO-IT Prof* project has made available to faculty self-paced, online instruction with comprehensive content that is tailored to faculty interests and needs. In addition, downloadable multimedia presentations and extensive lists of references and links to other useful web sites are available at the Faculty Room web site (www.washington.edu/doit/Faculty). This material is tailored specifically to postsecondary faculty and administrators. "The great strength of The Faculty Room concept lies in its quick and almost universal accessibility," according to John Pedraza, disabilities resource coordinator at Michigan State University (MSU). "The Faculty Room is a great site for faculty to learn more about students with disabilities at their own pace when they have immediate questions to be answered," Pedraza said. "MSU faculty find it extremely useful." Other reactions to this resource include:

- "[I learned] the DSS [Disabled Student Services] office is a resource for me as well as the student." (administrator)

- "I learned a lot about the technology that is available." (faculty member)

- "All the information was very informative! Thanks for the web site resources." (instructional designer)

- "I was really impressed with the system available on campus." (teaching assistant)

Responses to the question, Which parts of The Faculty Room were the most useful to you and why? included:

- "Overall descriptions and case studies because I could use them as links to our database!"

- "The case studies/FAQ's—but all of it really. I came across this web site today via a listserv I belong to, and so far I think it is a gold mine. It's very clearly presented and all useful information. I'm glad I found it."

- "I loved accessing it as it could be linked with our work! Perfect collaboration!"

- "I like that it's easy, convenient, that I can bookmark it, and go back to it when I need to—especially the case studies. There's nothing I really dislike . . . "

- "I am the disability services person at my school and I am very impressed with this site. I am considering notifying all the faculty about it via email so they can link up to it as needed."

- "Super resource. Please keep it going and do not change any of the URLs as you are firmly linked into our Learning and Teaching links throughout the database!! :>))."

Model 5. A distance any time, any where course provides lessons and discussion delivered via electronic mail. The lessons for this distance learning course can be obtained in the Faculty Room at www.washington.edu/doit/Faculty/Presentations/Distance/. They can by easily tailored to and delivered on any postsecondary campus, perhaps as part of orientations for new faculty.

Model 6. The televised instruction option uses a series of training videotapes to deliver professional development on public television stations hosted by institutions of higher education nationwide. As with the other models of instructional delivery, these tapes were developed in response to interests and needs expressed by faculty members and administrators. Videotaped presentations are downloadable from the Faculty Room and videotapes can be purchased from DO-IT.

CONCLUSION

Whether conscious or unconscious, the prejudicial attitudes and lack of knowledge and skills on the part of instructors may create barriers to the pursuit of educational opportunities for students with disabilities. Full access to postsecondary programs can be promoted through the increased knowledge and skills of all stakeholders and better coordination among faculty and support services. Ultimately, increased knowledge and skills of instructors regarding legal issues, accommodations, and resources can lead to more positive postsecondary and career outcomes for students with disabilities.

References

Addison, W. (1978). *Helping others learn: Designing programs for adults.* Reading, MA: McLagan.

Aksamit, D., Morris, M., & Leuenberger, J. (1987). Preparation of student services professionals and faculty for serving learning-disabled college students. *Journal of College Student Personnel, 28,* 53–59.

Alexander, C., & Strain, P. (1978). A review of educator's attitudes toward handicapped children and the concept of mainstreaming. *Psychology in the Schools, 15,* 390–396.

Anderson-Inman, L., Knox-Quinn, C., & Szymanski, M. (1999). Computer-supported studying: Stories of successful transition to postsecondary education. *Career Development for Exceptional Individuals, 22* (2), 185–212.

Blackhurst, A. E., Lahm, E. A., Harrison, E. M., & Chandler, W. G. (1999). A framework for aligning technology with transition competencies. *Career Development for Exceptional Individuals, 22* (2), 131–151.

Blackorby, J., & Wagner, M. (1996). Longitudinal post-school outcomes of youth with disabilities: Findings from the national longitudinal transition study. *Exceptional Children, 62* (5), 399–413.

Bowe, F. G. (2000). *Universal design in education: Teaching nontraditional students.* Westport, CT: Bergin & Garvey.

Brookfield, S. D. (1993). Self-directed learning, political clarity and the critical practice of adult education. *Adult Education Quarterly, 43* (4), 227–242.

Burgstahler, S. (2000). *Universal design of instruction.* Seattle, WA: University of Washington, DO-IT.

Burgstahler, S., Duclos, R., & Turcotte, M. (1999). *Preliminary findings: Faculty, teaching assistant, and student perceptions regarding accommodating students with disabilities in postsecondary environments.* Seattle, WA: University of Washington, DO-IT.

Caffarella, S., & Zinn, L. (1999). Professional development for faculty in higher education: A conceptual framework of barriers and supports. *Innovative Higher Education, 23* (3), 241–254.

Claxton, C. S., & Ralston, Y. (1978). *Learning styles: Their impact on teaching and administration.* Washington, DC: American Association for Higher Education.

Conti, G. J. (1998). Identifying your teaching style. In M. W. Galbraith (Ed.), *Adult learning methods* (pp. 73–77). Malabar, FL: Kreiger.

Dodd, J. M., Fischer, J., Hermanson, M., & Nelson, J. R. (1990). Tribal college faculty willingness to provide accommodations to students with learning disabilities. *Journal of American Indian Education, 30* (1), 8–16.

DO-IT. (2001a). *DO-IT Prof Annual Report.* Seattle, WA: University of Washington, DO-IT.

DO-IT, University of Washington (Producer), & Burgstahler, S. (Director). (2001b). *Building the team: Faculty, staff, and students working together* [Videotape]. Seattle, WA: University of Washington, DO-IT.

DO-IT, University of Washington (Producer), & Burgstahler, S. (Director). (2001c). *Working together: Faculty and students with disabilities* [Videotape]. Seattle, WA: University of Washington, DO-IT.

Dona, J., & Edmister, J. H. (2001). An examination of community college faculty members' knowledge of the Americans with Disabilities Act of 1990 at the fifteen community colleges in Mississippi. *Journal of Postsecondary Education and Disability, 14* (2), 91–103.

Fichten, C. S., Amsel, R., Bourdon, C. V., & Creti, L. (1988). Interaction between college students with a physical disability and their professors. *Journal of Applied Rehabilitation Counseling, 19,* 13–21.

Fichten, C., Barile, M., & Asuncion, J. V. (1999). *Learning technologies: Students with disabilities in postsecondary education.* Office of Learning Technologies. Montreal, Canada: Dawson College, Adaptech Project.

Fonosch, G. G., & Schwab, L. O. (1981). Attitudes of selected university faculty members toward disabled students. *Journal of College Student Personnel, 22,* 229–235.

Frank, K., & Wade, P. (1993). Disabled student services in postsecondary education: Who's responsible for what? *Journal of College Student Development, 34* (1), 26–30.

Gajar, A. (1998). Postsecondary education. In F. Rusch & J. Chadsey (Eds.), *Beyond high school: Transition from school to work* (pp. 383–405). Belmont, CA: Wadsworth.

Grasha, A. (1984). Learning styles: The journey from Greenwich Observatory to the college classroom. *Improving College and University Teaching, 22,* 46–53.

Hannah, M., & Pliner, S. (1983). Teacher attitudes toward handicapped children: A review and synthesis. *School Psychology Review, 12,* 12–25.

Henderson, C. (2001). *College freshmen with disabilities: A biennial statistical profile.* Washington, DC: American Council on Education.

Hill, J. L. (1996). Speaking out: Perceptions of students with disabilities regarding adequacy of services and willingness of faculty to make accommodations. *Journal of Postsecondary Education and Disability, 12* (1), 22–43.

Horn, L., & Berktold, J. (1999). Students with disabilities in postsecondary education: A profile of preparation, participation, and outcomes. *Education Statistics Quarterly, 1* (3), 59–64.

Houck, C., Asselin, S., Troutman, G., & Arrington, J. (1992). Students with learning disabilities in the university environment: A study of faculty and student perceptions. *Journal of Learning Disabilities, 25* (10), 678–684.

Jamieson, J. (1984). Attitudes of educators toward the handicapped. In R. Jones (Ed.), *Attitudes and attitude change in special education: Theory and practice* (pp. 206–222). Arlington, VA: The Council for Exceptional Children.

Knowles, M. S. (1980). *The modern practice of adult education: From pedagogy to andragogy.* New York, NY: Cambridge Books.

Leyser, Y. (1989). A survey of faculty attitudes and accommodations for students with disabilities. *Journal of Postsecondary Education and Disability, 7* (3 & 4), 97–108.

Leyser, Y., Vogel, S., Wyland, S., & Brulle, A. (1998). Faculty attitudes and practices regarding students with disabilities: Two decades after implementation of Section 504. *Journal of Postsecondary Education and Disability, 13* (3), 5–19.

Matthews, P., Anderson, D., & Skolnick, B. (1987). Faculty attitudes toward accommodations for college students with learning disabilities. *Learning Disabilities Focus, 3,* 46–52.

McCusker, C. (1995). The Americans with Disabilities Act: Its potential for expanding the scope of reasonable academic accommodations. *Journal of College and University Law, 21* (4), 619–641.

McNeil, J. M. (2000). Employment, earnings, and disability. Prepared for the 75th annual Conference of the Western Economic Association International, Vancouver, Canada.

Minner, S., & Prater, G. (1984). College teachers' expectations of LD students. *Academic Therapy, 20* (2), 225–259.

Moore, C. J., Newlon, B. J., & Nye, N. (1986). Faculty awareness of needs of physically disabled students in the college classroom. *Bulletin of the Association on Handicapped Student Services Programs in Postsecondary Education, 4,* 137–145.

National Center for the Study of Postsecondary Educational Supports (NCSPES). (2000a). *National survey of educational support provision to students with disabilities in postsecondary education settings.* Honolulu, HI: University of Hawaii at Manoa.

National Center for the Study of Postsecondary Educational Supports (NCSPES). (2000b). *Postsecondary education and employment for students with disabilities: Focus group discussions on supports and barriers in lifelong learning.* Honolulu, HI: University of Hawaii at Manoa.

National Council on Disability. (2000). *Transition and post-school outcomes for youth with disabilities: Closing the gaps to post-secondary education and employment.* Washington, DC: Author.

Nelson, J., Dodd, J., & Smith, D. (1990). Faculty willingness to accommodate students with learning disabilities: A comparison among academic divisions. *Journal of Learning Disabilities, 23* (3), 185–189.

Patrick, D. L. (1996). Correspondence to Senator Tom Harkin, September 9, 1996. Retrieved March 16, 2002 from www.usdoj.gov/crt/foia/cltr204.txt

Phelps, L. A., & Hanley-Maxwell, C. (1997). School-to-work transitions for youth with disabilities: A review of outcomes and practices. *Review of Educational Research, 67* (2), 197–226.

Pierce, G. (1998, Spring). Teaching teachers: A model for the professional development of new faculty. *Adult Learning,* 17–20.

Reskin, B., & Roos, P. (1990). *Job queues. Gender queues.* Philadelphia, PA: Temple University Press.

Schmetzke, A. (2001) Online distance education: 'Anytime, anywhere' but not for everyone. *Information Technology and Disability Journal, 7* (2). Available http://www.rit.edu/~easi/itd/itdv07n2/axel.htm

Stodden, R. A. (1998). School-to-work transition: Overview of disability legislation. In F. Rusch & J. Chadsey (Eds.), *Beyond high school: Transition from school to work.* Belmont, CA: Wadsworth Publishing.

Stodden, R. A., & Dowrick, P. W. (2001). Postsecondary education and employment of adults with disabilities. *American Rehabilitation, 25* (3), 19–23.

Thomas, A. M. (1991). *Beyond education: A new perspective on society's management of learning.* San Francisco, CA: Jossey-Bass.

Thompson, A., Bethea, L., & Turner, J. (1997). Faculty knowledge of disability laws in high education: A survey. *Rehabilitation Counseling Bulletin, 40*, 166–180.

Tight, M. (Ed.). (1981). *Adult learning and education.* Kent, England: Croom Helm.

Vogel, S., Leyser, Y., Wyland, S., & Brulle, A. (1999). Students with learning disabilities in higher education: Faculty attitude and practices. *Learning Disabilities Research & Practice, 14* (3), 173–186.

Waddell, C. D. (1999). *The growing digital divide in access for people with disabilities: Overcoming barriers to participation in the digital economy.* Retrieved from http://www.icdri.org/the_digital_divide.htm

Wagner, M., & Blackorby, J. (1996). Transition from high school to work or college: How special education students fare. *The future of children: Special education for students with disabilities, 6* (1), 103–120.

West, M., Kregel, J., Getzel, E., Zhu, M., Ipsen, S., & Martin, E. (1993). Beyond Section 504: Satisfaction and empowerment of students with disabilities in higher education. *Exceptional Children, 59* (5), 456–467.

Wooldridge, B. (1995). Increasing the effectiveness of university/college instruction: Integrating the results of learning style research into course design and delivery. In R. R. Sims & S. J. Sims (Eds.), *The importance of learning styles* (pp. 49–68). Westport, CT: Greenwood.

Yelin, E., & Katz, P. (1994). Labor force trends of persons with and without disabilities. *Monthly Labor Review, 117,* 36–42.

Yuker, H. (1994). Variables that influence attitudes toward people with disabilities. *Psychosocial Perspectives on Disability, 9* (5), 3–22.

ACKNOWLEDGMENTS

This chapter is based upon work supported by the National Science Foundation (grant #9800324) and the United States Department of Education, Office of Postsecondary Education (grant #P33A990042). Any opinions, findings, and conclusions or recommendations expressed in this material are those of the author and do not necessarily reflect the views of federal government.

Contact:

Sheryl Burgstahler
Director, DO-IT
4545 15th Avenue NE, Room 109
University of Washington
Seattle, WA 98105-4527
Voice   (206) 543-0622
Fax   (206) 685-4054
Email   sherylb@cac.washington.edu

Sheryl Burgstahler directs project DO-IT (Disabilities, Opportunities, Internet-working, and Technology) at the University of Washington. Dr. Burgstahler also co-directs the National Center on Accessible Information in Education (AccessIT) to promote the use of accessible technology in educational settings. She has published dozens of articles and delivered presentations at national and international conferences that focus on the full inclusion of individuals with disabilities in postsecondary education, distance learning, work-based learning, and electronic communities, and is the author or co-author of six books on using the Internet with pre-college students. She is Assistant Director of Information Systems and Affiliate Associate Professor in Education at the University of Washington.

11

Integrity in Learner-Centered Teaching

Douglas Robertson
Eastern Kentucky University

Learner-centered teaching challenges teachers with inherent conflicts and can be viewed as a conflicted educational helping relationship. This chapter explores fundamental conflicts in learner-centered teaching as well as ways to handle them constructively. Learner-centered teacher integrity is seen as the degree to which contradictory demands on the teacher (e.g., facilitating learning as well as evaluating it) are brought into synergistic relationship. A process for enhancing these synergies is suggested. This discussion emerges from a line of work that attempts to further develop the learner-centered teaching role in higher education (Robertson, 1996, 1997, 1999a, 1999b, 2000a, 2000b, 2000c, 2001).

> The test of a first-rate intelligence is the ability to hold two opposed ideas in the mind at the same time, and still retain the ability to function.
>
> —*Fitzgerald (1945, p. 69)*

INTRODUCTION

Learner-centered teaching requires the kind of intelligence that Fitzgerald (1945) mentions. It does so, in part, because the role of the learner-centered teacher has within it fundamental conflicts. For example, learner-centered teachers must serve as both facilitators and evaluators, if not simultaneously, then at least in uncomfortably close, temporal proximity, as in, "Tell me what *you* think . . . and forget that I'm grading you." Learner-centered teaching constitutes what could be called a conflicted helping relationship (Robertson, 1996, 2000a, 2000b). Conflict denotes contention, antagonism, incompatibility, or contradiction; paradox indicates things that appear contradictory but are nonetheless true. I think that to which Fitzgerald refers above is paradox, or being able to function within the context of things that seem antagonistic and incompatible but go together even so. Learner-centered teaching urges us to transform conflict that is inherent in this educational helping relationship into paradox.

Some everyday teacher questions motivated my exploration of conflict in learner-centered teaching: How can I give a student whom I have been mentoring a "D" on an exam and still have the student's trust? How can I deal with the many demands for my time and passion—my love of my own learning, my love of the subject, my love of the students and their learning? How do I go on with the material for the group because I know that most of them are ready and I know that we must but I also know that I am leaving a few individuals behind, perhaps forever? How do I harden my heart but keep it soft? How do I keep up with my subject area and also learn about teaching and learning? How do I care for myself and for my students at the same time? The following chapter answers each of these different questions with the same answer: I must transform conflict into paradox and thereby enhance my teacher integrity.

This chapter identifies some fundamental conflicts in the learner-centered teaching role and explores ways of achieving integrity (or paradox) in this conflicted educational helping relationship. Building on an extensive analysis of pertinent research, theory, and practice, this discussion emerges from a line of work that attempts to contribute to the further conceptualization and professionalization of the learner-centered teaching role in colleges and universities (Robertson, 1996, 1997, 1999a, 1999b, 2000a, 2000b, 2000c, 2001).

LITERATURE REVIEW

Scholarship on role conflict and successful coping in collegiate teaching and learning contexts has concentrated primarily on students, especially returning adult students with their notorious multiple role responsibilities (e.g., Anderson & Miezitis, 1999; Clouder, 1997; Harvey, & Wiebe, 1997; Home, 1998; Mallinckrodt & Leong, 1992; McBride, 1997; Mikolaj & Boggs, 1991; Widoff, 1999). Some scholarship has addressed conflicts within the overall professor role, especially those involving research versus teaching (e.g., Burroughs, 1990; Holly, 1990; Stark, 1986; Weimer, 1997; Wong, 1995). However, with a few exceptions (e.g., Palmer, 1998), little work appears to have focused on inherent conflicts in the work of professors-as-teachers, much less on how to handle those conflicts constructively.

CONFLICTS IN LEARNER-CENTERED TEACHING

The following five antagonisms serve to illustrate the conflicted nature of the educational helping relationship, or learner-centered teaching. These fundamental conflicts occur to me when I reflect on my teacher work. Readers should feel free to add and delete as they see fit.

Facilitator Versus Evaluator

Facilitator. As a facilitator of student learning, the learner-centered teacher is devoted to specific people who show up at the party (or enroll in the course). Learner-centered teachers teach students not subjects. They attend to those specific students' abilities and disabilities, experience or lack of experience; personality; learning style; gender, race, and class socialization; rhythms; learning traumas; and so forth. They attempt to help individuals to progress vis-à-vis the course objectives from where they entered the course to where they exit the course, regardless of where they started, how fast they progressed, or how far. Many learner-centered teachers even hope that the students develop overall as persons as well. The learner-centered teacher (an educational helping professional) is devoted to the students' learning and development.

Evaluator. As an evaluator of student learning, the learner-centered teacher represents a variety of constituents besides the individual learners. These other constituents may often have different agendas than the learners. Their agendas usually relate to maintaining standards and the meaning of course credit and degrees within various communities, while the students' agendas are much more personalized. Learner-centered teachers have an obligation to represent the standards of their regional accreditation associations, disciplines, departments, colleges, universities, alumna, and often, surrounding geographical region. Not to sound grandiose, teachers who issue grades in accredited institutions have a lot of company in their heads as they decide the grading fate of individual students.

Conflict. The learner-centered teacher must gain the trust from individual learners that a viable helping relationship requires while at the same time rendering for external communities summative evaluations that may be damaging to individual learners and their academic progress.

Loving the Subject (Teacher Learning) Versus Loving the Students (Student Learning)

> No wonder teaching was called an art, the most difficult kind of art in which the final expression depends upon a delicate and dangerous balance between two people and a subject. Eliminate the subject and the whole center collapses . . . (Sarton, 1961, p. 213)

Teacher learning. The educational helping relationship exists because the learner wants help learning a subject (Robertson, 2000b). Without the subject, the relationship ceases to have meaning and purpose, and it feels weird (Sarton, 1961). I admit that one of the things that attracted me about college teaching is that it required (I would say allowed, even promoted) me to keep learning. I love learning about things that interest me. It puts a spring in my step. If I have to stop, I can't wait to get back to it. I feel eternally grateful that I get paid to do something that I love so much.

Student learning. While my subject expertise plays a critical role in student learning, often it needs to be reined in so that I can serve as an effective educational helping professional. For example, students learn better with prompt and rich feedback vis-à-vis their active use of that which is to be learned. As a learner-centered teacher, my love of student learning requires me to plan into my schedule as much, or more, time to create active learning opportunities for students and to provide feedback to them about their learning as I include for my own ongoing learning of the subject.

Conflict. Learner-centered teachers must love their own subject learning and their students' subject learning simultaneously and equally, a challenge that expresses itself most tangibly in decisions about how teachers spend their time.

Subject Expert Versus Teaching and Learning Expert

Subject expert. As just discussed, the college teacher—learner-centered or not—is expected to be a subject expert. The pressure to keep up with one's subject comes from many sources outside of the self. Our colleagues, our administrators, our professional communities, our proximate geographical communities, our alumnae, those same students that want us to attend to them and only them, all want us to know our stuff.

Teaching and learning expert. Learner-centered teachers take on another subject besides their discipline. They define teaching as facilitating learning, which necessitates adding the subjects of what learning is and how it can best be facilitated to one's existing subject specialties.

Conflict. As mentioned previously, learner-centered teachers must deal with the conflict between their own learning and their students' learning. Additionally, with limited time and energy allocated to their own subject learning, learner-centered teachers add a competitor to their disciplinary subjects—namely, the subject of teaching and learning. Again, this conflict reveals itself most concretely in teachers' resource management (e.g., time and money allocations, which conferences or sessions to attend, which books and journals to read, and so forth).

Caring for Students Versus Caring for Self

Caring for students. Learner-centered teachers devote themselves to students as related to the students learning the subject. They care about the students, their abilities, experience, rhythms, potential, and welfare.

Caring for self. Learner-centered teachers must care for themselves so that they do not exhaust the fundamental resource that cares for the students (themselves). In an airline emergency, when oxygen masks are required, parents must remember that it is not a selfish act, but a vitally caring act, for them to put the mask on themselves first in order to care best for their children. In teaching, something similar is true: Teachers must care for themselves in order to care for the students. In addition, teachers are in a position to model healthy self-esteem and healthy caring. The way in which they care for students and for themselves may be one of the most important lessons that they have to teach.

Conflict. Like practitioners of any helping profession, learner-centered teachers have to care simultaneously for themselves and for their students. The exhausted teacher says, "If I read one more student essay, I'll scream!" and decides to rejuvenate with an afternoon devoted to her or his own work instead. Often, like so many of the learner-centered teachers' conflicts, the struggle is expressed in a competition for time, energy, and other teacher resources. In studying the development of caring, Gilligan (1982) theorized that developmental perspectives arranged themselves into three progressions, beginning with a focus on the self, shifting to a focus on the other, and resolving to a simultaneous focus on the welfare of self and other. Learner-centered teachers face this developmental press.

Individual Mentor Versus Group Learning Leader

Individual mentor. Learner-centered teachers practice a respect for diversity (writ large) that expresses itself as a devotion to each and every student's learning, not student learning as some kind of aggregate abstraction. I focus on individual abilities, experience, and rhythms. I try to mentor individuals.

Group learning leader. As a member of the teaching and learning system, teachers are learning leaders. They have the formal authority and responsibility to make decisions for the group regarding what to do, when to do it, and so forth.

Conflict. Learner-centered teachers can individualize courses, build in optimal flexibility, and respect difference in all ways. Notwithstanding this dedicated devotion to individual students progressing in different ways and rhythms, learner-centered teachers must sometimes make decisions on behalf of the group that they know will result in leaving an individual student behind while at the same time trying to mentor that individual student.

Exercise

Brainstorm. What conflicts do you experience as a teacher—conflicts that seem to go with that role for you?

Evaluate. How central (important) is that conflict to your work as a teacher? Rate each conflict in terms of its centrality, 1 to 5, low to high.

Share. Ask a colleague (or several colleagues) to do the same and explore your responses together.

Approaches to Conflicting Demands

Building on role theory (Goode, 1960; Levinson, 1959), empirical research on handling conflicting role demands suggests that strategies often fall into three categories (Beutell & O'Hare, 1987; Hall, 1972), which are briefly explained below (Figure 11.1).

FIGURE 11.1
Three Primary Strategies for Handling Conflicting Role Demands

Approach to role demands	Attempt Change		Do not Attempt Change
Locus of control	External	Internal	External or internal
Strategies	**Negotiate with others**	**Negotiate with self**	**React**

Negotiate with Others

I can address the conflicting demands overtly with people making the demands and collaborate to find new, more compatible role responsibilities. Also, I can cooperatively define different levels of acceptable performance in areas of role responsibilities.

Negotiate with Self

I can do with myself as I do with others, namely, redesign role responsibilities or acceptable levels of performance. I can change conception of the roles and then work to accept a less than perfect, but still excellent, performance in those roles.

Just React

I can avoid changing anything (role responsibilities or acceptable levels of performance) except my effort—that is, just try harder. The data suggest that this strategy may work in the short term, but over the long haul, it leads to burnout. A combination of the first two strategies—negotiating with self and others—appears to be the healthiest and most effective long-term strategy (Hall, 1972).

Exercise

Focus. Review the conflicts that you identified as central to your work as a teacher, and pick one.

Visualize. Imagine how you typically deal with that conflict.

Evaluate. What's good and not so good about your typical response.

Share. Request a colleague (or several) to do the same and discuss your responses together.

LEARNER-CENTERED TEACHER INTEGRITY

I began preparing this chapter thinking about conflict and coping and came to realize that I was really interested in paradox and harmony. Words and images matter, and briefly exploring these, and related, words (s.v., Webster, 1966) leads to a useful conceptualization—a continuum of learner-centered teacher integrity.

Conflict, Coping, Managing

Conflict, cope, and manage come from words that have to do with clashing, hitting, and controlling through force. These words imply forcefully overcoming antagonisms, subduing them, repressing their tension. This approach, outcome, and connotation are not what I had in mind as the optimal approach to the conflicted helping relationship that is learner-centered teaching.

Paradox, Harmonizing, Synergizing, Integrating

Words such as paradox, harmony, synergism, and integrate come from words that involve joining things together (in particular, things that appear incompatible) in ways that create entities that are more complete and significantly more empowered than before the joining. This approach, outcome, and connotation is, most certainly, what I had in mind as describing those occasions when I sense that I am functioning honestly and optimally as a learner-centered teacher.

Continuum of Learner-Centered Teacher Integrity

I began to realize that these words relate to different positions along a continuum that expresses the degree to which learner-centered teachers are integrating antagonistic role demands and transforming potentially paralyzing conflicts into generative paradox (Figure 11.2).

FIGURE 11.2
Learner-Centered Teacher Integrity

LOW ⟵⟶		HIGH
Disintegrating, not coping with conflicts, falling apart. For example, abdicating the role of learner-centered teacher and seeing oneself as a master learner who disseminates information and determines the degree to which that teacher-centered information is learned by students.	Coping with conflicts, managing, surviving. For example, compartmentalizing roles, as in now I am going to put on my grading hat, and now I have my facilitator hat on.	Integrating conflicts, synergizing solutions, achieving paradox. For example, introducing students to the facilitator/evaluator conflict and asking them how they would deal with it.

Low integrity. In this state, the teacher is not resolving contradictory pulls and pushes very well. The frustrated teacher may say, "To heck with it! Who has time for this grief!" This lack of resolution may lead to a complete disintegration of the learner-centered perspective, which is then replaced by the default college teaching perspective—teacher-centeredness.

Medium integrity. The learner-centered teacher may get contradictory roles and responsibilities to coexist, but not integrate, by techniques such as compartmentalizing. In this instance, the conflicting demands may be satisfied but not at the same time. Metaphorically, teachers use "hat talk," as in putting on my grading hat or my facilitator hat, for example. The teacher and students may not feel much resolution or energy from this approach, but it is workable and generally acceptable to teachers and students. Its effect on the teaching and learning environment is less than optimal because the consequences of teacher behaviors (such as grading) cannot be stopped simply by overtly changing the prevailing metaphor.

High integrity. Optimally, the teacher may achieve a resolution of conflicting demands that creates important synergies. For example, I bring the facilitator versus evaluator conflict into the classroom overtly in the first class meeting as a part of explaining the orientation of the course and my teaching philosophy to the students. I explain how I have tried to work with the conflict, and I invite them to enter a teacher's frame of reference and imagine how they would deal with it. Sometimes some great ideas result and sometimes they do not. Regardless, entering the teacher's frame of reference not only helps the students to understand (and often own) the grading system, it also has a developmental press for them. It encourages them not only to see situations from a variety of perspectives but also to take increasing responsibility for being an authority themselves and directing their own learning. A synergy is created. The conflicts resolve themselves, and cognitive development results. A generative paradox is achieved.

Steps Toward Integrity

The question becomes how do we achieve this high level of integrity—these synergistic harmonies arising from seemingly contradictory demands, these generative paradoxes? Parker Palmer (1998), one of the few authors to write about the vital role that paradox plays in college teaching, says that we must tap a larger love:

> If we are to hold paradoxes together, our own love is absolutely necessary—and yet our own love is never enough. In a time of tension, we must endure with whatever love we can muster until that very tension draws a larger love into the scene. (p. 85)

According to Palmer (1998), how we get that larger love is to wait and to suffer:

> There is a name for the endurance we must practice until a larger love arrives: it is called suffering. We will not be able to teach in the power of paradox until we are willing to suffer the tension of opposites, until we understand that such suffering is neither to be avoided nor merely to be survived but must be actively embraced for the way it expands our own hearts. (p. 85)

Regarding the significance of the need to be able to sit with tension, to endure discomfort, to be patient, to persist, I am in complete agreement with Palmer. In addition, I think that we can do things to facilitate the process of achieving integrity, of creating synergies, and of experiencing that larger love (Figure 11.3).

FIGURE 11.3
Steps Toward Learner-Centered Teacher Integrity

Step	Task
Identification	Identify specific conflict and sources of conflicting demands in self and environment
Intervention	Negotiate with self and environment toward harmony, synergy (adjust expectations, create alternatives, reach accord)
Integration	External and internal force field analysis, identify forces of harmony and discord (integration and disintegration, barriers and supports), enhance forces of harmony, diminish forces of discord

Identification

Our first task is to accept the conflict and to identify it. Denial of conflict may interfere with the work of this phase. (For purposes of illustration, we continue with the common facilitator versus evaluator conflict throughout this discussion of the process's three phases.) In groups of college teachers, when I bring up the facilitator versus evaluator conflict, normally heads start nodding in agreement, that particular tension being so ubiquitous among college teachers. Sometimes, one professor will argue that she or he does not experience a conflict among those functions. However, it soon becomes clear that the person does feel the conflict but simply does not want to call it one. For whatever reason, teachers may defend themselves psychologically through denial of conflict. We need to accept that our chosen teaching perspective—learner-centered teaching—has conflict inherent in it, and we need to be alert to identifying the most outstanding conflicts in our own particular teaching practice. We then need to identify the primary sources of the conflicting role demands. For example, in the conflict between the roles of facilitator and evaluator, who or what is asking us to behave as a learning facilitator and defining for us the specific expectations for that role? The same question can be asked for the role of evaluator.

Facilitator. We may have within our own minds a well-developed exemplar of the learning facilitator with which we compare ourselves. We may participate in professional communities, both directly and through print and electronic media, that have as the bedrock of their discourse facilitator exemplars such as Belenky, Clinchy, Goldberger, and Taurle's *midwife* (1986), Brookfield's *skilled teacher* (1990), Daloz's *mentor* (1986), Freiere's *partner* (1993), Knowles's *andragogue* (1975, 1989; Knowles & Associates, 1984), or Mezirow's *emancipatory educator* (1991). We may have departmental colleagues with whom we interact on a daily basis who articulate frequently exemplary images of college teachers as learning facilitators. Chairs, deans, provosts, and faculty development professionals may be sending messages to us that communicate the value of focusing on facilitating individual student learning rather than disseminating knowledge to the undifferentiated student masses. Students who have acquired a taste for instructional strategies that utilize active learning and a facilitative teaching paradigm may send the facilitator role demands to us.

Evaluator. Who is creating the expectation that we act as a learning evaluator? We can usually begin with ourselves. We carry with us into our college teaching at least 20 years of experience as a student in graded learning environments where it was the teacher's responsibility to evaluate our progress and render a grade. We expect of ourselves when we become the teacher to grade student performance. Students expect that of us as well. They have at least 12 years of experience in graded learning environments which has taught them that grading is an important part of what a teacher does, like it or not. Faculty colleagues, chairs, deans, provosts, and a whole bevy of other administrators, all expect us to serve as an evaluator. Some of them may even complain regularly in public and private about grade inflation and the dumbing down of the curriculum. Professional associations may rank institutions and programs based on reputation, and these rankings may affect not only our pride but also our funding, publication, and career advancement opportunities. Accreditation associations pay attention to our evaluation systems and results, and their messengers within our own institutions remind us of this fact regularly. The community in which we live talks about our institution, and we would like for them to convey respect for it. This ambient chatter sends messages to us regarding our need to be a responsible evaluator in our courses and to hold high our standards. The university's alumni want us to make sure that the value of their degrees are not eroded by lackadaisical, undemanding grading.

Intervention

Negotiate with self. The images that I have of the exemplary college teacher—the caring facilitator of individual student learning—may not be realistic, given the need to serve also as an evaluator of individual student learning. My image of the exemplary college teacher may be incomplete in the sense that it oscillates between images of either an exemplary facilitator or of an exemplary evaluator. I need to create an image of both together. Furthermore, I need to adjust the expectations that I am imposing on myself with regard to this synthesis. The exemplary image of the facilitator/evaluator cannot realistically involve the perfect expression of each conflicting role put together. I cannot expect myself to fulfill the purest image of each. I must become comfortable with this new exemplary image and set of expectations for myself.

Negotiate with others. In the information field that I inhabit, who is sending me the most important messages about my function as a facilitator and evaluator? One of the most constant and significant senders of role demands are the students. That means I need to negotiate with them. But I do not need to merely call the conflict to their attention. I need to invite them to enter the conflict from my perspective and to struggle with what they would do. I need to present my solution and request their response. This kind of process not only helps the students and the teacher to understand and share the same expectations for the teacher, it also stimulates development in the students by role playing the position of the formal authority in the learning environment.

Integration

Self. The work of the integration phase is to adapt to the ripple effects of whatever new was negotiated in the intervention phase and to take explicit actions to enhance supports of the novelty and to diminish hindrances (Robertson, 1988). In the locus of the self, we need to explore how the parts of our worldview relate to our conception of what we should be as a teacher.

For example, is our self-esteem highly invested in us aspiring to be Mother Theresa or Mahatma Gandhi in the classroom? If we change our conception of an exemplary teacher, how does that new conception ripple out through our self-esteem system of beliefs? And so forth. We may, over time, have a tendency to lose a fix on our new conception. Perhaps it would be useful once a week to set aside time to reflect on our sense of integration with regard to conflicts that we see as fundamental to our work as learner-centered teachers, in this case, facilitator versus evaluator.

Environment. In a Peanuts cartoon strip, Linus goes to the door and asks whether his friend still has the drawing that he had made. The person, who had thrown away the drawing, retrieves it from the trash and rolls it out to Linus on the porch, whereupon Linus says, "Great art should never be rolled across the porch. . . ." In the integration phase, we need to steer clear of folks who would roll our newfound integrity across the porch. We need to scan our environment for supports and hindrances of our new role definitions and expectations. Perhaps we should seek a consultative, confidential relationship with a colleague or faculty development professional in order to garner support for processing the ripple effects of our new image of learner-centered-teacher-as-facilitator/evaluator. Perhaps this would be a good time to reduce contact with colleagues who seem especially adept at finding flaws in our teaching philosophy and getting our goat.

CONCLUSION

Without Contraries there is no progression

—Blake (1963, p. 3.)

Perhaps what Blake (1963) had in mind was the possible synergies, the generative potential that comes from bringing contraries into harmony. Our discussion has explored this topic within the context of learner-centered teaching. We have examined conflicts that are fundamental to learner-centered teaching (at least for me); reviewed the scholarship on strategies for handling conflicts; explored the relationship between how we handle conflicts and the degree to which we have achieved teacher integrity, as expressed by a learner-centered teacher integrity continuum; and considered a method for enhancing our teacher integrity. The larger objectives of this discussion have been to help classroom teachers with this thorny problem of conflicting role demands as well as to develop further the conceptualization of college-level, learner-centered teaching.

REFERENCES

Anderson, B. J., & Miezitis, S. (1999). Stress and life satisfaction in mature female graduate students. *Initiatives, 59* (1), 33–43.

Belenky, M. F., Clinchy, B. M., Goldberger, N. R., & Tarule, J. M. (1986). *Women's ways of knowing: The development of self, voice, and mind.* New York, NY: Basic Books.

Beutell, N. J., & O'Hare, M. M. (1987). Coping with role conflict among returning students: Professional versus nonprofessional women. *Journal of College Student Personnel, 28* (2), 141–145.

Blake, W. (1963). *The marriage of heaven and hell.* Coral Gables, FL: University of Miami Press.

Brookfield, S. D. (1990). *The skillful teacher: On technique, trust, and responsiveness in the classroom.* San Francisco, CA: Jossey-Bass.

Burroughs, C. B. (1990). The new professionalism: Teaching and/or scholarship. *Liberal Education, 76* (5), 14–17.

Clouder, L. (1997). Women's ways of coping with continuing education. *Adult Learning, 8* (6), 146–148.

Daloz, L. A. (1986). *Effective teaching and mentoring: Realizing the transformational power of adult learning experiences.* San Francisco, CA: Jossey-Bass.

Fitzgerald, F. S. (1945). *The crack-up.* New York, NY: New Directions.

Freire, P. (1993). *Pedagogy of the oppressed* (rev. ed., M. B. Ramos, Trans.). New York, NY: Continuum.

Gilligan, C. (1982). *In a different voice: Psychological theory and women's development.* Cambridge, MA: Harvard University Press.

Goode, W. J. (1960). A theory of role strain. *American Sociological Review, 25* (4), 483–496.

Hall, D. T. (1972). A model of coping with role conflict: The role behavior of college educated women. *Administrative Science Quarterly, 17* (4), 471–486.

Harvey, C. D., & Wiebe, B. S. (1997). "I'm going to make the effort": How mothers become successful university students. *Canadian Home Economics Journal, 47* (4), 155–159.

Holly, C. (1990). The new professionalism: Changes and challenges. *Liberal Education, 76* (5), 17–19.

Home, A. M. (1998). Predicting role conflict, overload and contagion in adult women university students with families and jobs. *Adult Education Quarterly, 48,* 85–97.

Knowles, M. S. (1975). *Self-directed learning: A guide for learners and teachers.* Chicago, IL: Association/Follett.

Knowles, M. S. (1989). *The making of an adult educator: An autobiographical journey.* San Francisco, CA: Jossey-Bass.

Knowles, M. S., & Associates (1984). *Andragogy in action: Applying modern principles of adult learning.* San Francisco, CA: Jossey-Bass.

Levinson, D. J. (1959). Role, personality, and social structure in the organizational setting. *Journal of Abnormal and Social Psychology, 58* (2), 170–180.

Mallinckrodt, B., & Leong, F. T. (1992). Social support in academic programs and family environments: Sex differences and role conflicts for graduate students. *Journal of Counseling and Development, 70* (6), 716–723.

McBride, M. C. (1997). Counseling the superwoman: Helping university women cope with multiple roles. *Guidance and Counseling, 12,* 19–23.

Mezirow, J. (1991). *Transformative dimensions of adult learning.* San Francisco, CA: Jossey-Bass.

Mikolaj, E. L., & Boggs, D. L. (1991). Intrapersonal role conflicts of adult women undergraduate students. *Journal of Continuing Higher Education, 39* (2), 13–19.

Palmer, P. J. (1998). *The courage to teach: Exploring the inner landscape of a teacher's life.* San Francisco, CA: Jossey-Bass.

Robertson, D. L. (1988). *Self-directed growth.* Muncie, IN: Accelerated Development.

Robertson, D. L. (1996). Facilitating transformative learning: Attending to the dynamics of the education helping relationship. *Adult Education Quarterly, 47* (1), 41–53.

Robertson, D. L. (1997). Transformative learning and transition theory: Toward developing the ability to facilitate insight. *Journal on Excellence in College Teaching, 8* (1), 105–125.

Robertson, D. L. (1999a). Unconscious displacements in college teacher and student relationships: Conceptualizing, identifying, and managing transference. *Innovative Higher Education, 23* (3), 151–169.

Robertson, D. L. (1999b). Professors' perspectives on their teaching: A new construct and developmental model. *Innovative Higher Education, 23* (4), 271–294.

Robertson, D. L. (2000a). College teaching as an educational helping relationship. *Toward the Best in the Academy, 13* (1).

Robertson, D. L. (2000b). Enriching the scholarship of teaching: Determining appropriate cross-professional applications among teaching, counseling, and psychotherapy. *Innovative Higher Education, 25* (2), 111–125.

Robertson, D. R. (2000c). Professors in space and time: Four utilities of a new metaphor and developmental model for professors-as-teachers. *Journal on Excellence in College Teaching, 11* (1), 117–132.

Robertson, D. R. (2001). Beyond learner-centeredness: Close encounters of the systemocentric kind. *Journal of Faculty Development, 18* (1), 7–13.

Sarton, M. (1961). *The small room.* New York, NY: Norton.

Stark, J. S. (1986). Administrator and faculty views of scholarly performance. *New Directions for Institutional Research, No. 50,* 59–74.

Webster's third new international dictionary of the English language, unabridged. (1966). Springfield, MA: Merriam.

Weimer, M. (1997). Integration of teaching and research: Myth, reality, and possibility. *New Directions for Teaching and Learning, No. 72,* 53–62.

Widoff, J. C. (1999). The adult male undergraduate student experience: Real men do return to school. *Journal of Continuing Higher Education, 47* (2), 15–24.

Wong, E. D. (1995). Challenges confronting the researcher/teacher: A rejoinder to Wilson. *Educational Researcher, 24* (8), 2–23.

Contact:

Douglas Reimondo Robertson
Professor and Director
Teaching and Learning Center
Eastern Kentucky University
2 Keen Johnson Building
521 Lancaster Avenue
Richmond, KY 40475
Voice   (859) 622-6517
Fax   (859) 626-6518
Email   douglas.robertson@eku.edu

Douglas Reimondo Robertson is Professor of Geography and Educational Leadership and founding Director of the Teaching and Learning Center at Eastern Kentucky University. He has published 35 scholarly articles, most recently on college teaching and learning, as well as a well-received book on intentional change in adult life which has entered its third printing (*Self-Directed Growth*). Dr. Robertson has helped to start three university faculty development centers and has served as the founding director at two of them. He serves as Senior Editor for the New Forums Press Book Series on Practices for Better Teaching, as well as on the Editorial Board of the *Journal on Excellence in College Teaching*. Also, he reviews manuscripts for *Innovations in Higher Education* and *To Improve the Academy*. Dr. Robertson has provided over 100 trainings, consultations, and speeches to a wide variety of educational, business, governmental, human service, and health care organizations. His current scholarship focuses on building two interrelated theories—a developmental model of professors-as-teachers and a conceptualization of college teaching as an educational helping relationship. He taught his first college course in 1971.

12

Something More: Moments of Meeting and the Teacher-Learner Relationship

Richard G. Tiberius
John Teshima
Alan R. Kindler
University of Toronto

The Boston Group, drawing upon developmental and clinical research, has identified special moments in human interaction that they call "moments of meeting." These moments occur spontaneously within the context of ongoing relational interaction and can effectively restructure relationships. We think of these moments of meeting as pivotal moments because of their potentially pivotal effect on relationships. In this chapter we briefly describe the theory underlying these moments of relational change, using examples from education. Then we suggest strategies that may help teachers participate creatively in such moments. Finally, we explore the implications of this theory for the concept of authenticity.

INTRODUCTION

Educators have come to appreciate the powerful role of the teacher-learner relationship in facilitating learning. Indeed, Joseph Lowman (1984) concludes that the teacher-learner relationship is as important to the facilitation of learning as are the traditional skills of the trade such as clarity of expression and organization. Until recently, the process of building and maintaining teacher-learner relationships has been understood as a gradual process of building an alliance through trust, a safe environment, and negotiation (Tiberius & Billson, 1991).

Recently, a group made up of psychiatrists, psychoanalysts, child development researchers, and pediatricians has been studying the process of change in normal development and, by analogy, in psychoanalytic or psychotherapeutic treatment. Working within that frame of reference, this group has described what they call "something more" than the traditional intervention of interpretation, which may be effective in contributing to the change process. They describe a process of change that occurs in the interactive relational domain, rather than in the domain of verbal and cognitive transactions, a process of relational restructuring that goes beyond the accepted one.

The elements of this new process are sudden, spontaneous, and dramatic in their impact. These moments of change are located in the microscopic study of the interaction between the patient and therapist. The Boston Group (Stern et al., 1998), drawing upon developmental and clinical research, has identified special moments in human interaction that they call "now moments." These moments occur spontaneously within the context of ongoing relational interaction and can lead to significant restructuring of relationships. From discussions with dozens of teachers, we are convinced that such moments also occur within the teacher-learner relationship. Whether these now moments lead to positive or negative restructuring of the relationship, or are just missed and have no impact whatsoever, depends largely on the ability of the teacher to seize—to authentically and personally respond to—these opportunities. The work of the Boston Group, therefore, suggests a mode of action through which teachers' authentic responsiveness in teacher-learner relationships may contribute positively to the learning process.

In this chapter we briefly describe the theory underlying these now moments, using examples from education. Then we explore the implications of this theory for the concept of authenticity as it is used in the higher education literature today. To anticipate our conclusion, authentic responses by teachers to now moments can have a powerful positive effect on the teacher-learner relationship—but at the price of increasing the teacher's vulnerability. We describe some exercises, taken from improvisational theater and meditation, aimed at enhancing our ability to recognize now moments and respond to them in ways that enhance the teacher-learner relationship. We also consider the risks faced by the teacher in such interactions, including the sense of increased vulnerability associated with exposure of his or her authentic self. Finally, using Parker Palmer's (1998) language, we explain the tension between the attraction of authenticity and the fear of vulnerability.

PRESENT MOMENTS, NOW MOMENTS, AND MOMENTS OF MEETING

A relationship can be understood as an ongoing process of mutual regulation toward some kind of inter-subjective goal. Relationship building is a trial and error process of negotiating, readjusting, and correcting, a process that Stern et al. (1998) call "moving along" (p. 909). Moving along consists of a string of present moments (see below) in which the participants interact as they attempt to fulfill the mutual goals of the relationship. These goals may range in complexity from the mundane, such as explaining the time and place of the next meeting, to the abstract and complex negotiation of intimacy.

When a present moment becomes emotionally "hot," it is a "now moment." We can recognize a now moment because it feels different from those that have gone before. This different quality may include positive feelings of increased intensity, excitement, and curiosity, or negative feelings of increased anxiety weirdness, or uncertainty. In other words, the minute you start to sweat in a teaching relationship, you have likely hit a now moment. Such interactive moments, whether colored by positive or negative affective tone, demand a unique and often personal response. If this moment is seized, that is, authentically and personally responded to by each person, it becomes a moment of meeting. The Boston Group's proposals suggest that these moments of meeting contribute to changes in the deeper relationship between teacher and student, changes that we believe may, in turn, positively affect the learning process. The Boston Group suggests that following such moments of meeting, a transient "disjoin" occurs between the two participants, an open space which allows new rules about how to be together to be creatively constructed between the pair. These new rules allow for a new kind of relationship to go forward, with unpredictable but often mutually rewarding consequences.

We will use two examples to illustrate the application of this theory. In the first one the teacher failed to seize a now moment and in the second the teacher succeeded and created a moment of meeting. Although the examples are from medical teaching, similar scenarios are common to any subject area.

Example 1: Failure to Seize a Now Moment

[Scene: An attending physician-teacher (T) and medical student (S) are talking directly after the student has seen a patient.]

Present moment	T: So the patient is jaundiced? What are the causes of jaundice?
Present moment	S: Gallstones?

Present moment	T:	Yes, gallstones. And what is the mechanism behind gallstones causing jaundice?
Present moment	S:	Could be a problem with the biliary tract.
Present moment	T:	A *problem* with the biliary tract? What kind of problem?
Now moment	S:	[Smiling slightly, with a playful look.] Are you playing the game "Guess what's on my mind"?
Failing response	T:	[Staring coldly] I'm not playing any games. I'm teaching. In fact, I'm using the Socratic technique, one of the most effective teaching strategies in medical education.
Present moment	S:	[Subdued; continues answering the questions without enthusiasm.] Yes, well, maybe some kind of *blockage* of the biliary tract?

The above example illustrates the normal process of interaction, which is made up of a string of so-called present moments. Present moments occur within a framework defined by the nature of the relationship between this teacher and learner, and by the technique that the teacher is using. The Socratic technique required the teacher to ask questions and the student to answer them. This exchange moved along routinely until the student departed from the rules of taking turns (questions from the teacher followed by answers from the student) by asking a question ("Are you playing the game 'Guess what's on my mind'?"). With that question the student provoked a special kind of present moment, one that signaled a challenge to the familiar teaching strategy and to rules of the current teacher-student relationship. The dyad was pulled into the present, creating a now moment that was too specific and personal to be handled by a standard teaching strategy or script. Now moments force the teacher to change in some way, to improvise, usually with a novel response with respect to their previous relationship. If the teacher is able to do this, if he or she recognizes and seizes the now moment, it can lead to a moment of meeting which could expand his or her relationship (e.g., deepen the trust, increase the safety, etc.) with the student.

In the case described above, the teacher's response was more likely to constrict than to expand the relationship. The teacher's response clearly told the student that challenges to the teaching method were not allowed and that humor was not appreciated in this teacher-student relationship. The student felt chastised and became resigned to playing out this game in a mechanical fashion, according to the old rules. In the future, this student would be less likely to engage openly with this teacher, and their relationship might stagnate. As a consequence, learning would be stifled rather than facilitated.

Example 2: Success in Seizing a Now Moment

Present moment	T:	So the patient is jaundiced? What are the causes of jaundice?
Present moment	S:	Gallstones?
Present moment	T:	Yes, gallstones. And what is the mechanism behind gallstones causing jaundice?
Present moment	S:	Could be a problem with the biliary tract.
Present moment	T:	A *problem* with the biliary tract? What kind of problem?
Now moment	S:	[Smiling slightly] Are you playing the game "Guess what's on my mind"?
Seizing the moment	T:	[Laughing, slapping hand on face.] Uhh...yeah, you got me! Guilty as charged. Was it that obvious? But I had noble intentions. I was trying to use the Socratic technique where I ask you questions to lead you to the answer instead of telling you the answer. I am told that it's a superior strategy to just telling students the answers. Doesn't it work for you?
Moment of meeting	S:	Well, maybe, but it makes me feel foolish. Like I really can't think. I have to follow the breadcrumbs that you're laying down. I don't want to just listen passively. That's no good either. It wouldn't stay with me.
Moment of meeting	T:	I hadn't thought of it that way. I can see how my method could drive you a bit mad. How about if I just ask you to tell me what you know about obstructive jaundice and then I'll give it a critique. And if that's not useful let's change it again. Don't be afraid to speak up. It's your education.
Moment of meeting	S:	That's a phrase I haven't heard very often.

In this second example, the teacher responded to the student in a spontaneous and authentic way. In doing so, the teacher and student both now realize that 1) "It's okay to joke around in a teaching session" and 2) "It's okay for
the student to question the teaching method." More fundamental is the realization that "It's okay to bring my own discomfort into the discussion and expect my teacher to be interested and responsive." As a result, the teacher-student relationship has been expanded in that both know more about each
other's experience of the relationship. The teacher and student also know im-
plicitly, in a way that may not available to verbal description, that they can relate to each other in new ways, ways that can allow the student to learn more
effectively.

The exciting possible outcome of a moment of meeting is the expansion
of the inter-subjective space. That is, the implicit teacher-student relationship
temporarily loses its constraints—its hitherto unspoken and unrecognized
rules—and is able to expand to accommodate a greater range of possibilities.
Future interaction takes place within this context of these expanded possibilities (Stern et al., 1998). How can a moment of meeting precipitate such a sudden and dramatic change in the relationship? The Boston Group rely on non-
linear systems theory to conceptualize these events. The self-organizing
feature of our minds tends to create progressively coherent relational knowledge from each relational experience throughout life. We bring these assumptions and expectations with us to each new relationship and the two new systems shape each other and organize a set of expectations or implicit knowledge
of how it is to be with each other, in the context of our current goals. Each moment of meeting precipitates a process of shaping interpersonal knowledge
about the other. The result is a modification of each relational partner's implicit relational knowledge of the other person. With each shift in the implicit
rules of the relationship, new and unpredictable possibilities emerge and new
relational systems are created.

The following features summarize the essential characteristics of a moment of meeting (Stern et al., 1998, p. 913):

• They are novel happenings, the opposite of business as usual

• They require a personal, specific response, not a routine, technical
  response

• They require spontaneity and improvisation; they cannot be planned or
  scripted

- They have affective qualities which may include heightened intensity, discomfort excitement, arousal, strangeness, or disorientation—they deal with something important and different than business as usual happening now in the relationship between two people

- They need not be verbally explicated

- They are unique and cannot be repeated. They are not "tricks of the trade" that can be used in other situations with other people

- They require a sensibility, namely to be able to allow oneself to respond in a personal and spontaneous manner

ENHANCING THE ABILITY TO CREATE MOMENTS OF MEETING

When we presented these ideas at workshops (at the annual meetings of POD and the Association of Academic Psychiatrists), participants found them gripping. Most of the participants easily identified situations in their teaching that were emotional, weird, uncomfortable, and difficult. They also had no trouble confirming the findings from the therapeutic literature regarding the powerful effects of these moments on their subsequent relationship with students. Virtually all participants were eager to learn how to respond constructively to such moments—to seize the moments, using the language of the theorists. We introduced three training methods that are particularly suited to this task.

The first of these methods borrows from the theatrical discipline of improvisation. Originally intended for actors, these skills assist teachers to develop flexibility and spontaneity in their roles. To respond constructively within a now moment the teacher may need to expand beyond his or her usual role responsiveness. Now moments require unique responses that are not formulaic but are constructed spontaneously to fit the specific situation. The ability to engage in a spontaneous response, to be in the moment, is precisely what improvisational theater is about. Our belief is that training in improvisational theater skills can enhance our ability to respond constructively at these unpredictable moments in the course of teaching.

Of course, teaching strategies are also essential to effective teaching. Irby (1994) has described "scripts" as mini teaching packages that comprise the best strategy to use in a situation defined by a particular teaching situation. Scripts help teachers become both effective and efficient. We, on the other hand, are arguing that sometimes teachers must be able to depart from their familiar scripts or their usual roles, in order to participate in these now moments effectively. This is especially true when the teacher is inclined to enact roles that are protective of the teacher's self-esteem or defensive of teachers' power and authority. Such teachers are more likely to miss the opportunities offered by now moments when they arise. Improvisational theater allows people to practice being spontaneous enough so that they overcome their fear of being vulnerable, of screwing up in front of the other person. It is all about an experiential process of developing the confidence to follow instincts, not technique. Our objective in providing practice in improvisational theater is to enhance the teachers' ability to be in the moment, to be flexible, to temporarily suspend their teaching strategies or their rules about their relationship with the student in order to enter into an authentic, personal interaction.

The second of these methods is mindfulness training (e.g., Kabat-Zinn, 1990). Mindfulness training may have an equally promising role to play in helping teachers seize now moments. Mindfulness training helps us preempt stereotypic responses like deeply ingrained teacher roles or habits. Such stereotypic responses prevent us from noticing the opportunity afforded by a now moment. Mindfulness releases a person's attention from captivity by these habitual thought trains. The objective of mindfulness training is not the development of automatic reflexes but something more like giving yourself the psychological space to make a decision based upon self-reflection, knowing when to allow yourself to step out of role and follow your instincts. This is the key point. Both mindfulness training and improvisational theater should provide teachers with increased confidence and the readiness to be spontaneous and authentic. Seizing the moment requires a kind of sensitivity to the subjective qualities of relational events rather than a skill brought objectively to bear on a specific situation.

A third method we would suggest, extrapolated from Teasdale, Segal, and Williams's (1995) clinical work on attention control training of consists of practicing new trigger responses to compete with habitual ones. Assume that our first Socratic teacher, while rushing to class, had an angry altercation with another driver in the parking lot, who chucked the finger at him. He was primed for anger. The student who challenged his teaching method may have been the final straw. This teacher could make up positive responses and practice them in situations in which unhelpful reflexes are provoked. For our Socratic teacher, these situations may be ones in which students challenge him. He needs new trigger responses. An analogy given by Teasdale, Segal, and Williams (1995, p. 32) is as follows: Most people would complete MOU_ _ with SE. But this tendency can be reversed by presentations of the word MOUND. The object of this practice is to raise the likelihood that you will complete the pattern that begins with an emotional trigger in a different way.

Teachers would need to practice the new patterns on many occasions, in many different contexts.

FEAR OF RESPONDING IN AN AUTHENTIC MANNER

Although the most common reaction to our workshops was eagerness to learn strategies for seizing now moments, the second most common reaction was apprehension. Participants expressed their fear of becoming vulnerable should they become more authentic in their responses. Some of the workshop participants had hoped that improvisational theater would provide them with a means of acquiring lightning quick reflexes that they could call upon in psychologically perilous situations. They were looking for the teacher's equivalent of martial arts training—skills that would protect them from attack by their students.

We have been impressed with the intensity of the fear expressed by participants each time we have presented these ideas to a group. One participant told us that the teacher role is protective. He feels safe while he is in the role of authority, talking about the subject without disclosing his own personal attitudes or weaknesses. Disclosures of a personal nature may invite reciprocation by the student. Boundary issues lie in this direction, he pointed out. He was not prepared to engage in a conversation with a student concerning his private life, his real beliefs about the subject, or his weaknesses. Yet, all of these interactions that invoke his vulnerability are also authentic interactions according to the educational literature.

Honesty about what one knows, for example, is one of the central characteristics of authenticity. A teacher who does not know something about a subject and admits it publicly is authentic. Another characteristic of an authentic response to students is "integrity" (Brookfield, 1990, p. 164), the congruence between a teacher's words and actions. A third is the teacher's connection with the subject matter that the student is trying to learn. It is essential that teachers reveal to students their actual connection to the subject, including their emotional responses to it. Authentic teachers, according to Chickering and Reisser (1993), have a well-integrated system of values and behaviors of their own, but they do not impose them on the learners. They disclose the basis of their beliefs and values so that the learners can reflect on their choices and make their own decisions. Finally, authentic teachers respect learners by hearing their personal concerns and by receptivity to learners' ideas (Brookfield, 1990). These types of responses put the teacher at psychological risk.

Parker Palmer (1998), in his enormously popular book, *The Courage to Teach,* analyzed the fear that paralyzes authentic teaching. One of the deepest human fears, he writes, is the fear of a live encounter with what he calls "alien otherness" (Palmer, 1998, p. 37). The "other" can be a student who speaks her or his own truth, telling us what we may not want to hear and threatening our view of the world or self—as in our example: "Are you playing the game 'Guess what's on my mind'?" Palmer (1998) argues that we rather control the outcomes of encounters with students. He goes on to describe various teaching roles that insolate teachers from confrontation with such live encounters: hiding behind notebooks, podiums, credentials, power, the pretence of objectivity, or silence (Palmer, 1998). Teaching requires an act of courage because teachers expose themselves in very personal ways—they are vulnerable (Palmer, 1998).

In her book, *Teaching to Transgress: Education as the Practice of Freedom*, bell hooks (1994) addresses similar themes. She states that she was helped the most by teachers "who have had the courage to transgress those boundaries that would confine each pupil to a rote, assembly-line approach to learning" (hooks, 1994, p.13). She argues that teachers should not operate in a position of safety and power and encourages them to bring their own personal experiences into teaching situations (hooks, 1994). She emphasizes that teachers must be willing to take the same personal risks that they expect of their students—they need to be able to "practice being vulnerable in the classroom" (hooks, 1994, p. 21).

INDUCING THE CREATIVE TENSION

We have begun to appreciate a conflict inherent in these moments of meeting. The joy of the moments of meeting was as palpable as the fear. When participants at our workshops spoke about their moments of meeting, they were excited. They were not driven to engage in moments of meeting out of some theoretical obligation to authentic teaching; they were drawn to the moments. They got an emotional jag, a kind of high, from expanding their relationship with their students. The expansion of a relationship is exciting. It's like seeing something in a new light, a brighter light. The romantic literature is full of this kind of imagery, of course, but the same phenomenon happens in other areas such as appreciation of art, music, the natural world, or, as we are observing, in the world of teacher-student relationships. This is the positive pole. The negative pole, as we discussed above, is fear.

The two conflicting motivations create what Parker Palmer (1998) has called a paradoxical tension, the creative tension that exists within each of the dimensions of a successful teacher-learner relationship. This tension is not something to avoid or eliminate. It is one of the characteristics of effective teaching. In Parker Palmer's (1998) words:

> Teaching and learning require a higher degree of awareness than we ordinarily possess—and awareness is always heightened when we are caught in a creative tension. Paradox is another name for that tension, a way of holding opposites together that creates an electric charge that keeps us awake. Not all good teachers use the same technique, but whatever technique they use, good teachers always find ways to induce this creative tension. (pp. 73–74)

Creative tension is a good thing, but debilitating conflict is not. Some of our colleagues, in responding to the theory, challenged us with cases that clearly gave us reason for concern. One of the early and most frequent examples raised by our audience was a sexual harassment example. Another involved a physical threat. We should have anticipated it. After all, we told them that the key to recognition of these moments was a situation that was affectively hot, weird, uncomfortable, and difficult. This fits perfectly their experience of a sexually inappropriate comment. Their point was that they could not follow our advice to this kind of comment because it would be dangerous to respond in a genuine and personal manner to sexual harassment. They clarified that the moments of which they spoke with concern were not merely naively inappropriate, as in the case of a student with a crush on his teacher. They were referring to power moves meant to control the teacher. All of the speakers who voiced these concerns were women who were speaking from personal experience and obviously deeply troubled by them.

These examples are from relationships in which the mutual goals have changed to render them outside the teacher-student range of mutual influence. Threats of harm or attempts at sexual involvement by either participant are not, by definition, part of the educational relationship. It may be true that a sequence of moments of meeting, or now moments, could be identified leading up to these phenomena; however, the improvisational freedom to respond with authenticity no longer applies when the relationship has altered in these ways. On the contrary, it now behooves the teacher to recognize the altered state of the student, be it sexual arousal or destructive rage, and respond in very measured and specific ways that set limits and protect the participants' personal and physical integrity. The theory we are offering here has nothing to contribute to the strategies necessary to manage these emergent and potentially dangerous situations. We learned from our workshop experience how important it is to clarify this limitation and to clearly delineate our focus on the well-functioning educational dyad.

The teacher-learner relationship is set apart from other kinds of relationships such as romantic relationships and abusive relationships by the unique set of obligations and expectations that define it. Although teacher-learner relationships can be accommodating of growth and change they also presume certain ground rules that are not open for negotiation, such as safety and appropriate boundaries.

A useful analogy might be one of two of musicians jamming with each other. They both understand that they must play together in a certain way, each respecting the other's role and contribution to the music. Either one of them can then take the playing in a new direction, establishing a new theme or groove. But the same principles of cooperatively playing a piece of music together would still exist. However, if one musician decided to drown out the other on purpose or somehow ruin their contribution to the music, the basic ground rules would be broken and the musicians might not be able to play together any more. In a teacher-student relationship, moving along (Sterns et al., 1998) occurs much like these musicians jamming. Each can take the relationship in a new direction, within certain limits. A student who threatens his teacher by failing to play along with the Socratic method is merely challenging a variation of the expectations making up the relationship. But a student who threatens his teacher with physical harm is going much further. He or she is changing the very nature of the relationship to one that is no longer cooperative and mutually respectful—from an educational one to an abusive or sexual one.

We have suggested exercises aimed at helping teachers learn how to respond more effectively to now moments that challenge the teacher-learner relationship. But for other, more fundamental challenges to the interpersonal relationship, different responses may be warranted. Even an effective, authentic teacher would handle differently a challenge to the teacher-learner relationship such as, "You don't really care about me," versus a challenge to the basic safety or stability of the interpersonal relationship such as, "You'd better watch your back when you leave your office tonight."

There is a sense in which the teacher can say, with respect to the first case, that the student was a very challenging student to teach but the student was not uncivil, rude, or violent. The teacher responding to the second case may say that the student was way beyond a teaching-learning contract; he or she was not even civil. There was no way this student should be in this university. There is a lot of writing coming out these days on uncivil behavior. It is a big issue because it frightens teachers. It is not surprising that teachers want to use our microanalysis to understand incivility and to learn ways to cope with it. Although this need is understandable, it is probably not a useful application of these proposals.

We are not discussing strategies for dealing with inappropriate student behavior. Our analysis is focused on the ability to de-center from business as usual and to get enough psychological distance from our performances that we can recognize an unusual interpersonal situation when it occurs within the context of the teacher-student relationship. What we are arguing is that there are different kinds of unusual situations. It is possible for someone to respond in a personal, constructive manner to one type of now moment, while at the same time refusing to do so for another now moment because he or she recognizes the latter as beyond the allowable zone for teacher-student relationships. The former challenges the techniques that we are using but not to the normal civility that is accorded another person in our society. The latter, like the sexual examples given by some of the participants in our workshops, were clearly beyond the acceptable teacher-student relationship in our society. We agree with Palmer (1998) that fear is part of good teaching, but not fear for your life.

CONCLUSION

In this chapter we described how the theory underlying now moments might be usefully applied to teacher-student relationships and we suggested three strategies for training teachers in responding to now moments more effectively. We hope that we have opened an important discussion. However, there is very little evidence, as yet, to support our suggestions. Early in our investigation of this topic, experienced teachers, who were as enthusiastic about the theory as we were, encouraged us. They told us that the theory helped them understand some of their most troublesome teaching moments, ones that both confused and distressed them. They also found their new understanding to be quite unsettling. Some teachers literally gasped when they imagined how many now moments they might have missed. Teachers were eager to know how they could use the theory to become more aware of now moments and to respond to them more effectively. Therefore, in preparation to conduct workshops on this topic, we searched the literature for strategies that might help teachers. Participants with experience in improvisational theater and mindfulness agreed that these training methods were particularly suited to the task.

The next step, certainly, is to study the phenomenon in an educational setting. We must attempt to document, in a detailed descriptive fashion, now moments occurring in typical educational settings. Are they common occurrences or rare? How frequently are they missed either by the teacher or the learner? And we must attempt to measure the effect of knowledge of the theory or skills training on success in addressing such moments. Does knowledge of the theory itself or skills acquired in any of the training methods confer any benefit? We welcome any colleagues who are interested in joining us in this exciting phase.

REFERENCES

Brookfield, S. D. (1990). *The skillful teacher: On technique, trust, and responsiveness in the classroom.* San Francisco, CA: Jossey-Bass.

Chickering, A. W., & Reisser, L. (1993). *Education and identity.* San Francisco, CA: Jossey-Bass.

hooks, b. (1994). *Teaching to transgress: Education as the practice of freedom.* New York, NY: Routledge.

Irby, D. M. (1994). What clinical teachers in medicine need to know. *Academic Medicine, 69,* 333–342.

Kabat-Zinn, J. (1990). *Full catastrophe living: Using the wisdom of your body and mind to face stress, pain, and illness.* New York, NY: Delta Press.

Lowman, J. (1984). *Mastering the techniques of teaching.* San Francisco, CA: Jossey-Bass.

Palmer, P. J. (1998*). The courage to teach: Exploring the inner landscape of a teacher's life.* San Francisco, CA: Jossey-Bass.

Stern, D. N., Sander, L. W., Nahum, J. P., Harrison, A. M., Lyons-Ruth, K., Morgan, A. C., Bruschweiler-Stern, N., & Tronick, E. Z. (1998). Non-interpretive mechanisms in psychoanalytic therapy: The "something more" than interpretation. *International Journal of Psycho-Analysis, 79,* 903–921.

Teasdale, J. D., Segal, Z., & Williams, J. M. G. (1995). How does cognitive therapy prevent depressive relapse and why should attentional control (mindfulness) training help? *Behavior Research and Therapy, 33* (1), 25–39.

Tiberius, R. G., & Billson, J. M (1991). The social context of teaching and learning. In R. J. Menges & M. Svinicki (Eds.) *College teaching: From theory to practice* (pp. 67–86). New Directions for Teaching and Learning, No. 45. San Francisco, CA: Jossey-Bass.

Contact:

Richard G. Tiberius
University of Toronto Faculty of Medicine
Centre For Research in Education at the University Health Network
200 Elizabeth Street
1ES 583, Toronto, Ontario M5G 2C4 Canada
Voice   (416) 340-4194,
Fax   (416) 340-3792
Email   r.tiberius@utoronto.ca

John Teshima
Department of Psychiatry, University of Toronto
Sunnybrook and Women's College Health Sciences Centre
2075 Bayview Avenue, F-Wing
Toronto, Ontario M4N 3M5 Canada
Voice   (416) 480-6100 ext. 3077
Fax   (416) 480 6818
Email   john.teshima@utoronto.ca

Alan R. Kindler
Department of Psychiatry and St. Michael's Hospital
University of Toronto
Toronto, Ontario M5G 2C4 Canada
Voice   (416) 923-8868
Fax   (416) 920-2483
Email   kindler@istar.ca

Richard G. Tiberius has a PhD in Applied Psychology from the Ontario Institute for Studies in Education/University of Toronto. He holds the position of professor in the Department of Psychiatry and the Centre for Research in Education where he collaborates with medical faculty in designing and conducting educational research and faculty development activities. His scholarly work and consulting practice focuses on the improvement of the teaching and learning process, especially the role of the teacher-student relationship in learning. He has authored numerous journal articles, book chapters, and books in United States, Canadian, and British journals, and has conducted workshops and lectured throughout North America and Europe.

John Teshima completed medical school and his psychiatry residency at the University of Toronto. He is currently completing an M.Ed. at the Ontario Institute for Studies in Education/University of Toronto. He is a staff psychiatrist at Sunnybrook and Women's College Health Sciences Centre, where he is the undergraduate education coordinator for psychiatry. He is a lecturer in the University of Toronto's Department of Psychiatry. He is also the education coordinator for a telehealth project that provides children's mental health services to underserviced communities across Ontario. His main educational interests are in undergraduate medical education and also in continuing education for health professionals.

Alan R. Kindler is a Training and Supervising Analyst with the Toronto Institute of Psychoanalysis and past president of the Toronto Psychoanalytic Society. He is an Assistant Professor of Psychiatry at the University of Toronto, a staff psychiatrist at the Wellesley and St. Michael's Hospitals and is on the faculties of the Toronto Institute of Contemporary Psychoanalysis, the Toronto Child Psychotherapy Program, and the Advanced Training Program in Psychoanalytic Psychotherapy. He is in private analytic practice and has a special interest in self psychology. He is on the International Council for Psychoanalytic Self Psychology and a board and faculty member of the Institute for the Advancement of Self Psychology in Toronto. His recent publications include an edition of *Psychoanalytic Inquiry on Psychoanalytic Supervision* (co-edited with Dr. Joshua Levy) and "Optimal Responsiveness and Psychoanalytic Supervision" (in *Optimal Responsiveness: How Therapists Heal Their Patients,* edited by H. Bacal, 1997).

13

Undergraduate Students as Collaborators in Building Student Learning Communities

Candyce Reynolds
Portland State University

Colleges and universities have recently used the concept of learning communities as a strategy to improve undergraduate student learning. This chapter describes a learning community approach where upper-division undergraduates serve as mentors for freshman and sophomore students and develop and sustain learning communities with faculty partners. The impact of this program is described and implications are discussed.

INTRODUCTION

Increasingly, colleges and universities are recognizing the importance of developing new curricular structures to enhance undergraduate student learning in response to criticism (e.g., Astin, 1993; Boyer, 1987; Coles, 1993) that higher education has not addressed the needs of a new generation of students. The Wingspread Group in Higher Education (1993) called for higher education institutions to build communities that develop an informed and involved citizenry that can assume leadership roles in American society. One strategy that colleges and universities have developed to meet this challenge is the creation of learning communities.

Shapiro and Levine (1999, p. 3) outline the following basic characteristics that define a learning community:

- Organizing students and faculty into smaller groups

- Encouraging integration of the curriculum

- Helping students establish academic and social networks

- Providing a setting for students to be socialized to the expectations of college

- Bringing faculty together in more meaningful ways

- Focusing faculty and students on learning outcomes

- Providing a setting for community-based delivery of academic support programs

- Offering a critical lens for examining the first-year experiences

Colleges and universities have developed a variety of models that incorporate these characteristics into an institution's unique culture. For example, the University of Washington and the University of Oregon utilize a freshman interest group (FIG) program where students are involved in a living/learning environment (Bennett, 1999; Tinto & Goodsell, 1993). Temple University and University of Maryland, College Park have developed learning community programs that address student needs through academic freshman seminar courses (Shapiro & Levine, 1999). Other campuses, such as The Evergreen State College (Youtz, 1984) and Portland State University (White, 1998) integrate learning communities into their interdisciplinary general education curriculum. This chapter will describe the use of upper division undergraduate students in developing learning communities within its general education program at Portland State University (PSU) and discuss implications for other campuses.

THE PORTLAND STATE UNIVERSITY MODEL

The faculty senate at PSU initiated a new general education program, University Studies, in 1994. A faculty working group developed the four-year general education plan based on higher education research on student success. The creation of intentional academic learning communities was at the forefront of the reform. Alexander Astin's work (1992, 1993) figured prominently in the development of the program as a whole, and specifically in the development of a student mentor program that involved using upper division students as mentors in support of the general education reform. Astin (1992, p. 30) described several factors that were correlated with positive effects in general education:

- Student-student interaction

- Faculty-student interaction

- Discussing racial/ethnic issues with other students

- Hours devoted to studying

- Tutoring other students

- An institutional emphasis on diversity

University Studies was developed to address these issues within its curricular design. (See White [1994] for a more detailed description of the general education reform at Portland State University as a whole.)

The general education program at PSU spans across an undergraduate's entire academic career, starting with a year-long Freshman Inquiry and ending with a Senior Capstone, where interdisciplinary groups of students engage in a community-based learning course that addresses community issues. During the year-long freshman level course (Freshman Inquiry), undergraduate mentors are partnered with faculty to deliver these courses. In many other academic settings, a mentor is an experienced student who works with new students to aid in the adjustment to college. In our setting, the role of mentor is much broader. Mentors are role models, teachers, community builders, translators, and more. The use of these mentors has contributed to the success of the Freshman Inquiry program in ways that we had not anticipated at the inception of the program.

The role of peer mentor was created to enhance student experiences in these areas. Peer mentors were assigned to individual faculty teaching Freshman Inquiry. Peer mentors, who are upper-division undergraduates, attend the three-hour main section of the course and lead mentor sessions one hour twice a week with smaller groups of students. Originally, the primary role of mentor was to serve as a tutor of sorts for the main class. The mentor session would provide students opportunities to connect with each other in a smaller context and receive help from the mentors and fellow students on the coursework and in adjusting to college. As a student moved into Sophomore Inquiry, they would work with a graduate mentor in a similar fashion. (Students are required to take three interdisciplinary term-long courses to fulfill their Sophomore Inquiry requirement).

Portland State University's general education reform is entering its ninth year. Mentors have played an increasing role in transforming the curriculum, faculty practices, and students during this time.

THE CURRENT ROLE OF THE MENTOR

As mentioned earlier, the role of the peer mentor in Freshman Inquiry has evolved to include a multitude of tasks and functions. While being sensitive to the primacy of the faculty role in Freshman Inquiry, mentors now engage fully in a partnership with faculty to deliver the curriculum. Not only are they teachers, they are friends, facilitators of discussion and activities, technology trainers, role models, and guidance counselors.

During the first years of University Studies, it became evident that mentors were more than just tutors and guides. As with any institutional transformation process, the first years were a bit rocky. Faculty in Freshman Inquiry learned quickly that their mentors were valued colleagues in developing and delivering curriculum, managing classroom conduct, and providing collegial support as faculty endeavored to transform their own teaching strategies. Of significant importance in the first years, mentors served as a communication bridge between faculty and students aiding faculty and program administrators with valuable feedback on the impact of the program on students.

The mentor role today continues to be broad and multidimensional. As program administrators saw the role expanding, specific training and mentor support mechanisms were instituted. Currently, the program employs 45 upper-division undergraduate peer mentors and 38 graduate mentors. The positions are highly competitive and draw some of PSU's most talented and well-rounded students. Peer mentors are chosen for their academic skills (3.0 minimum GPA is required), interpersonal skills, problem solving skills, and commitment to program goals. At this point in the development of the University Studies program, the majority of the peer mentors have been enrolled in the University Studies general education classes and describe part of their motivation to be mentors as a way to give back to a program what was helpful in their own academic and personal development. Peer mentors receive a Laurel's Scholarship (a state-funded academic scholarship) that pays for their tuition and a small monthly stipend as compensation.

Writing an inclusive job description for mentors is difficult. All mentors are trained in collaborative/cooperative teaching methods, community building techniques, diversity education, teaching of writing, technology applications, and group/team development skills. Mentors are also trained in accessing campus and community resources. Minimally, mentors attend the main class sessions as an active participant in the course. Peer mentors meet with small groups of students twice a week for one hour. Faculty and mentors ideally meet at least once a week to plan curriculum and discuss course and student progress. Peer mentors have input into the mentor session portion of student grades.

Because faculty and mentors enter into a partnership to work on a particular course, the role of the individual mentor is dependent on what each brings to the enterprise. In some ways, this is what makes the mentor program so unique and successful. There is not one correct way for a mentor to work. Faculty and mentors work together to create strategies that incorporate their personalities and strengths in order to contribute to their students' success. Mentors, in collaboration with faculty, often bring their unique talents and experiences into the classroom and the mentor sessions. For example, faculty can assign more complex technology assignments when they have a mentor who has extensive technology experience. A faculty member with an English major mentor can confidently assign peer review during the mentor session. Mentors often influence the choice of texts and assignments. Mentors always provide valuable feedback to the faculty member about how the course is being perceived by students and how the courses and assignments could be improved.

IMPACT OF THE MENTOR PROGRAM

We have observed that the mentor program has had an enormous impact on the students, the faculty, and the mentors themselves. Again, it would have been hard to predict the breadth and extent of the impact of mentors at the inception of the program.

Impact on Students

Students often speak during focus groups and in their course evaluations about the role of their mentor in their success and comfort level at the university. As PSU is an urban institution that attracts first-generation college students or other nontraditional students, student retention and success is often dependent on how comfortable a student feels in this particular academic environment. Mentors, just by their presence, are strong role models of success in the university and a sign that students are valued by the university.

In addition, mentors role model and teach students academic coping skills. There are not many places today where students can get such pragmatic help as how to approach a complex text, how to read an assignment, and how to see the broader and personal implications of any given topic. Time and stress management are often topics of discussion, and mentors can speak from a uniquely current place about how to balance the multiple roles of a modern, urban student. Mentors share what does and does not work in academia.

Perhaps anyone new to a challenging endeavor (as in being a freshman university student) is likely to have difficulty interacting with those they perceive as having power over him or her. Mentors hear honest reflections from students about their experience at the university, in the class, and in their personal lives. Faculty in the first years were shocked by the information that their students shared with mentors about their lives, things they did not often hear about in other types of general education courses. Domestic violence, homelessness, mental illness, lack of parental support, and lack of academic preparation are all issues that mentors tend to learn about due to their in-between status. Knowing what a student is dealing with empowers both faculty and mentor to help the student, thus aiding in student academic progress.

Faculty also learned that students are much more likely to approach an in-between person regarding their concerns about the course, the assignments, and their grade. The just-in-time feedback that mentors have been able to provide faculty has greatly enhanced student success in a course. How often do faculty explain away the lack of class enthusiasm and success to lack of motivation on the students' part? Mentors' timely, but diplomatic, feedback has enabled faculty to adjust their teaching to better meet students' needs.

Mentors also serve as a bridge to faculty by encouraging and modeling discussion with faculty. Students new to academia are often intimidated by faculty and have difficulty engaging the faculty-student interactions that are so important to their success. Mentors often walk that fine line between providing for the baby bird and nudging them out of the nest.

Students often describe finding a first friend at PSU in their mentor and making connections with fellow students in their Freshman Inquiry mentor sessions. In a large urban university that serves primarily commuter students, Freshman Inquiry, and especially the mentor sessions, offer some sense of home on campus.

Impact on Faculty
While this area has not been studied systematically, there is evidence that mentors have had a significant impact on faculty development. Many faculty have talked about the unique opportunity to have a "colleague" to discuss their course with. Often for the first time, faculty have someone they can muse with about why a certain student seems to respond adversely to certain content and why that lecture did not quite captivate their audience in the way they had planned.

Faculty report that their teaching and their own learning have improved because of their work with a mentor. The continuous feedback loop allows them to continually fine-tune their curriculum. Often, input from mentors allows faculty to see the topic of their course with a fresh eye. In addition, faculty report that they enjoy getting to know their students better through their input and the mentor's encouragement of students to use their office hours. Mentors help faculty reconnect with why they decided to teach in the first place.

Impact on Mentors
As with many peer helping programs, the greatest impact of the mentor program may be on the mentors themselves. While mentors, as a whole, are extremely successful students before they become mentors, they seem to become even better students. In spite of increased commitments and incredible challenges, mentors' GPAs, in general, improve. Mentors describe that mentoring forces them to organize themselves and their schoolwork. They have little free time and they also feel the pull to be an example for their students. Academics also seem to improve because not only are the students in the course learning to approach academic material in new ways, mentors are, too. They often describe understanding material at a much greater depth than they had previously.

Because mentors are aware of the goals of University Studies, they become keenly aware of the presence or lack of presence of these qualities in their own learning. Mentors report significant improvement in the achievement in the four University Studies goals. Mentors describe being better writers, better critical thinkers, and better citizens as part of being a mentor.

CONCLUSION

Learning communities have the potential of having a huge impact on student learning and retention as well as the way faculty approach student learning through their teaching (Shapiro & Levine, 1999). Institutions of higher education need to continue to create models for developing learning communities that work on their individual campuses. Using undergraduates in building and sustaining learning communities is one way that institutions can tap into the rich resource in their students, while contributing to faculty development and overall student learning. Although the Portland State University model may not be one that institutions can adopt completely, it seems important for institutions to seriously consider how they could use undergraduate students in building and sustaining learning communities. As one can see, the use of undergraduate and graduate mentors can have a far-reaching impact on students, faculty, and mentors themselves.

REFERENCES

Astin, A. W. (1992). What really matters in general education: Provocative findings from a national study of student outcomes. *Perspectives, 22* (1), 23–46.

Astin, A. W. (1993). *What matters in college: Four critical years revisited.* San Francisco, CA: Jossey-Bass.

Bennett, J. (1999). Learning communities, academic advising, and other support programs. In J. H. Levine (Ed.), *Learning communities: New structures, new partnerships for learning.* Columbia, SC: National Center for the First-Year Experience and Students in Transition.

Boyer, E. L. (1987). *College: The undergraduate experience in America.* New York, NY: HarperCollins.

Coles, R. (1993). *The call to service: A witness to idealism.* Boston, MA: Houghton Mifflin.

Shapiro, N. S., & Levine, J. H. (1999). *Creating learning communities: A practical guide to winning support, organizing for change, and implementing programs.* San Francisco, CA: Jossey-Bass.

Tinto, V., & Goodsell, A. (1993). *A longitudinal study of freshman interest groups at the University of Washington.* University Park, PA: National Center for Postsecondary Teaching, Learning, and Assessment.

White, C. R. (1994). A model for comprehensive reform in general education: Portland State University. *The Journal of General Education, 43* (3), 167–228.

White, C. R. (1998). Placing community-building at the center of the curriculum, *Metropolitan Universities, 9* (1), 55–62.

Wingspread Group in Higher Education. (1993). *An American imperative: Higher expectations for higher education.* Racine, WI: Johnson Foundation.

Youtz, B. (1984). The Evergreen State College: An experiment maturing. In R. M. Jones & B. L. Smith (Eds.), *Against the current.* Cambridge, MA: Schenkman.

Contact:

Candyce Reynolds
Director of Mentor Programs
Portland State University
17 PO Box 751—UNST
Portland, OR 97207
Voice   (503) 725-8367
Fax   (503) 725-5977
Email   reynoldsc@pdx.edu

Candyce Reynolds is the Director of Mentor Programs and Associate Professor in University Studies at Portland State University. A PhD in Counseling Psychology from the University of Oregon, she focuses her work with mentors and her scholarship on the development of reflective teaching practices.

14

Improving Teaching and Learning: Students' Perspectives

X. Mara Chen
Ellen M. Lawler
Elichia A. Venso
Salisbury University

Despite much debate among educators over methods to improve the climate and effectiveness of teaching and learning, very limited effort has been directed toward seeking input from students. In this study, a survey of students' opinions regarding college teaching and learning was given in six courses with 163 students completing the survey. This chapter analyzed the survey results and proposed specific strategies that professors can use to make teaching engaging as well as informative, and thus, to enhance student learning.

INTRODUCTION

A majority of educators in a recent California survey claimed critical thinking as the primary instructional objective (Elder & Bartell, 1997; Haas & Keely, 1998). Understanding of material presented is no longer the only educational objective; college students should be able to apply their knowledge and perform in an outstanding manner in the real world (Havanek & Brodwin, 1998; Taylor & Marienau, 1997). However, college-level education has long focused on providing content instruction rather than promoting learning, and often the present way of teaching does not stimulate active learning (Barr & Tagg, 1995; Lord, 1994). Teaching has traditionally been practiced as a teacher-centered, teacher-to-learner knowledge transfer process. But today's teaching and learning process has become increasingly complex. The profile of student body has become more diverse in terms of experiences, stages of intellectual development, emotional maturity, background, and learning styles. College student diversity calls for effective approaches that take students' learning styles and instructional preferences into account (Cherif, 1994; Nelson, 1996).

Too often, students have been functionally invisible in the classroom (Fabry, Eisenbach, Curry, & Golich, 1997). The only method used to determine whether a student is engaged intellectually in the classroom is by examination. While more instruction does not necessarily produce and guarantee more learning, effective teaching does promote better learning. There is a growing debate regarding which teaching methods best develop an effective undergraduate learning environment and promote learning excellence. Effective classroom interaction appears to be the key to learning effectiveness. College teaching must appreciate students' preferences in learning environment and teach to their strengths (Cannon, 1997; Krause, 1998). Teaching should no longer be a one-way linear flow, but rather a flexible and interactive process that must engage students at several levels. Hall (1994) points out that we need to be concerned not only about the content we deliver, but also the way in which the learning process takes place.

Many researchers have indicated the need for college teachers to learn about teaching. "Prevailing wisdom is that we teach as we were taught, or if we've given any pedagogical consideration, we teach as we learn. But we must do better than that. We must consider the ways our students need to learn, and teach to their strengths" (Krause, 1998, p. 61). Understanding those differences in which individual students learn will make us more effective teachers. College professors, unlike secondary school teachers, have little formal education and training in teaching methods. Collaborative teaching may provide a good approach to this learning process by sharing experiences and insights (Darling-Hammond, 1998; Quinlan, 1998). Effective instruction should promote students' active involvement in the learning process, and emphasize students' critical thinking and problem solving skills through a provocative inquiry approach (Kronberg & Griffin, 2000; Mills, 1998; Sternberg, 1998).

Today's workplace demands good analytical and interpersonal skills more than ever, and education should help students develop the skills needed to solve problems effectively as team players, rather than as isolated individuals. Cooperative and collaborative learning and research experiences help students overcome the fear of technical courses while gaining interpersonal skills in teamwork (Metheny & Metheny, 1997; Nikolova Eddins, Willams, Bushek, Porter, & Kineke, 1997). What we teach and how we teach are important, but what is actually learned by students is more important (Zoller, 2000). College education should incorporate a series of increasingly sophisticated learning processes to foster the development of the students' knowledge pyramid, which consists of a broad conceptual foundation, solid information processing and analytic skills, creative problem solving capabilities, critical thinking, and applied intelligence. Students often engage in learning in response to external pressures (good grades, awards, jobs, etc.). All of these may be valid motivators; however, teachers should add to those motivators and encourage students to get personally and passionately involved in learning for the sake of knowledge and intellectual development (Child & Williams, 1996).

The above challenges and suggestions from educators have little direct input from students. In particular, there have been no opinions sought from students regarding specific measures teachers can take to make teaching and learning more engaging and effective. In this study, we present students' opinions on ways in which instructors can improve teaching and learning effectiveness.

STUDENTS' PERSPECTIVE

As recipients of information, knowledge, and skills, college students should have a strong voice about the teaching and learning process. Students can present a general framework of teaching effectiveness from the learner's point of view.

Traditionally, student input with regard to teaching consists of end-of-semester teacher and course evaluations, which, while limited, do provide some valuable information. Studies have suggested that students' evaluations of a teacher's overall teaching effectiveness are largely objective and not significantly influenced by knowledge of their grades (Baird, 1987; Ikponmwosa, 1986). Tang (1997) found that students' evaluations help to outline the important predicators of an instructor's overall teaching effectiveness. The top four factors outlined in his regression model include informative presentation of subject matter, effective answers to students' questions, a courteous professional manner of treating students, and preparedness for each class.

Our study goes beyond semester evaluations by seeking and analyzing students' opinions regarding teaching in general, not just in response to a particular teacher in a specific course. Our different disciplines—geography, biology, and environmental health programs—furthered our interest in gaining a better understanding of students' perspectives about college teaching and learning.

Survey Design

The survey questionnaire that we designed and conducted consists of three major sections: student profile, objective questions regarding teaching format, and open-ended questions seeking input on desirable attributes of teachers and the classroom environment (Appendix 14.1). Four questions in the student profile section were designed to ensure that the participants are representative of our student body and to identify potential similarities and differences in the responses from the different groups of students to questions relating to the teaching format. The questions in the teaching format section constitute the core of this survey. They are designed to quantify students' preferences regarding teaching styles and format, out-of-classroom activities, the use of technology, and learning responsibility. The last section contains three open-ended questions designed to seek the students' desired optimum extrinsic factors in their learning. These questions focus on what they perceive as the important qualities of teachers and the classroom environment.

Survey Administration

The survey was given in the six courses we were teaching at approximately mid-semester in an anonymous and volunteer fashion. We gathered data from students in our courses during class time to ensure independent opinions from each student that were free of other students' influence. Students who were taking two or more courses with us were asked to participate only once. Of the 163 students who participated in the survey, a majority (147) had enrolled in college within two years of their high school graduation. In terms of their class status, 67 were seniors, 45 juniors, and 51 were freshmen and sophomores.

Survey Results and Interpretation

In processing and analyzing the survey, we have summarized the overall pattern of student opinions, as well as the opinion pattern by student class status, specifically freshmen-sophomore, junior, and senior. The freshmen and sophomore students were combined because few freshmen were enrolled in the majors' classes chosen for the survey. The following important themes were drawn from the responses to the survey's multiple-choice questions (Table 14.1).

Most students (145) prefer a flexible and dynamic lecture format to traditional straight lecturing (see question 5 in Table 14.1). They like lectures that incorporate the use of visual aids with a moderate amount of classroom discussions and student group work. Only 17 of the students prefer a teacher-centered lecture format, which uses 95% of the class time for straight lecturing. This

TABLE 14.1
Survey Summary of College Students Opinions Regarding Teaching

Question #	Number and Percent of Surveyed Students in Each Answer Category					
	Answer (a)	Answer (b)	Answer (c)	Answer (d)	Answer (e)	No Answers
1.	25 15.3%	26 16.0%	45 27.6%	67 41.1%	n/a n/a	0 0
2.	106 65.0%	25 15.3%	16 9.8%	10 6.1%	n/a n/a	6 3.7%
3.	147 90.2%	16 9.8%	n/a n/a	n/a n/a	n/a n/a	0 0
4.	152 93.3%	11 6.7%	n/a n/a	n/a n/a	n/a n/a	0 0
5.	17 10.4%	56 34.4%	15 9.2%	74 45.4%	n/a n/a	1 0.6%
6.	26 16.0%	110 67.5%	27 16.6%	n/a n/a	n/a n/a	0 0
7.	19 11.7%	6 3.7%	138 84.7%	n/a n/a	n/a n/a	0 0
8.	41 25.2%	71 43.6%	10 6.1%	40 24.5%	n/a n/a	1 0.6%
9.	32 19.6%	8 4.9%	25 15.3%	98 60.1%	n/a n/a	0 0
10.	58 35.6%	105 64.4%	n/a n/a	n/a n/a	n/a n/a	0 0
11.	73 44.8%	11 6.7%	4 2.5%	61 37.4%	13 8.0%	1 0.6%
12.	39 23.9%	14 8.6%	22 13.5%	74 45.4%	14 8.6%	0 0
13.	60 36.8%	49 30.1%	8 4.9%	45 27.6%	n/a n/a	0 0
14.	56 34.4%	8 4.9%	15 9.2%	26 16.0%	58 35.6%	0 0
15.	142 87.1%	15 9.2%	2 1.2%	2 1.2%	n/a n/a	2 1.2%

preference suggests that classroom interactions involving more components of the central nervous system promote better learning. Increased sensory input (vision as well as hearing), increased motor output (speaking as well as writing), and increased internal processing (interactive discussions and group work) work together to increase overall learning effectiveness.

The majority of students prefer an instructor who moves about the front of the room and gives an interesting and informative lecture embedded with an occasional pace breaker, such as a joke or a story (110 students answering question 6 and 73 students answering question 11 in Table 14.1). This response indicates that both the content of lecture and method of delivery are important. Instructors can deliver their lectures in a traditional way, in front of the classroom. But they should consciously try to give their presentations with a variety in movement, style, and pace to maintain students' attention and interests.

Most students (98) welcome an inquiry-based teaching approach. They prefer the teacher to ask many questions, and even more important, students want to be encouraged to ask more questions themselves (see question 9 in Table 14.1). In addition, they would like to have guided and structured group activities to reinforce the lectures. These preferences suggest that college students' critical thinking and teamwork skills need to be fostered and promoted. These higher-level learning skills may not be easily developed from a passive learning environment.

Most of the students surveyed (118) welcome the use of technology beyond the classroom, but a sizable group is still not as enthusiastic as we have assumed. Contrary to our common perceptions, most students prefer to have traditional homework and team projects/reports (see question 13 in Table 14.1). This response, we believe, reflects the students' desire for more feedback than they get from exams or peer electronic discussions about how they are doing in the learning process. In some cases, however, it may reflect some students' desire to have exam grades diluted by graded homework. It is still obviously important for instructors to use their judgment in determining the correct balance of various graded exercises to enhance learning without decreasing course rigor. In addition, the mixed attitude toward the use of technology may also reflect lack of confidence among some students regarding computer technology and highlight the need for activities that produce technologically confident students.

Generally speaking, the students of different class status (senior, junior, sophomore, and freshmen) expressed similar opinions on most of the survey questions. Class status did not appear to affect student perceptions of teaching and learning, with the following two exceptions:

- There were striking differences in students' opinion in the desired format of student group work in classroom. Significantly more freshmen and sophomore students preferred structured group discussion than did juniors and seniors, who preferred classes without such group work. This difference may suggest that higher-level students are more mature and ready for more independent learning coupled with direct intellectual exchange in the classroom.

- There were also significant differences in responses regarding learning activities other than group discussion. Most seniors welcome a combination of different learning activities, including homework, presentation, and team projects, while most students from other class status groups prefer homework. This difference may indicate that senior students would like to have the learning opportunities that allow them to sharpen their problem solving and teamwork skills.

Finally, most of our students (142) seemed to have a mature attitude toward their learning and believed that they themselves hold the ultimate responsibility in achieving a high GPA (see question 15 in Table 14.1). Although this attitude may be a comfort to us and is a good beginning, it is still our professional obligation to foster generations of responsible and effective learners.

In addition to multiple-choice questions, our survey contained three open-ended questions designed to identify 1) the common characteristics of instructors perceived as outstanding, 2) the specific things students believe instructors can do to make lectures interesting and informative, and 3) the ideal classroom environment envisioned by students.

Over half the students surveyed identified similar characteristics as outstanding in both high school and college instructors. Characteristics, such as dedicated, honest, fair, patient, understanding, and reasonable, were cited more frequently than other characteristics, such as knowledgeable, experienced, and organized. Furthermore, a quarter of the students surveyed specifically mentioned the importance of teachers getting to know them as individuals and being accessible outside the classroom. Good communication skills were highly valued, and being interesting was cited almost twice as often as being informative. Being knowledgeable and professionally experienced was cited three times as often as innate intelligence. Students put an increased emphasis on teacher's interpersonal qualities, concerns for students, presentation, and communication skills.

Instructors can make lectures interesting and engaging, as well as inform-ative, by using visual aids, actively involving students in the classroom, and presenting related personal experiences and anecdotes. Demonstrating the rel-evance of the course material to the real world was specifically mentioned by over one-third of the respondents. As stated in Lowman's (1996) observational study, exemplary college teachers have a strong power to promote learning by making their courses clear and engaging.

The ideal components of a classroom learning environment include fre-quent teacher-student interactions, caring and skilled teachers, a small num-ber of students per class, a relaxed atmosphere, and a comfortable, well-equipped classroom. Obviously, students prefer an active learning environment in a well-equipped setting. Although this list does not contain any new revela-tions, creating such a teaching and learning environment remains challenging.

DISCUSSION ON TEACHING STRATEGIES

Achieving educational excellence has called for an integrated curriculum, qual-ity instruction based upon active learning, in- and out-of-class interactions, a stimulating environment with an emphasis on higher expectations, and an un-derstanding and flexible teaching approach for diverse learning styles (Ewell, Jones, & Lenth, 1996). The results from our study have reinforced these gen-eral guiding principles. However, we need to address specific strategies or ap-proaches to fulfill the general educational goals. Based on our survey study, we have come to identify the following specific aspects that can be emphasized to improve the climate and effectiveness of teaching and learning.

- The overall theme of students' responses suggested that teaching-learn-ing interactions that can truly engage the student are critical for effective teaching. Most teachers would probably understand what makes teach-ing informative, but may not have the concrete ideas about making teaching engaging. Education should focus not only on teaching stu-dents what to learn, but also on how to learn (learning to learn). The inquiry-based and student-centered interaction between teacher and stu-dents provides students time to process the concepts (Leonard, 2000) and digest the delivered data and information.

- Making teaching interesting does not mean entertaining students. On the contrary, we suggest that we should promote a higher learning standard through a flexible teaching approach, which reduces students' learning stress and improves their learning productivity. As the cognitive content in a course decreases, the teacher should focus more on facilitation rather than content delivery (Hall, 1994). Effective teaching requires imagination and creativity in classroom delivery, including the use of humor to reduce anxiety and improve students' ability to learn (Berk, 1996). In addition, Berk (1996) also argues that some of us rarely succeed at anything unless we have fun doing it. We can embed some "fun" things into our teaching to generate and maintain our students' interest and attention in learning, especially in courses that students perceive as boring and difficult. For example, if Fridays appear to be days with a lower attendance, it may help the learning atmosphere to let students have a group discussion on what they have learned during the whole week and/or inject some brief pace breaker stories or a joke into the lectures to stimulate the students. If students see our extra efforts in our teaching, they may be more likely to put extra effort in their learning.

• Active learning results from active teaching. Inquiry-based teaching is suggested to produce a classroom atmosphere marked by intellectual vitality and emotional vigor and promote students' critical thinking (Ahern-Rindell, 1999; Mills, 1998;). Giving students a voice in a course empowers their enthusiasm and improves their attitude about learning (Fabry, Eisenbach, Curry, & Golich, 1997). Our survey indicates that effective teaching should get students involved by encouraging them to ask/answer more questions in the classroom and by facilitating them to discuss with and learn from their fellow students. However, the survey does not suggest that there is a single best teaching style from which active learning will take place. The effectiveness of teaching in a specific situation is contingent on its relation to students, course content, and learning objectives (Hall, 1994).

• Learning is a dynamic and complex process. The student's intelligence, academic preparedness, mental motivation, emotional desire for knowledge, and maturity for challenge often affect the outcome. Effective learning occurs in a zone of novelty, where students are challenged but not overwhelmed (Sternberg, 1998). Because of this very complexity in learning, effective teaching requires a teacher to play multiple roles in their learning: instructor, facilitator, and mentor in and out of the classroom. Too often, teachers spend much time and effort on content preparation, but too little time and effort on designing and understanding the associated learning process to accomplish teaching objectives. Many of us often play the all-knowing authority figure and believe students lack the potential for a high-level intellectual exchange. This teaching practice allows us to recycle our lecture notes, perhaps making our teaching easier, but creating the kind of students we do not respect. Encouraging students to intellectually engage in the classroom creates mutual respect between faculty and students (Giampetro-Meyer, & Holc, 1997). Only a few students in our survey use words such as "strict," "control," "good disciplinarian," and "complete authority" to describe the characteristics of an outstanding teacher. This may indicate that strict, teacher-centered teaching produces learning apathy. College students welcome freedom and the associated responsibilities in their learning. We must encourage, reward, and guide their engagement in learning, rather than force them to attend classes with an apathetic learning attitude or resentment toward teachers.

• Technology has become a key component in education. Nantz and Lundgren (1998) suggested that the use of technology allows learning across the barriers of time and space by enabling students' access to course materials whenever and wherever they desire. Based on our survey, students welcome the use of videos and computer programs in lecturing, email communication, and the Internet in delivering course materials. However, these same students also stress the importance of an understanding, approachable, and available teacher in their learning. Therefore, the use of technology should be designed and used with care. If the use of email replaces face-to-face interactions, students may have the feeling that the teacher is too busy or does not care enough for them. The use of visual aids, such as videos and the Internet, should be coupled with structured classroom discussion. Otherwise, students certainly enjoy the multimedia show but are unlikely to fully remember or understand what they have seen and heard.

CONCLUSION

In light of the results from this survey, it becomes apparent that students perceive the key to effective learning lies in interactive teaching. Teachers should emphasize student-oriented active learning, instead of teacher-centered lecturing. In particular, it is important to provide a stimulating, yet relaxed, learning climate: making instructions engaging, interesting, as well as informative. Effective communication between the teacher and students in and out of the classroom is critical to learning efficiency. The teaching and learning process is analogous to a computer network in which efficient network communications between the server and its node computers becomes impossible without effective protocols, regardless of the speed and capacity the individual computers might have. In the classroom, a lack of good rapport and mutual respect between teachers and students rarely results in learning excellence, despite well-educated teachers, eager-to-learn students, and well-equipped classrooms.

Although each individual student may not be capable of telling us what we should be doing as effective teachers, students' collective voice can give us a better understanding of their learning process and preferences. From the students' perspective, teachers should encourage them to ask many questions, design more classroom discussions, lecture with the aid of technology, and use occasional pace breakers, such as jokes and stories. In all, effective teaching should focus as much on how to motivate students to learn as on what they should be taught.

REFERENCES

Ahern-Rindell, A. J. (1999). Apply inquiry-based and cooperative group learning strategies to promote critical thinking. *Journal of College Science Teaching, 28* (3), 203–207.

Baird, J. S. (1987). Perceived learning in relation to student evaluation of university instruction. *Journal of Educational Psychology, 79* (1), 90–91.

Barr, R. B., & Tagg, J. (1995). From teaching to learning: A new paradigm for undergraduate education. *Change, 27* (6), 12–25.

Berk, R. A. (1996). Student rating of 10 strategies for using humor in college teaching. *Journal on Excellence in College Teaching, 7* (3), 71–92.

Cannon, J. R. (1997). The constructivist learning environment survey may help halt student exodus from college science courses. *Journal of College Science Teaching, 27* (1), 67–71.

Cherif, A. H. (1994). Instructional strategies that never fail us. *Journal of College Science Teaching, 24* (1), 55–58.

Child, M., & Williams, D. D. (1996). College learning and teaching: Struggling with/in the tensions. *Studies in Higher Education, 21* (1), 31–45.

Darling-Hammond, L. (1998). Teacher learning that supports student learning. *Educational Leadership, 55* (5), 6–12.

Ewell, P. T., Jones, D. P., & Lenth, C. S. (1996). What research says about improving undergraduate education: Twelve attributes of good practice. *AAHE Bulletin,* 5–8.

Fabry, V. J., Eisenbach, R., Curry, R. R., & Golich, V. L. (1997). Thank you for asking: Classroom assessment techniques and students' perceptions of learning. *Journal on Excellence in College Teaching, 8* (1), 3–21.

Giampetro-Meyer, A., & Holc, J. (1997). Encouraging students to demonstrate intellectual behavior that professors respect. *College Teaching, 45* (3), 92–96.

Haas, P. F., & Keely, S. M. (1998). Coping with faculty resistance to teaching critical thinking. *College Teaching, 46* (2), 63–68.

Hall, F. S. (1994). Management education by design. *Journal of Management Education, 18* (2), 182–198.

Havanek, J. E., & Brodwin, M. G. (1998). Restructuring university and colleges: The student-focused paradigm. *Education, 119* (1), 115–119.

Ikponmwosa, O. S. H. (1986). Knowledge of grades and student evaluation of university instruction. *Indian Journal of Psychometry and Education, 17* (1–2), 47–52.

Krause, L. B. (1998). The cognitive profile model of learning styles. *Journal of College Science Teaching, 28* (1), 57–61.

Kronberg, J. R., & Griffin, M. S. (2000). Analysis problems: A means to developing students' critical-thinking skills. *Journal of College Science Teaching, 29,* 348–352.

Leonard, W. H. (2000). How do college students best learn? An assessment of popular teaching styles and their effectiveness. *Journal of College Science Teaching, 29* (6), 385–388.

Lord, T. (1994). Using constructivism to enhance student learning in college biology. *Journal of College Science Teaching, 23,* 346–348.

Lowman, J. (1996). Characteristics of exemplary teachers. In M. D. Svinicki & R. J. Menges (Eds.), *Honoring exemplary teaching* (pp. 33–40). San Francisco, CA: Jossey-Bass.

Metheny, D., & Metheny, W. (1997). Enriching technical courses with learning teams. *College Teaching, 45* (1), 32–36.

Mills, J. (1998). Better teaching through provocation. *College Teaching, 46* (1), 21–26.

Nantz, K. S., & Lundgren, T. D. (1998). Lecturing with technology. *College Teaching, 46* (2), 53–57.

Nelson, C. E. (1996). Students diversity requires different approaches to college teaching, even in math and science. *American Behavioral Scientist, 40* (2), 165–177.

Nikolova Eddins, S. G., Willams, D.G., Bushek, D., Porter, D., & Kineke, G. (1997). Searching for a prominent role of research in undergraduate education: Project interface. *Journal on Excellence in College Teaching, 8* (1), 69–81.

Paul, R. W., Elder, L., & Bartell, T. (1997). *California teacher preparation for instruction in critical thinking: Research findings and policy recommendations.* Sacramento, CA: California Commission on Teacher Credentialing.

Quinlan, K. M. (1998). Promoting faculty learning about collaborative teaching. *College Teaching, 46* (2), 43–47.

Sternberg, R. J. (1998). Principles of teaching for successful intelligence. *Educational Psychologist, 33,* 65–72.

Tang, T. L. (1997). Teaching evaluation at a public institution of higher education: Factors related to the overall teaching effectiveness. *Public Personnel Management, 26* (3), 379–390.

Taylor, K., & Marienau, C. (1997). Constructive development theory as a framework for assessment in higher education. *Assessment and Evaluation in Higher Education, 22* (2), 233–244.

Zoller U. (2000). Teaching tomorrow's college science courses: Are we getting it right. *Journal of College Science Teaching, 29* (6), 409–414.

Contact:

X. Mara Chen
Department of Geography and Geosciences
Salisbury University
Salisbury, MD 21801
Voice   (410) 546-6202
Fax   (410) 548-4506
Email   mxchen@salisbury.edu

Ellen M. Lawler, Chair
Department of Biological Sciences
Salisbury University
Salisbury, MD 21801
Voice   (410) 543-6496
Fax   (410) 543-6433
Email   emlawler@salisbury.edu

Elichia A. Venso, Director
Department of Environmental Health Science
Salisbury University
Salisbury, MD 21801
Voice   (410) 543-6499
Fax   (410) 543-6433
Email   eavenso@salisbury.edu

X. Mara Chen is Associate Professor in the Department of Geography and Geosciences at Salisbury University.

Ellen M. Lawler is Associate Professor in the Department of Biological Sciences at Salisbury University.

Elichia A. Venso is Associate Professor and Director of the Environmental Health Science Program at Salisbury University.

APPENDIX 14.1

A SURVEY OF STUDENTS' OPINIONS REGARDING COLLEGE TEACHING

For questions 1–4, select the choice that describes your current status and fill in on scantron.

1. Your Classification
   (a) Freshman   (b) Sophomore
   (c) Junior   (d) Senior

2. Your major is within which school
   (a) Henson School of Science and Technology
   (b) Fulton School of Liberal Arts
   (c) Perdue School of Business
   (d) Seidel School of Education and Professional Studies

3. Did you enroll in college within two years of high school graduation?
   (a) yes   (b) no

4. You are
   (a) full-time   (b) part-time

For questions 5–15, select your TOP PREFERENCE (select ONE only and fill in on scantron).

5. Lecture format
   (a) 95% of time for straight lecturing
   (b) lectures supported with visual aids (slides and VCR tapes)
   (c) lectures with student discussions/group work
   (d) lectures with visual aids, questions/discussions, and student group work

6. Presentation style of instructor
   (a) instructor stays at front of room, usually remaining in one area
   (b) instructor moves about front of room
   (c) instructor moves about room, in amongst students

7. Which is more critical to your classroom learning
   (a) a lecture that is interesting
   (b) a lecture that is informative
   (c) a lecture that is both interesting and informative

8. Format of student group work in classroom
    (a) structured group discussion with given topics
    (b) work on solving/answering problems/questions given by instructor
    (c) unstructured group discussion (no detailed instructions from the instructor)
    (d) I prefer classes without group work

9. Number of questions
    (a) Instructor should ask a few questions of students
    (b) Instructor should ask many questions of students
    (c) Instructor should not ask questions, but encourage students to do so
    (d) Instructor should ask many questions and encourage students to do the same

10. Who should ask more questions in classroom?
    (a) instructor
    (b) students

11. Lecture pace breakers
    (a) a story/ joke
    (b) a break in lecture to allow for students to have a short discussion
    (c) a break to allow students to stretch
    (d) combination of above
    (e) no pace breaker is necessary

12. Methods for transmission of notes (to supplement traditional use of the blackboard and overheads)
    (a) use of instructional technology (videos, computer projections)
    (b) use of Internet
    (c) use of a course booklet (purchased at university bookstore)
    (d) combination of the above
    (e) none of the above are necessary

13. Use of technology outside the classroom
    (a) course related information available on the web
    (b) communications from instructor via email
    (c) students required to find related information on the Internet
    (d) none of the above

14. Related activities
    (a) homework   (b) student presentations
    (c) project report/term paper   (d) team reports/projects
    (e) combination of the above

15. For you to achieve a high GPA in your college learning, who plays the most responsible role?
    (a) myself   (b) professors
    (c) parents   (d) others (specify)

    _____.

16. List below four characteristics (based on your own experience) that you think make outstanding high school teachers and college professors.

    High School Teacher   College Professor
    (a) _____   (a) _____
    (b) _____   (b) _____
    (c) _____   (c) _____
    (d) _____   (d) _____

17. List three major things, which in your opinion professors can do to make lectures interesting as well as informative.
    (a)
    (b)
    (c)

18. On the back of this page, please describe your ideal college classroom learning environment (Please UNDERLINE your key words).

Section IV

Philosophical Issues in Faculty Development

15

The Essential Role of Faculty Development in New Higher Education Models

Devorah A. Lieberman
Portland State University

Alan E. Guskin
Project on the Future of Higher Education
Antioch University

There is a growing interest in and active discussion about new educational environments, which shift the emphasis of education from faculty and their teaching to students and their learning. This shift enables us to view the education of students in multiple educational environments beyond the traditional model of faculty teaching students in a classroom. Combining both different instructional roles and educational settings into new higher education models of undergraduate education will demand that faculty learn new roles. It also holds out the hope that reducing the demands on faculty time and increasing the availability of other institutional resources will enhance the quality of faculty worklife. To successfully address factors like financial constraints and accountability while creating, implementing, and sustaining new higher education models will require the commitment of a number of significant groups in the institution. Among the most important will be the work of faculty development professionals and the centers they lead.

INTRODUCTION

In the next ten years, the academy will undergo major reforms as institutions strive to deal with significant reductions in financial resources and increases in costs, demands for accountable student learning outcomes, and stable—or increased—student enrollment. These conditions raise serious concerns about our present educational delivery system that is primarily limited to faculty teaching students in classroom settings in traditional institutional structures.

Decreases in financial resources convert directly into budget reductions and personnel cuts. Stated bluntly, more students must be taught with fewer faculty and fewer support personnel. In traditional higher education settings, this would mean sharp increases in faculty workload and, most probably, decreases in student learning outcomes.

There is a growing and vocal interest in new educational environments, which shift the emphasis of education from faculty and their teaching to students and their learning. This shift enables us to view the education of students in multiple educational environments beyond the traditional model of faculty teaching students in a classroom. This shift in thinking to student learning-focused environments creates the foundation for the reform of undergraduate education, even its transformation.

THE NEW HIGHER EDUCATION MODELS

Peter Ewell (2002) predicts this shift will focus on a move from course-based credits and seat time to assessment-based mastery of recognized bodies of knowledge and skills. Students would be accountable for "attainment of common outcomes, not on common content or curricular structure" (Ewell, 2002, p.5). Specifically, this shift will require major changes in how institutions are organized and the systems used to count and measure what they do. It will also require various new pedagogies within these learning environments. Furthermore, formative institutional and programmatic assessment will be an expectation and an obligation. All participants in these environments will be involved in the assessment of student learning. Marie Eaton (2002), in summing up how the new higher education models could change how faculty work, writes, "In the new university, faculty will relinquish some of their responsibility for *delivery* of instruction to become *designers* of learning environments" (p. 3).

The higher education setting of the next ten years will be marked by a host of new instructional roles in many new educational settings. Table 15.1 highlights a few examples of these changes.

TABLE 15.1
Changing Roles in the New Higher Education Models

Instructional Roles	Educational Arenas
• Expert/presentation/discussion	• Partner with other institutions
• Mentoring/reflection	• Partner with community and work environments
• Information guide/guide to resources	• Partner with nonfaculty and co-curricular educators
• Facilitator of group discussions	• Partner with the library as key learning center
• Intensive workshop leader	• Function in settings that integrate students' academic learning experience (across disciplines/courses, etc.)
• Research project leader	
• Consultant project leader of problem-based experience	
• Development of content software/adaptation of off-the-shelf software to local institutional needs	• Function in settings that integrate academic and experiential learning
• Partnership between faculty and co-curricular educators	• Establish intense faculty-student interactions outside of formal classes
	• Establish peer learning environments
	• Establish faculty-led courses/traditional and technology enhanced
	• Create accelerated learning courses
	• Outsource parts of curriculum
	• Develop off the shelf material/software
	• Prepackaged total course material prepared inside/outside institution
	• Integration of Hi Tech/Hi Touch

Many or most of the new higher education settings will combine some or many of these different instructional roles and educational settings in order to refocus on student learning while reducing instructional costs. Put another way, by utilizing these new roles and settings, the institution will be able to reduce the cost of educating an individual student.

A major strategy for accomplishing this would be reducing the time an individual faculty member spends with any single group of students, while concurrently increasing the exposure of students to sources of learning other than the traditional faculty member. Some of these instructional roles and settings will actually provide more intense faculty-student interactions that occur over shorter periods of time than they do presently.

A key to the learning and financial success of any of the emerging higher education models will be the capability to use new information technologies and software in sophisticated ways, and to integrate, as partners, individuals and groups that have only rarely been so involved. An example of this might mean that librarians (and the library) would be key educators and key learning centers. Another example may well be the integration of student service personnel into the educational process. External to the institution, this will mean that community members and work site supervisors become partners in the student learning process.

The role of technology is beginning to change how students learn and, it is likely, will transform student learning experiences in the future. The recent improvements in information and computer technologies are likely to continue to develop at an ever-increasing pace over the years ahead—especially in the area of sophisticated content-oriented software—which will enable institutions of higher education to further integrate technology into the core of the educational process. Newman and Scurry (2001) emphasize this point in a recent article:

> As the inexorable improvement in digital technology continues, and we gain a better understanding of how to use it, we will experience further improvements in the capacity, reliability, cost effectiveness and ease of use. Soon it will be impossible, even with great effort, to achieve the same learning results without the use of technology that we can achieve with it. (p. B7)

New higher education models of undergraduate education that combine different instructional roles and educational settings will require more faculty to learn new skills in order to succeed in the new instructional roles. At the same time, these new models hold out the hope for reducing the demands on faculty time and increasing the availability of other institutional resources that will enhance the quality of faculty work-life. There will be reduced pressure to teach more students and to add additional classes, there will be time for faculty members to pursue their professional and scholarly passions, and there will be potential for increased stimulation from faculty-student interaction, increased excitement from being involved in new educational environments, and increased availability of resources for decent salaries.

Such major and widespread institutional reform of faculty roles and student learning will not be successful without major efforts to provide faculty with the necessary skills, training, technology, and support to perform their new roles. As important, these new roles will only be successful if 1) the institutional rewards for faculty are aligned with their new roles, and 2) the faculty, academic, and administrative decision-makers understand and provide resources for the new faculty roles and the support necessary to implement and sustain them.

To successfully address factors like financial constraints and accountability while creating, implementing and sustaining new higher education models will require the commitment of a number of significant groups in the institution. Among the most important will be the work of faculty development professionals and the centers they lead.

FACULTY DEVELOPMENT AND NEW HIGHER EDUCATION MODELS

As faculty development professionals position themselves to support the continuing needs of faculty members and administrators to think differently about delivery, assessment, scholarship, and demographics, they will need to address some major issues. Table 15.2 begins to address some current responsibilities of faculty developers and how their expertise will be needed to implement the new higher education models:

TABLE 15.2
Ways to Support Faculty in Current and New Higher Education Models

Current/Traditional Support	To Implement New Higher Education Model
Developing effective classroom techniques	Learning how to effectively mentor students, to lead intensive discussion/workshop-type sessions

Increasing effectiveness of classroom evaluation systems	Creating assessment instruments to measure student learning
Creating new courses and syllabi	Creating standards for student learning outcomes to be measured by assessment tools independent of faculty teaching students
	Creating alternatives to present calendar for offering student learning experiences— e.g., accelerated learning formats
Implementing problem-based learning in classroom	Creating community learning experiences that are problem-based where faculty members act as lead consultants working with community partners
Utilizing technology to assist classroom teaching	Development of content software/ adaptation of off-the-shelf software to provide options beyond the traditional classroom environment
	Development of online learning environments
Enabling students to do library research	Working in partnership with librarians to provide individualized learning environments for students; partnership with librarians who serve as the primary guide to information resources
Creating internship experiences for students	Creating service-learning and community engagement experiences and the means for students to reflect on these experiences for college credit
	Developing partnerships with community agencies and individuals to create learning environments for students

Working with other faculty in joint interdisciplinary courses	Developing learning communities that integrate a number of different learning environments—community engagement, individualized and peer learning formats, integration of technology—and utilizing assessment of student learning outcomes rather than grades and credit hours
Encouraging faculty to integrate their research interests into their teaching	Encouraging and helping faculty expand conceptions of scholarship to include the scholarship of teaching and learning as well as the scholarship of community engagement
Helping faculty develop their portfolios for tenure and promotion	Facilitating faculty rewards for participating in new higher education model development by persuading faculty and academic leaders to align rewards and new faculty roles

Inherent in these shifts is a new perspective in the role of faculty developers within the institution. Much like librarians, faculty developers will have to shift their thinking from being providers of good and important technical services to professionals whose work is critical for the transformation of the institution. Also like librarians, faculty developers will move from the periphery of the academic enterprise to the core—focusing on strategies that enable students to learn more effectively and efficiently within many different arenas and for faculty skills and expertise to be focused and used efficiently.

In order to accomplish these critical functions, faculty developers must perceive themselves as institutional change agents. Rather than directing support activities to individual faculty, faculty developers will also need to take responsibility for supporting administrators and faculty leaders, who have some sense that significant change is needed, by providing access to new conceptions of educating students, new institutional forms to enable them to occur, and the change process needed to accomplish both.

The following questions identify some goals of the faculty developer in supporting new higher education models:

• How are faculty supported as they explore multiple pedagogical needs?

- How are faculty supported as they deal with the new learning environments of the new models of higher education?

- How are faculty supported as they expand their definitions and forms of scholarship?

- How are individuals educated to evaluate faculty involved in new instructional roles and expanded forms of scholarship?

- How are part-time and adjunct faculty assisted in their teaching roles at the institution?

- How are faculty, staff, and students supported as they partner with members of the surrounding and international communities as well as diversifying and internationalizing?

SUPPORTING MULTIPLE TEACHING AND LEARNING PEDAGOGIES

In the new higher education model, faculty and students are expected to be scholarly. Scholarly, in this context, means that learning environments will include course content that is not only current and topical within the discipline, but engages students in an interdisciplinary approach, focuses on students' developing inquiry and critical thinking skills, and emphasizes student learning with peers as well as spending more time learning independently. Traditionally, the focus has been on the teacher and the process through which the course content is delivered. The students' responsibilities have been to learn the content, regardless of delivery mode or style. With the shift in roles and responsibilities, for faculty and learner, the emphasis will rest on the scholarly approaches to teaching and learning by all participants in the learning environment.

LEARNING ENVIRONMENTS IN THE NEW MODEL FOR HIGHER EDUCATION

In the past, institutions of higher education touted their low faculty-to-student ratio. However, as institutional budgets decrease, it is becoming critical for funding streams to increase. To meet expenses, institutions have turned to increasing tuition and increasing numbers of students. This has occurred without significantly enhancing tenure-track faculty ranks. Consequently, class sizes have increased exponentially both in face-to-face classes as well as in online course delivery.

Working with faculty members and academic administrators, faculty development offices are indispensable for developing these new learning environments in ways that the faculty and student relationships are created that reflect small student-to-faculty ratios. A common assumption is that as student enrollment increases and faculty numbers do not, the frequency of faculty/student interaction and accessibility of faculty member to student are significantly compromised. These outcomes are not inevitable but they do require important changes. Faculty developers can help provide support strategies that can enhance the feeling of connection between each student and the faculty. In this process, faculty developers can assist faculty to: 1) identify student learning outcomes in the course and the particular learning environment, 2) consider alternative learning environments in which students can access the information, 3) assist with various pedagogies that focus on student learning, 4) assist with assessment strategies, 5) suggest ways to be efficient in order to reduce faculty time on task, and 6) assist faculty and students in encouraging student learning by the development of individualized student learning plans to meet individualized needs (Ewell, 2002, p. 5). The following are specific examples of ways faculty developers can meet these needs.

The electronic learning environment requires thinking differently about delivery, content, and student feedback. It is critical that the academy focuses not only on the importance of the technological delivery, but also on the pedagogy involved in this process. The literature on the relationship between student learning and technology has emphasized that technology is a tool that provides a learning environment in which students learn. How learning is framed within that environment is critical (Laurillard, 1993). Faculty developers working together with instructional designers can provide that learning environment by integrating student learning, course delivery, and technology. They can also enhance student learning and faculty effectiveness by integrating librarians and other important institutional members involved in the educational process.

Whether students are spending time learning by themselves or with peers as well as interacting with faculty in new ways, clarity of student learning outcomes and their assessment are critical. Also, formative assessment of student learning is needed as well as assessment of the learning environment itself.

Intensive faculty-student interaction over short periods of time. While the 12- to 16-week course and lecture are the major modes of teaching and learning in higher education, most learning outside of colleges and universities occurs in shorter and more intensive periods of time. Utilizing this learning environment within higher education can increase faculty-student interaction and connection, even in large institutional settings. Such learning environments will require faculty to be skilled in facilitating group process and methods for working in intensive group settings. These intensive workshop-type settings will also require faculty and academic administrators to rethink the nature of the weekly and term academic calendar. Faculty developers can help both faculty and administrative leaders deal with the structures, learning processes, and skills needed to implement these types of learning environments.

Faculty developers have a significant role in supporting the hybrid course. Pedagogical principles that apply to the face-to-face environment do not necessarily apply to the electronic environment. The hybrid course spans both those environments; thus, the instructor has the opportunity to focus on student learning differently in two different environments. In this case, the instructor can answer the following questions: "What can the student learner achieve in the face-to-face environment that is impossible in the electronic environment?" and "What can the student-learner achieve in the online environment that would be impossible in the face-to-face environment?" The answers to these questions coupled with specific student learning outcomes for this course guide the learning activities and pedagogies that shape each aspect of the course. Faculty developers and instructional designers working in concert provide indispensable support for faculty teaching in this environment.

Faculty developers assist faculty in pedagogies appropriate for community-based learning. When learning outcomes are achieved through interaction with a carefully considered community-based experience, nontraditional pedagogies may be appropriate. "In the new university, a significant part of a faculty member's time will be allocated to cultivating both research field sites and community based learning environments in which undergraduates can observe and participate in the process of discovery" (Eaton, 2002, p. 5). Faculty developers will become brokers between the faculty/student and the community partner as well as between faculty and institutional partners such as librarians and student affairs professionals. Ewell (2002) coins the phrase "learning broker" (p. 11). This "involves identifying and setting up appropriate field settings or on-line opportunities for learning, as well as organizing the kind of monitoring and feedback support that such settings demand" (Ewell, 2002, p. 11).

Creating alternative times and days of course delivery. While at present all courses are offered in set time slots during the weekly and term calendars, there is considerable new evidence that accelerated courses (e.g., six weeks) are effective in producing student learning (Wladkowski & Westover, 1999). As discussed earlier, intensive, short-term workshop-type learning environments also offer alternatives to the present course settings. Faculty developers will assist in developing courses that are offered on weekends, in shortened terms, on nontraditional days, and in a myriad of other times and formats (Guskin & Marcy, 2001; Guskin & Marcy, in press).

Expectations for skills such as critical thinking, problem-based learning, reflective practice, and intercultural competence thread throughout the curriculum. Employers assert that these are usually the types of skills they seek in their new hires. Eaton (2002) claims that faculty spend most of their instructional time in classrooms or labs, either lecturing or facilitating discussions. "Largely untapped are other potential avenues for student learning and strategies to engender the kinds of thinking and skills that our graduates need to face in the complexities of today's society" (Eaton, 2002, p. 2). Faculty developers can assist campus-wide in supporting appropriate pedagogies that can be adapted to both face-to-face, electronic, and community-based learning environments.

FACULTY RECOGNITION IN PROMOTION AND TENURE

Institutions are addressing issues of faculty recognition in the promotion and tenure process. Educators seeking to think differently about teaching, learning, and scholarship responded positively when Rice (1991) encouraged scholars to reexamine the traditionally recognized definitions and forms of scholarship. Boyer (1990), along with Glassick, Huber, and Maeroff (1997), continued the discussion by exploring multiple forms of scholarship. As institutions expect faculty to focus more on student learning outcomes and course delivery, it is also imperative that an expanded definition of scholarship be recognized in the academy. Expanded definitions of scholarship readily include the scholarship of teaching, the scholarship of engagement, and discipline-based scholarship. The assumption is that expanded forms of scholarship will contribute new knowledge to an existing body of literature. The expected outcome from this scholarship is that those who teach will enhance their own practice by learning from others who have studied the interactions between the learning environment, the learner, and the instructor. With increased demands on teaching faculty, and the permission to pursue diverse forms of scholarship, it is important that no scholarship "be privileged over another with respect to rewards" (Ewell, 2002, p. 12). Eaton (2002) claims,

> The reward structures in the new university need to reflect the synergy of teaching, scholarship and learning. "In the new university, department chairs, deans and professional organizations have to pay attention to this trend and to give significant rewards for the effort required

to design and manage inquiry based learning environments, develop community based partnerships for learning, and create a collaborative and interdisciplinary program. (pp. 10–11)

As faculty choose to undertake expanded forms of scholarship, faculty developers can help them to 1) frame appropriate research questions, 2) design research, 3) assist with data collection and analysis, and 4) to identify appropriate public dissemination outlets. Colleagues in different disciplines are usually not as familiar with these outlets as are faculty developers.

Faculty seeking to broaden scholarship interests do not have models for documenting their scholarship in promotion and tenure materials. Faculty developers, who are outside the evaluation system in the promotion and tenure process, have the opportunity to provide assistance to faculty in preparing their promotion and tenure materials. This assistance can be in the form of one-on-one feedback, workshops for untenured faculty, workshops for departments, and online materials (http://oaa.pdx.edu/cae).

Administrators and faculty need a common understanding of their institution's definitions of scholarship as well as how to evaluate them. If faculty believe that expanded definitions of scholarship are recognized equally with traditional scholarship, they will be more inclined to undertake new and often untested forms of research design and scholarship. The information gathered through these expanded forms of scholarship would be critical for the continual assessment of the different learning environments and delivery model designs. Because faculty developers are not part of the evaluative process of the promotion and tenure review process, they are ideally positioned to assist deans, department chairs, and promotion and tenure committees in understanding the expanded definitions of scholarship.

ASSESSING THE CLASSROOM, THE PROGRAM, AND THE INSTITUTION

Palomba and Banta (1999) define assessment as " . . . the systematic collection, review and use of information about educational programs for the purpose of improving student learning development" (p. 4). Assessment must be threaded throughout the new higher education model, from the singular learning environment, to learning communities, to program review (Rhodes, 2002), to institutional assessment.

In the traditional learning environment, feedback from students about course content is gathered at designated junctures throughout the term (e.g., quizzes, exams, term papers, and projects). Little attention is paid to assessment of the learning environment or specific pedagogies. In the new higher education model, with multiple learning environments, the instructor will gather formative assessment throughout the term that informs him or her both on what the students are learning and how they are learning. These data will allow the instructor to be more nimble in making mid-course changes in the learning environment and will help with designing future courses. In the traditional learning environment, course data was collected for student and personnel purposes. In the new higher education model, course data will also inform and help shape program and institutional goals (Angelo, 2001).

ASSISTING PART-TIME AND ADJUNCT FACULTY IN THEIR INSTITUTION TEACHING ROLES

As institutions of higher education strain to meet the needs of increasing student enrollment, they often hire more adjunct and part-time faculty. Because these faculty are not faced with promotion and tenure issues, they are hired to teach multiple classes and more students. In the traditional higher education model, faculty developers spend more time assisting tenure-track faculty, leaving the adjunct faculty feeling marginalized and truly adjunct to the institution. In the new higher education model, faculty developers can provide institutional support around teaching and learning needs for tenure-track, adjunct, and part-time faculty. Data from the National Study of Postsecondary Faculty, 1987, 1992, and 1998 (United States Department of Education, National Center for Educational Statistics), cited in Guskin and Marcy (2001), reported that the percentage of tenure-track faculty decreased 12% between 1987 and 1998 while the percentage of nontenure-track faculty increased by 149% between 1987 and 1998. If this trend continues, the nontenure-track faculty will far surpass the tenure-track faculty across higher education. Faculty developers are the support providers for these faculty.

SUPPORTING FACULTY, STAFF, AND STUDENTS AS CAMPUSES DIVERSIFY AND INTERNATIONALIZE

As the demographics in the United States population change, so are the demographics changing among students and faculty. In efforts to achieve greater international and domestic diversity among students and faculty, representative of diversity within the region, institutions have a responsibility to provide support in outreach for faculty and students as well as intercultural communication and communication competence (Kardia, 1998). Faculty developers are critical for providing course and curriculum support and faculty recruitment and retention.

CONCLUSION

The future will not be an easy one for faculty nor for their institutions. Driven by reducing financial resources, increasing expenses, increases in the diversity and size of the student population, as well as demands for accountability of student learning, alternatives to present teaching and learning structures and processes will be more acceptable and necessary. New models of undergraduate education that will deal with these pressures will lead to significant changes in how faculty teach and students learn. In these new settings, the role of faculty developers will be critical. There will be the increased need for centralized faculty development to support the campus broadly in everything from individual faculty support, to program review, to campus wide assessment (Rhodes, 2002).

While, at present, others may question of the allocation of scarce resources to fund faculty development activities, faculty developers must anticipate these pressures and the future needs of new higher education models and lead both faculty and administrative leaders to deal with the demands of the future. As faculty, staff, and administrators address how they expect to meet the realities of the future by creating new learning environments, it is important for the success of the institution that faculty developers position themselves as key players in enabling faculty to become effective in these new settings.

REFERENCES

Angelo, T. A. (2001). Doing faculty development as if we value learning most: Transformative guidelines from research to practice. In D. Lieberman & C. Wehlburg (Eds.), *To Improve the Academy: Vol. 19. Resources for faculty, instructional, and organizational development* (pp. 97–112). Bolton, MA: Anker.

Boyer, E. L. (1990). *Scholarship reconsidered: Priorities of the professoriate.* Princeton, NJ: The Carnegie Foundation for the Advancement of Teaching.

Chickering, A. W., & Gamson, Z. F. (1987). Seven principles for good practice in undergraduate education. *AAHE Bulletin, 39* (7), 3–7.

Eaton, M. (2002). Searching for the 'new university': Changing faculty roles. *Project on the Future of Higher Education.* Available: http://www.antioch.edu/pfhe

Ewell, P. (2002). Three dialectics in higher education's future. *Project on the Future of Higher Education.* Available: http://www.antioch.edu/pfhe

Glassick, C. E., Huber, M. T., & Maeroff, G. I. (1997). *Scholarship assessed: Evaluation of the professoriate.* San Francisco, CA: Jossey-Bass.

Guskin, A., & Marcy, M. (2001). Facing the future: Faculty work, student learning and fundamental reform. *Project on the future of higher education.* Available: http://www.antioch.edu/pfhe

Guskin, A., & Marcy, M. (in press). Pressures for fundamental reform: Creating a viable academic future. In R. Diamond (Ed.), *Field guide to academic leadership.* San Francisco, CA: Jossey-Bass.

Kardia, D. (1998). Becoming a multicultural faculty developer: Reflections from the field. In M. Kaplan & D. Lieberman (Eds.), *To Improve the Academy: Vol. 17. Resources for faculty, instructional, and organizational development* (pp. 15–33). Stillwater, OK: New Forums Press.

Laurillard, D. (1993). *Rethinking university teaching: A framework for the effective use of educational technology.* London, England: Routledge.

Marincovich, M., Prostko, J., & Stout, F. (Eds.). (1998). *The professional development of graduate teaching assistants.* Bolton, MA: Anker.

Newman, F., & Scurry, J. (2001, July 13). Online technology pushes pedagogy to the forefront. *The Chronicle of Higher Education,* p. B7.

Palomba, C. A., & Banta, T. W. (1999). *Assessment essentials: Planning, implementing, and improving assessment in higher education.* San Francisco, CA: Jossey-Bass.

Rhodes, T. (2002). Could it be that it does make sense? A program review process for integrating activities. In D. Lieberman & C. Wehlburg (Eds.), *To Improve the Academy: Vol. 20. Resources for faculty, instructional, and organizational development* (pp. 49–64). Bolton, MA: Anker.

Rice, E. (1991). The new American scholar: Scholarship and the purposes of the university. *Metropolitan Universities, 1* (4), 7–18.

Wladkowski, R. J., & Westover, T. (1999). Accelerated courses as a learning format for adults. *The Canadian Journal for the Study of Adult Education, 13* (1), 1–20.

Contact:

Devorah A. Lieberman
Vice Provost and Special Assistant to the President
Portland State University
Center for Academic Excellence
Box 751
Portland, OR 97207
Voice   (503) 725-5642
Fax   (503) 728-5262
Email   Liebermand@pdx.edu
Web   http://www.oaa.pdx.edu/cae

Alan E. Guskin
Co-Director and Senior Scholar
Project on the Future of Higher Education and
Distinguished University Professor
Antioch University
Home Address:
7724-171st St SW
Edmonds, WA 98026
Email   aguskin@university.atioch.edu

Devorah A. Lieberman is Vice Provost and Special Assistant to the President at Portland State University. She received her PhD (1984) in Intercultural Communication. She directs the Center for Academic Excellence that supports all areas of teaching/learning, community-university partnerships, and assessment. She is also responsible for four campus-wide Presidential Initiatives: Assessment, Student Advising, Diversity, and Internationalizing the campus. Her scholarly research interests include institutional change, the scholarship of teaching/learning, teaching/learning and technology, and intercultural communication. Her participation in Al Guskin's Project for the Future of Higher Education is helping shape her current research agenda and scholarly activities.

Alan E. Guskin became Distinguished University Professor and University President Emeritus of Antioch University on October 1, 1997. He has served as president and chancellor of two universities (Antioch University from 1985 to 1997 and the University of Wisconsin, Parkside from 1975 to 1985) and has held faculty positions at the University of Michigan as well the University of Wisconsin, Parkside and Antioch University. He is presently co-directing the Project on the Future of Higher Education, which, along with 14 leading thinkers and practitioners, is developing new models for the future of undergraduate education. He recently received the 2001 Morris T. Keeton Award from the Council on Adult and Experiential Learning "for his long and noteworthy history in higher education as an administrator, teacher, writer, consultant, and speaker and his demonstrated commitment to student learning and innovation and change in higher education."

16

Are They Really Teachers? Problem-Based Learning and Information Professionals

Michael Anderson
Virginia Baldwin
University of Nebraska, Lincoln

Traditionally, working with teaching faculty is the primary consulting role for most faculty development professionals. The boundaries, however, are not always clear regarding instructional assistance that is provided to other personnel. This chapter demonstrates how collaboration among faculty consultants and information specialists can result in enhanced library utilization and better research-related instruction. Our model uses problem-based learning (PBL) as a vehicle for teaching research and retrieval skills in either a single class experience or in multiple classroom visits with an engineering librarian.

INTRODUCTION

Traditionally, working with teaching faculty is the primary consulting role for faculty development professionals. However, the boundaries are not always clear regarding instructional assistance given to other personnel such as those who provide information services. Does the scope of faculty development include the providing of service to nonteaching faculty or to those who teach infrequently? Searching relevant literature provided some guidance about faculty development roles but the definitions are, perhaps necessarily, general. For example, in Morrison (1997), we found the following: "faculty developers provide consultative assistance to faculty members and teaching assistants in such varied domains as research, scholarly writing, and career planning" (p. 122). Is an engineering librarian, generally not considered teaching faculty, who instructs single sessions about the utilization of a technical library and multiple databases really teaching? Moreover, is working with an information specialist within the domain of faculty consulting? In short, are they really teachers and how should an instructional consultant address the needs of nonteaching faculty?

This chapter describes the collaboration between a faculty teaching consultant and an engineering librarian. The librarian is a new faculty member who made initial contact with the teaching and learning center after the annual new faculty orientation. The center participates in the orientation and shares information about services supportive of faculty teaching efforts. Our initial contact concerned short-term (one or two class sessions) teaching assignments where teaching about engineering library utilization was the curriculum. Initially, we discussed teaching tactics and strategies for designing courses as any consultant and client would. However, the fact that the course under consideration was, historically, a single session taught in each of several engineering courses about conducting library research, seemed to stretch the consulting boundaries. The result was a mutually beneficial experience regarding the impact of informed pedagogy, specifically problem-based learning (PBL), on nontraditional instructional settings. The librarian requested information on innovative practices that could enhance the more traditional instructional methods that she used at a previous institution. She felt that the old methods were ineffective and sought a method that was more motivational for students. During our consultation process, we developed a set of general teaching questions about library research instruction: What are the objectives for the instruction sessions? How will our methodological choices help students accomplish the objectives? How will we know if the students learn the requisite skills? If it is correct that learning that happens in the natural setting is more authentic (Brown, Collins, & Duguid, 1989; Lave, 1988; Vygotsky, 1986), then how can one or two classroom visits, with the intent of teaching about engineering research strategies, best emulate the library research environment?

THE OBJECTIVE

Graduates of university engineering programs in today's information age will find continuing education and research a necessity. Engineers will need to use information resources when solving design problems and for tracking new discoveries and ideas that are developed by other engineers and scientists. The Accreditation Board for Engineering and Technology (ABET) recognizes this and requires every engineering curriculum to include a lifelong learning component (Engineering Accreditation Commission, 1995). For civil engineering, which is one of the mainstream engineering fields, lifelong individual learning is considered the core issue (Grigg, 1998). With this in mind, we discussed the objectives for the engineering library session extensively, paying particular attention to the fact that students would receive limited exposure to the material. Moreover, if the primary objective is for the students to be able to apply what they have learned in their current or future engineering coursework, then we should not become bogged down with a laundry list of topics. McKeachie (1994) advises the same, saying that objectives should not cover a certain set of topics, but learning that can be applied and used in situations outside the course. Our overarching objective is for students to be able to construct a research query and conduct a complex library search for engineering information that is useful both in the classroom and for lifelong learning.

Once this objective was established, the challenge was designing a session(s) that incorporated the necessary content databases and information formats while, at the same time, helped the students learn to use and apply the research process. We know that in courses where both content and process are valuable, the principles of problem-based learning are often used to organize the curriculum. So, why not pose actual problems used by engineering professors to more closely emulate classroom objectives and career objectives? We believe that this method more closely reflected the real work of engineers.

The Method

Engineering education literature stresses teaching techniques that address various student learning styles. Maskell and Grabau (1998) stress the importance of problem-based cooperative learning and conclude that this mode provides an environment that builds students' motivation and morale. The result is a better attitude toward learning that enhances students' sense of achievement associated with completion of the project. Further, Bakos (1997) directly ties the lifelong learning component to web-based Internet resources and the ability of the engineering student/practitioner to access and critically evaluate them. He refers specifically to the multitude of government agencies that are organizing and posting information that has potential use in the field of civil engineering. Bakos (1997) also gives examples of freely available information from other sources, namely research results and specialized collections from universities and libraries. The use of problem-based learning for library instruction accommodates learning styles and mimics the process of continued learning.

A general principle supporting PBL is that learning is initiated by posing problems that the students want to solve (Boud & Feletti, 1991). While we know that solving library-based problems may not be highly motivating to undergraduate engineering students, we believe when faced with the alternative (a lengthy lecture on how you might use an engineering library), posing actual problems will produce more energetic and authentic student responses. Another PBL principle, cooperative learning, suggests that students find better solutions when they collaborate and will be better prepared for the workforce if they can work with others (Duch, Allen, & White, 2000). Our idea was that when students work together on real engineering questions the result will be a more thorough understanding of engineering library resource utilization. Exposure to PBL literature provided by the teaching consultant and attendance at PBL related workshops helped to convince the librarian that this method would be more effective than traditional approaches.

> Good problems require students to make decisions based on facts, information, logic, and/or rationalization. Problems should require that students define what assumptions are needed, what information is relevant, and what steps or procedures are required to solve the problem. (Duch, Allen, & White, 2000, p. 1)

For example, a student may pose the simple question, "What are the different designs for mobile phones?" Knowing how to separate relevant information from less important data may not be as difficult as in the case of a more complex question such as, "What are the design characteristics of a model web search engine interface?" In both questions, the student will need experience at narrowing the search to find salient information, but in the latter question, many more complex decisions are needed. Posing a problem that students will have to solve and discuss, as in our model, during a second session with the librarian, is active and experiential. Further, this assignment allows the librarian an opportunity to track student success and field questions about barriers (learning issues) that arose during the research process.

THE MODEL

We believe that students, while perhaps Internet savvy, are not as disposed to identifying accuracy in nonlibrary sources; moreover, many students do not know what scholarly journals are or how to use them. As a practicing engineer, in keeping with a lifelong learning mission, these resources will be important on an ongoing basis. Some of these resources are available freely over the Internet. Advanced methods that can be used to more precisely search the Internet, when learned as concepts, can be applied equally to periodical indexes and are transferable from one index to another. In addition to learning these concepts and how to use them, students will need some tools for evaluating the information. These tools will enable them to distinguish web site information sources from published sources, scholarly resources from nonscholarly resources, and more highly researched and accepted information sources from those less researched.

Our model uses a two-session format in which the librarian visits classes for the purpose of instruction about engineering research and library utilization specific to that course. During the first session, the librarian introduces a sample problem, based on those developed by engineering professors, and a flowchart (Figure 16.1) that outlines the basic types of information sources, categorizes the sources, and indicates source reliability (Flow of Scientific Information, n.d.). In addition, students are introduced to the database web sites so as to familiarize them with specific database interface structures that they will use when they search in groups. And finally, students are given a resource utilization assignment.

For each class, we consulted in advance with teaching faculty about possible topics that are typical either for a research project, thesis, dissertation, or a topic of professional interest, depending upon course content and level. Six topics were identified for each class. The topics were listed on the assignment and the students were given a choice of the six topics. Once the topic was selected, the next task was to formulate a research question associated with a specific research task that requires the students to identify relevant information sources. The following are examples of research questions and the keywords actually used in student searches in two engineering classes:

- *Mechanical Engineering*
  Topic: Liquid fueled rocket engines
  Research Question: (What has been published about liquid) "rocket fuel efficiency and performance?"
  Keywords Used: Liquid fuel rocket, efficiency, and performance

- *Construction Management*
  Topic: Concrete admixtures
  Research Question: "I would like to find out what amounts of the different aggregates makes concrete the strongest."
  Keywords Used: Concrete, admixtures, strength

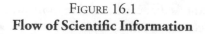

FIGURE 16.1
Flow of Scientific Information

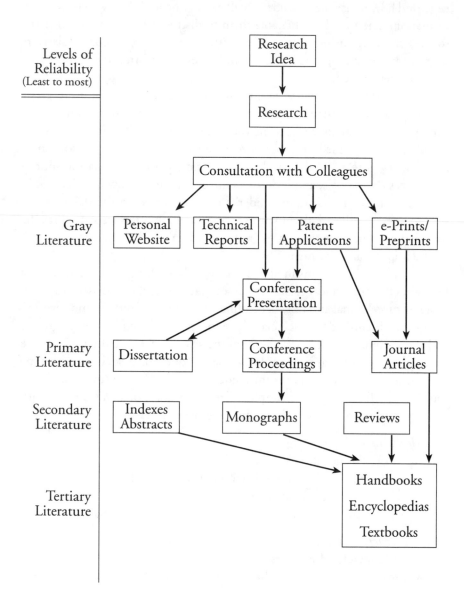

Students then select (or are assigned) partners. In these small groups they will be expected to research their query and report the details of their search. Group members must visit the library facilities, physically examine print journals, and use pertinent online sources to gather information. Each group is expected to record the steps taken to either narrow or broaden a search and the search terms they used. They must also explain how they determined the reliability of the information they gathered. The assignment questions are representative of the categories shown in Figure 16.1, such as technical reports and patent information (gray literature), conference proceedings and journal articles (primary literature), and reference resources (tertiary literature). Secondary sources such as periodical indexes, used to find a citation in a specific journal and issue, are introduced as tools to facilitate access to the primary literature (Solla, 2000). Questions are included that require student evaluation of information sources using criteria learned through actual examination of issues of two journals selected by the librarians/instructor. Figure 16.2 represents an example of a decision-making guide meant to show the reader how students might conduct their search assignment.

The goal of the second session is to use student search results to enhance instruction. Students discuss their searches, share the barriers that prevented successful searches, and exchange strategies and tactics that were helpful in completing the assignment. The library specialist uses student examples to reemphasize the key concepts, clarify learning objectives, and teach to issues left unresolved by student searches. The librarian can extend the learning process by inviting students or entire groups to the engineering library for more in-depth instruction or to solve specific problems that arose during the exercise.

A one-session model was also developed because some engineering professors will not commit more than one class day to library instruction. In the single session model, the librarian emphasizes the value of research skills to student coursework and future careers, provides instructions about completing the assignment, and introduces the mechanics and fundamental concepts involved in completing it. The searches are completed cooperatively in small groups and submitted to the course professor the following week for grading by the librarian and library staff. The limitations of a single session are mitigated when written feedback about the assignment is included. In the single session, students are afforded the same opportunity for personal assistance in the engineering library, again, to enhance the students' ability to learn the research process.

FIGURE 16.2
Assignment Decision-Making Guide

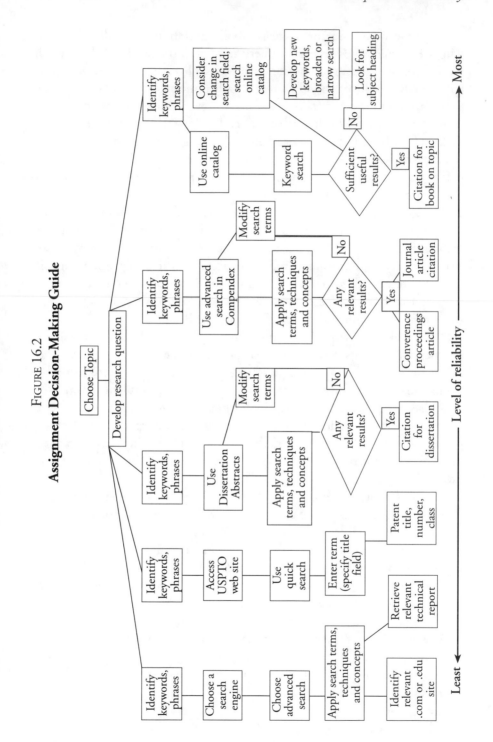

THE RESULTS

Teaching that accomplishes learning objectives is desirable in any form of instruction but it is more difficult when class time is limited. The constraint of posing library research problems within two class sessions means that assessing student work must be part of the instruction. Often, assessment is designed as a summative apparatus rather than formative, but in this model, the second session utilizes assessment for learning rather than assessment of learning (Stiggins, 2001). The completion of the assignment does provide a limited evaluation of the learning and, more important, the projects create a focus for student discussion and are used as a teaching device in the second session. During the second session, students are asked conceptual questions such as, "What are some of the techniques that you used on your assignment to narrow your search or to make it more precise?" After sufficient prompting in some classes, several students responded based on how they completed the assignment by citing a variety of methods, such as adding a term with the Boolean operator "and" or searching in a more restricted field such as title or subject. Students are encouraged to notice the transferability of this knowledge from one engineering topic to another and to other search engines and databases.

In addition, a one-minute evaluation was administered that included writing a sentence describing any new concepts that were learned. The results indicated that many students felt more comfortable with using periodical indexes, recognized their usefulness, and learned how to evaluate information sources. A second question asked students to write a sentence describing something that is still unclear. Results provided additional ideas for future sessions. The one-minute evaluation included responses regarding the usefulness of this knowledge during their educational and professional careers. The responses indicated that students did expand their information gathering techniques and found the experience and knowledge gained to be useful. See the appendices for the complete results for one engineering class.

CONCLUSION

The benefits of the consultation process and our collaboration extend beyond the development of a successful PBL teaching model for engineering library instruction. The engineering students and professors involved provided positive feedback about the changes and the impact on learning; however, other secondary effects may be just as significant as improved student research skills. For example, our collaboration helped a newly hired engineering librarian make connections with other engineering faculty who were impressed with faculty comments about the research skills lessons. The PBL library assignment is now included in more of the College of Engineering and Technology courses. In addition, other engineering faculty members who were trying to implement a problem-based approach in their courses have asked for library support and collaboration.

Another benefit of our partnership is a broader shared understanding of the role of faculty development. For a faculty consultant, making connections with an information specialist is helpful in understanding the role of the librarian as a part of the overall education experience. Our university is a land grant institution, a research level one institution, and an Association of American Universities institution, and as such, has dual missions: One goal is teaching and another is maintaining a commitment to a high research standard. With this in mind, library and information specialists could be considered integral with respect to achieving both goals. Librarians have the ability and impetus to categorize information sources, and a librarian working with a faculty consultant can develop methods that will use these organizational skills more effectively to improve student learning.

REFERENCES

Bakos, J. D., Jr. (1997). Communication skills for the 21st century. *Journal of Professional Issues in Engineering Education and Practice, 123* (1), 14–16.

Boud, D., & Feletti, G. (1991). Introduction. In D. Boud & G. Feletti (Eds.), *The challenge of problem-based learning* (p. 12). New York, NY: St. Martin's Press.

Brown, J. S., Collins, A., & Duguid, P. (1989). Situated cognition and the culture of learning. *Educational Researcher, 13,* 32–41.

Duch, B. J., Allen, D. E., & White, H. B. (2000, October). Problem-based learning: Preparing students in the 21st century. In *Teaching at UNL, 22* (2). The newsletter of the UNL Teaching and Learning Center. Used with permission of *Teaching Excellence,* a service of POD member services.

Engineering Accreditation Commission of the Accreditation Board for Engineering and Technology (ABET). (1995). *ABET engineering criteria 2000.* Baltimore, MD: Author.

Flow of Scientific Information. (n.d.). Retrieved December 12, 2001, from http://www.lib.uwaterloo.ca/usered/grad/researchskills/flow_of_info.htm

Grigg, N. S. (1998). Universities and professional associations: Partnerships for civil engineering careers. *Journal of Management in Engineering, 14* (2), 45–55.

Lave, J. (1988). *Cognition in practice: Mind, mathematics and culture in everyday life.* New York, NY: Cambridge University Press.

Maskell, D. L., & Grabau, P. J. (1998). A multidisciplinary cooperative problem-based learning approach to embedded systems design. *IEEE Transactions on Education, 41* (2), 101–103.

McKeachie, W. J. (1994). *Teaching tips* (9th ed.). Lexington, MA: D. C. Heath.

Morrison, D. E. (1997). Overview of instructional consultation in North America. In K. T. Brinko & R. J. Menges (Eds.), *Practically speaking: A sourcebook for instructional consultants in higher education* (pp. 121–129). Stillwater, OK: New Forums Press.

Solla, L. (2000). *Chem 602: Lecture, week one.* Retrieved December 10, 2001, from http://www.library.cornell.edu/psl/chem602/lectures/lecture1.htm

Stiggins, R. (2001, November 8). *Assessment and state performance standards.* Workshop presented by the Nebraska State Department of Education, University of Nebraska, Lincoln.

Vygotsky, L. (1986). *Thought and language.* Cambridge, MA: MIT Press.

Contact:

Michael Anderson
115 Benton Hall
University of Nebraska, Lincoln
Lincoln, NE 68588
Voice   (402) 472-9766
Email   manderson6@unl.edu

Virginia Baldwin
Associate Professor
Engineering Library
W204 Nebraska Hall
University of Nebraska, Lincoln
Lincoln, NE 68588-0516
Voice   (402) 472-3412
Fax   (402) 472-0663
Email   vbaldwin2@unl.edu

Michael Anderson is a Faculty Instructional Consultant for the University of Nebraska, Lincoln Teaching and Learning Center. The center is the second oldest in the United States and is currently being disbanded for budgetary reasons after 32 years of service to the faculty. Dr. Anderson has been with the center for three years.

Virginia Baldwin joined the faculty of the University Libraries at the University of Nebraska, Lincoln as Associate Professor and Head of the Engineering Library on September 1, 2000. On September 1, 2001, she was also appointed Head of the Physics Library. Ms. Baldwin is a member of the American Society for Information Science and the American Society for Engineering Education. She is also the Editor of the journal *Science and Technology Libraries.*

APPENDIX **16.1**

LIBRARY INSTRUCTIONS SESSIONS

Write a sentence describing one new concept that you learned in these sessions.

Response	Number
How to broaden and narrow searches	3
How to use Compendex	7
The variety of available resources	3
How to search for tech reports	1
Nothing	3
Truncation	3
How to find periodicals	3
How to use the UNL Libraries and the Eng. Library	7
Available Internet resources	3
How to do patent searches	2
How to use Boolean logic in searches	3
How to use Academic Search Elite	1
Techniques in slowing steel corrosion	1

APPENDIX 16.2

Write a sentence describing something that was presented in these sessions that is still unclear to you.

Response	Number
Abstracts	1
Use of the UNL catalog	1
Truncation	3
Nothing	13
Differences between scholarly and nonscholarly resources	1
Use of Academic Search Elite	5
Use of Compendex	2
How to find journal articles	1
How to find reference books	2
How to use the UNL web site	2
How to use advanced search features	3
The setup of the library	2
How to do patent searches	1

APPENDIX 16.3

What is your perception of the value of these exercises:

a. In your coursework at UNL

Response	Number
Will be useful in research and assignments	30
Came too late in my student career	1
Unsure	3
It will be of some use	5

b. In your professional career

Response	Number
Unsure	6
It should be helpful	17
It will help me keep up to date on technology	9
It will help to show what journals professionals use	1
It will be little or no help	7

17

Embracing a Philosophy of Lifelong Learning in Higher Education: Starting with Faculty Beliefs about Their Role as Educators

Carolin Kreber
University of Alberta

Recent events on the international political scene point to a need to teach course content and learning skills that focus on issues of equity and diversity, understanding of the local culture and differences among cultures; learning for ethics, citizenship, and democracy, interpersonal skills; and an ability to make informed and responsible value judgments. These, among others, are important aspects of lifelong learning. To embrace a philosophy of lifelong learning in higher education it seems paramount to focus on faculty beliefs about teaching to encourage a critical interrogation of course and program goals. The chapter concludes with several suggestions for the practice of faculty development.

INTRODUCTION

In this chapter, I will first suggest that there are two different ways of learning about teaching, which, by extension, represent two different approaches to faculty development. Subsequently, I will review some literature on the meaning of lifelong learning and show how a philosophy of lifelong learning is linked to one's goals and purposes of college and university teaching. Finally, I will highlight the practical implications of what has been suggested for the practice of faculty development.

288

When thinking about the type of learning that educational developers may opt to foster among faculty, we can distinguish two different approaches. The first could be seen as being aimed at encouraging faculty to reflect on, and learn about, how to promote certain skills, knowledge, and attitudes in their students. This approach understands learning about teaching as a process that occurs within a given framework of predetermined educational goals and purposes. The goal is to work toward to these given ends, not to question them. The second approach would be aimed at encouraging faculty to reflect on, and learn about, the educational goals themselves. This approach understands learning about teaching as questioning of a given framework of educational goals and purposes and as determining the goals of higher education. Certainly, no one would deny that once educational goals and purposes have been identified and deemed valuable, helping students develop in the direction of these goals becomes paramount. Thus, it would seem that both types of learning about teaching—how to promote certain skills, knowledge, and attitudes in students and identifying meaningful educational goals, are important. While the importance of these two types of learning about teaching have long been recognized—there have always been educational philosophers (asking what and why) and instructional designers (asking how)—their implications for faculty development to date have not been fully realized. In further illustrating the fundamental difference between these two types of learning about teaching, the contributions of German critical social theorist Jürgen Habermas (1971, 1981) and American adult education scholar Jack Mezirow (1991) seem particularly helpful. In briefly summarizing the most significant points of their work, an effort is made to highlight its practical implications.

DIFFERENT WAYS OF LEARNING

In his classic *Knowledge and Human Interests,* Habermas (1971) argues that there are three basic human interests: controlling nature, social harmony, and individual growth. Over the course of human evolution, these three interests have given rise to three different kinds of knowledge—the instrumental, the communicative, and the emancipatory. Each kind of knowledge is generated by a certain form of science, together with its corresponding procedures for testing the validity of truth claims—hypothesis testing through the scientific method (empirical-analytical science), reaching understanding through consensus (hermeneutics), and emancipation through critical reflection (critical science), respectively. Though Habermas never discusses learning as such, his theory of knowledge-constitutive interests has provided the basis for Mezirow's (1991, 2001) model of perspective transformation or transformative learning, a well-developed construct in adult learning theory (e.g., Cranton, 1994, 1996; Marsick, 1990).

According to Mezirow (1991), the three forms of science Habermas distinguished—the empirical-analytical, the hermeneutic, and the critical—can also be interpreted as three different forms of learning. Learners, like scientists, approach problems in ways that seem most promising to meet desired goals, or interests. If the interest it to establish cause and effect relationships, learning follows the empirical-hypothetical method and it is *instrumental* in nature. If the interest is to reach greater understanding of what others mean through the written word or dialogue, learning it is *communicative*. Finally, if the interest is freedom from coercion and distorted ideology, learning becomes *emancipatory*. As I will show next, it is these three forms of learning that are also present when faculty learn about teaching.

As we saw earlier, faculty may follow the footsteps of the instructional designer and ask, "How can we best promote certain skills, knowledge, and attitudes in my students?" They may also follow the footsteps of the educational philosopher and ask, "Which educational goals are worth our intentional pursuit, and why?"

Instrumental Learning

When goals and purposes are considered as given, learning is primarily of an instrumental nature. Faculty may wish to learn how to enhance students' reading skills, how to encourage greater motivation, how to increase students' memory of facts and algorithms, how to foster deep-level learning, or how to create more culturally responsive classrooms or appreciation of different lifestyles. In pursuing such endeavors, a faculty member may decide on a particular approach or strategy to be used, develop a set of hypotheses as to what might happen as a result, implement the strategy, collect some data on the way, and interpret these data against the hypotheses. These hypotheses may be derived from personal teaching experience, discussions with colleagues at teaching-related conferences, or knowledge of some of the relevant literature on teaching and learning in higher education. Examples of such hypotheses may include:

- If I provide my students with advance organizers they will achieve better results in summarizing and critiquing the assigned reading materials.

- If I convey the relevance of the material through application to real-life issues students will feel more motivated.

- If I use quizzes students will remember facts and algorithms better.

- If I base my course on a series of case studies and have students work in small groups to discuss and solve them on their own, they will seek an understanding of important principles and thus engage in deep-level learning.

- If I have course participants share their experiences, allow for discussion, and use examples illustrative of different lifestyles, students will report on this favorably.

Investigations of this kind are very valuable to teachers and students alike as they enhance our understanding of what practices better facilitate student learning. Present initiatives to promote faculty engagement in the scholarship of teaching tend to fall into this domain of learning. The goal is to have faculty consult and contribute to the knowledge base on how to best teach certain subjects by collecting data, interpreting these, and sharing their findings with the larger community. The ultimate purpose of such inquiry, of course, is the enhancement of student learning.

A good example of such an initiative is the Pew National Fellowship Program for Carnegie Scholars (Cambridge, 2000; Hutchings, 1999) offered by the Carnegie Academy for the Scholarship of Teaching and Learning (CASTL). The purpose of the Pew Fellowship program is described as creating

> a community of scholars, diverse in all the ways that matter in teaching and learning, whose work will advance the profession of teaching and deepen student learning. The central work of the Carnegie Scholars is to create and disseminate examples of the scholarship of teaching and learning that contribute to thought and practice in the field. (CASTL, n.d.)

Pew scholars are trained in the practice of the scholarship of teaching as they engage in research on teaching and learning within their discipline. Their work is expected to have 1) clear goals, 2) require adequate preparation, 3) make use of appropriate methods, 4) produce significant results, 5) demonstrate effective presentation, and 6) involve reflective critique (Glassick, Huber, & Maeroff, 1997).

It is the first of these criteria that seems particularly important for the present discussion. What does having clear goals mean? I take clear goals to mean a precise articulation of a purpose or problem to be solved. I do not take it to mean, however, a critical interrogation of one's goals. An important question, therefore, is at what point, and by whom, are the goals themselves being examined? I suggest that college and university teaching, or the scholarship thereof, can be approached from either a micro or a macro perspective. If we choose to take a micro perspective on (the scholarship of) teaching, we may conclude that goals instructors set for their courses, or certain segments thereof, are determined to a large extent by the field or discipline itself. Few colleagues would deny that each field has its own knowledge base with its own methods of inquiry, and one important goal of instructors, therefore, should be to ensure students are exposed to both the content and ways of thinking aligned with this field. As for one of my own courses on adult developmental/learning theory, for example, one clear goal of mine that likely would remain uncontested, if shared with my peers, is that students understand the major differences between the various developmental/learning theories studied. This goal is deceivingly neutral in a sense that the assumptions, beliefs, and values that underlie it, namely that teaching of content is important, is one that is deeply ingrained in the academy and thus is taken for granted.

However, if we choose to take a macro perspective on (the scholarship of) teaching, the question of what are clear goals reveals itself as being more complex. A macro perspective, the way I define it for the purpose of this chapter, would take into account the broader context in which teaching and learning take place. This context, to a large extent, is defined by the educational philosophical stance of the instructor and the institution. From a macro perspective, the question of clear goals becomes one of desirable goals. Questions that would be asked are, "What, according to the instructor and the institution, is the purpose of higher education, what are the goals, and why are the goals this way?" and only later "How can they best be achieved?" A macro perspective, therefore, includes a critical interrogation of goals. While the Carnegie standards are indeed important—stating one's goals in clear terms and showing evidence of adequate preparation, using appropriate methods, showing significant results, and demonstrating effective presentation and reflective critique on the process and the results—I propose that what has not received sufficient attention to date is reflective critique of the educational goals themselves.

When faculty learn about the meaningfulness, appropriateness, or desirability of educational goals, the learning they are engaged in is not instrumental but communicative in nature (Mezirow, 1991).

Communicative Learning

Communicative learning is not about testing hypotheses but about reaching greater understanding among individuals. The purpose is "learning to understand what others mean and to make ourselves understood as we attempt to share ideas through speech, the written word" (Mezirow, 1991, p. 75) and interactions with others. Once a common understanding or consensus has been achieved, on the basis of existing social norms and moral understandings, this is considered valid knowledge. In an article on the scholarship of teaching, Kreber and Cranton (2000) showed that much of faculty learning about teaching falls in the domain of communicative learning. Obviously, when faculty ask, "Which educational goals are worth our intentional pursuit?" this question cannot be answered through instrumental learning but calls for communicative learning. When faculty engaged in communicative learning reach understanding of what are valuable goals, they engage in dialogue framed by their assumptions of what the university as an institution, or perhaps a particular discipline, stands for. Goals are being determined on the basis of consensus. Very important learning can be achieved this way. Such learning is present, for example, when program or course planning committees get together to determine the content of a particular course. These committees are usually formed for large mandatory introductory courses offered in several sections, therefore requiring more than one instructor. Consensus is reached, as we have seen, within a framework of existing assumptions. What is particularly interesting about Habermas's (1971) work is that it suggests these existing assumptions that we hold about university teaching and learning, however, are socially and historically constructed. Consequently, Habermas (1971) encourages people to critically question these long-held assumptions by tracing their origins. When this happens, learning may become emancipatory.

Emancipatory Learning
When individuals engage in emancipatory learning, the goal is to overcome the limitations of self-knowledge and the social constraints on one's thoughts and actions. Mezirow (1991) suggests that in emancipatory learning "Knowledge is gained through critical self-reflection . . . the form of inquiry in critical self-reflection is appraisive rather than prescriptive or designative" (p. 87). One may argue that when faculty critically question why they have certain goals and purposes they engage in emancipatory learning. Such learning may include realizing that educational goals and purposes that seemed very meaningful at some earlier time have outlived their day. It may include realizing that goals have been considered only through the lens of the discipline but not through the lens of the broader learning experience that colleges and universities should provide.

Let us now explore why attending to educational goals and purposes seems important and why colleges and universities should commit themselves to a philosophy of lifelong learning.

LIFELONG LEARNING

Clearly, lifelong learning is not a new concept. So why should lifelong learning be any more significant today than it was when John Dewey discussed learning as a lifelong process in the first quarter of the 20th century? Is it?

When discussed in the context of higher education, a commitment to lifelong learning is usually seen in educational policies that provide regulations on issues of access, inter- and intra-sector arrangements of credit transfer, prior learning assessment or arrangements for learning at a distance, and continuing education. Basically, these are regulations that permit people to engage in formal learning throughout their adult years. The focus on these discussions is not on what students should learn in order to be successful lifelong learners but on how they could become involved in continuous learning. However, in our rapidly changing world, the development of lifelong learning skills has been recognized as an important goal and responsibility of higher education (Boud, 1997; Candy, 1991; Knapper & Cropley, 2000). According to this literature, skills and competencies for lifelong learning that should be explicitly taught include communication skills, the ability to think critically, knowledge and skills necessary for working life, and the ability to learn how to learn. In our increasingly complex global society, additional skills and knowledge areas seem important. Recent events on the international political scene call for a much stronger focus in our curricula and programs on issues of equity and diversity; understanding of the local culture and differences between cultures; learning for ethics, citizenship, and democracy; and environmental and health issues. Skills to be learned to function responsibly in such a world would also encompass, I would think, interpersonal skills including empathy and tolerance, integrity, and an ability to make informed and responsible value judgments.

Let us now explore what a few selective scholars of education suggest are important skills and knowledge to be acquired to engage in lifelong learning.

Writing about the necessity to help students self-direct their learning, Bandura (1997) argues that

> Good schooling fosters psychosocial growth that contributes to the quality of life beyond the vocational domain. A major goal of formal education should be to equip students with the intellectual tools, efficacy beliefs, and intrinsic interests to educate themselves throughout their lifetime. These personal resources enable individuals to gain new knowledge and cultivate skills either for their own sake or to better their lives. (p. 17)

Speaking specifically to the role of higher education institutions, Knapper and Cropley (2000) suggest that

Institutions have an important part to play in promoting the development of the personal prerequisites and competencies for lifelong learning. This could be done partly by training people in lifelong learning competencies, and partly by providing them with opportunities to exercise skills they had already acquired. The major purpose would be to equip people in such a way that they wanted to continue learning and believed they could do so. Achieving these goals would require teaching and learning activities that depart from the norms of conventional classrooms. (p. 56)

Knapper and Cropley (2000) also cite Little's (1983) work, who suggested that if Cardinal Newman's beliefs about (liberal) education were translated into statements regarding course content,

he can be seen as advocating that students acquire communication skills, ability in critical thinking, understanding of the local culture and differences between cultures, interpersonal skills (including empathy and tolerance), integrity and an ability to make informed and responsible value judgements, as well as knowledge and skills necessary for working life and the ability to learn how to learn. (p. 57)

Of particular interest are also the areas of knowledge Lengrand (1986), in a document prepared for United Nations Educational, Scientific, and Cultural Organization (UNESCO), identified as minimum content necessary in a system of education that is committed to lifelong learning. These knowledge areas are knowledge of communication, science and technology, the fine arts, ethics and citizenship, time and space, and how to care for one's own body. Environmental education, too, has long been recognized as another important area students in schools, colleges, and universities should be exposed to (Knapper & Cropley, 2000). Discussing their vision of how universities and colleges could respond to these learning demands, Knapper and Cropley (2000) argue that "the themes in question should run through all courses and programmes, to the maximum extent possible" (p. 58).

And what about educating for citizenship and democracy? Schapiro (1999) raises our awareness of the role contemporary higher education institutions need to play in educating students about and for democracy—that is for liberty, equality, and community. Among the questions education should concern itself with are (Shapiro, 1999, p. 8):

- How can we help students to acquire the skills, attitudes, dispositions, and knowledge they will need in order to be active and responsible democratic citizens?

- How can we create democratic learning communities which recognize and affirm the diversity of all our members?

- How can we affirm and develop each student's individual and particular identity while also helping each of them to develop a commitment to a common good?

- How can we help students to work for social, political, and environmental reconstruction?

- How can we affirm new epistemologies and new ways of constructing meaning, while maintaining a common discourse and common standards of scholarship?

Schapiro (1999) contends that in responding to these questions to achieve a democratic education for our times, our practice should be guided by four democratic principles as they have evolved over the past 25 years. These are the critical, feminist, and multicultural pedagogies as well as the notion of a participatory democracy (as achieved, for example, through participation of students and teachers in curriculum planning, in mutual evaluation, etc.).

FOCUSING ON EDUCATIONAL GOALS

In the remainder of this chapter I will focus on what faculty developers can do to promote a learning culture that embraces lifelong learning, broadly conceived. As we have seen, a philosophy of lifelong learning is based on an understanding that promoting those attitudes, skills, and knowledge that individuals need to function fully and responsibly in a democratic society, and to engage in continued learning throughout their lives, is an important goal of college and university teaching. Rather than focusing faculty development initiatives exclusively on how to facilitate student learning, the question that needs addressing first is that of what kind of learning to promote.

When faculty engage in learning about curricular and program goals and purposes, their learning is either communicative or emancipatory, or both (Kreber & Cranton, 2000). Goals and purposes of teaching are the foundations of one's philosophy of teaching. A philosophy of teaching, generally speaking, provides a rationale for educational practice (Lawson, 1991; Ozmon & Graver, 1990). Goodyear and Allchin (1998) suggest that "articulating an individual teaching philosophy provides the foundation by which to clarify goals, to guide behaviour, to seed scholarly dialogue on teaching, and to organise evaluation" (p. 103). Philosophies, therefore, are not something esoteric, abstract, and intangible that only those engaging in the formal study of education should be concerned with. Rather, educational philosophies are the roadmap to what we do as trainers or educators, and therefore are important for all instructors.

Whether we call it teaching philosophies, teaching perspectives, goals and values clarification, or conceptions of teaching and learning, the important point is that any professional practice is guided by certain goals, whether they are explicit or implicit. Helping others making their goals explicit and encouraging reflection on these, I would suggest, is an important aspect of faculty development, yet one that has received only marginal attention to date.

IMPLICATIONS FOR PRACTICE

As for concrete ways by which faculty developers could promote attention to faculty beliefs about education and their roles as educators, discussion forums and reading circles seem particularly meaningful. As a start, faculty could also be encouraged to complete any of the inventories now available that identify one's beliefs about education. Examples include the "Philosophy of Adult Education Inventory" (Zinn, 1990), the "Teaching Perspectives Inventory" (Pratt & Associates, 1998), or the "Approaches to Teaching Inventory" (Prosser & Trigwell, 1996). Each of these instruments is easy to complete, requires little time for analysis, and is a powerful heuristic if the goal is to encourage reflection. They could be used in individual as well as group settings. Mezirow (1990), in his edited volume *Fostering Critical Reflection in Adulthood,* discusses many strategies faculty developers could use to further stimulate the reflective process. Among the strategies featured in the book are the use of critical incidents, metaphor analysis, repertory grids, and concept mapping. While the purpose in this chapter is not to discuss these strategies in detail (interested readers are referred to Mezirow's book) it may suffice to say that each of these strategies has as its goal to make one's underlying assumptions explicit and to trace their origins. They are, therefore, perfectly suited if the goal is to encourage emancipatory learning among faculty.

Once beliefs, assumptions, and values on teaching and on one's roles as educators have been identified, they would need to be compared to and assessed against a philosophy of lifelong learning. Faculty developers would play an important role in exploring together with faculty the meaning of lifelong learning and the implications of lifelong learning with respect to the design of programs, curricula, and courses so that these reflect course content and learning skills needed for lifelong learning. Such discussions should emphasize the importance of teaching knowledge and skills necessary for working life and the ability to learn how to learn. It seems equally important to encourage faculty to explore whether issues of equity and diversity' understanding of the local culture and differences between cultures—broadly conceived as including all areas of difference in gender, religion, disability, class, learning styles, race, age, ethnicity, culture, and sexual orientation—learning for ethics, citizenship, and democracy; environmental and health issues; interpersonal skills; and the ability to make informed and responsible value judgments are important skills and knowledge areas to consider in a system that commits itself to lifelong learning. Once faculty, through critical questioning and emancipatory learning, conclude that these are important skills and knowledge areas and that an important goal of college and university education is to teach these, how these issues could run as themes throughout their courses would be the next problem to tackle. Earlier I suggested that most of the studies currently done under the umbrella of the scholarship of teaching pay little attention to a critical interrogation of program and curricula goals. A meaningful project of involving faculty in the scholarship of teaching would be to explore together with them, perhaps in the form of an action research project, just how the goals associated with lifelong learning could be pursued across the curriculum.

CONCLUSION

While I believe that a philosophy of lifelong learning has the greatest potential to strive when it gains the support of the faculty, I also see a role of faculty developers in becoming agents of institutional change. As change agents, faculty developers would advocate a general learning climate on campus that is conducive to lifelong learning. Such a climate would value diversity (broadly conceived as including all differences in lifestyle and identity) and equity across all activities on campus.

REFERENCES

Bandura, A. (Ed.). (1997). *Self-efficacy in changing schools.* Cambridge, MA: Cambridge University Press.

Boud, D. (1997). *Providing for lifelong learning through work-based study. Challenges for policy and practice.* Paper presented at the International Conference on Lifelong Learning, Guildford, Surrey, England.

Cambridge, B. L. (2000). The scholarship of teaching and learning: A national initiative. In M. Kaplan & D. Lieberman (Eds.), *To Improve the Academy: Vol. 18. Resources for faculty, instructional, and organizational development* (pp. 55–68). Bolton, MA: Anker.

Candy, P. (1991). *Self-direction for lifelong learning.* San Francisco, CA: Jossey-Bass.

Carnegie Academy for the Scholarship of Teaching and Learning (CASTL). (n.d.). Available: http://www.middlesex.cc.ma.us/carnegie/

Cranton, P. A. (1994). *Understanding and promoting transformative learning.* San Francisco, CA: Jossey-Bass.

Cranton, P. A. (1996). *Professional development as transformative learning.* San Francisco, CA: Jossey-Bass.

Glassick, C., Huber, M., & Maeroff, G. (1997). *Scholarship assessed: Evaluation of the professoriate.* Princeton, NJ: The Carnegie Foundation for the Advancement of Teaching.

Goodyear, G. E., & Allchin, D. (1998). Statements of teaching philosophy. In M. Kaplan (Ed.), *To improve the academy: Vol.17. Resources for faculty, instructional, and organizational development* (pp. 103–122), Stillwater, OK: New Forums Press.

Habermas, J. (1971). *Knowledge and human interests.* Boston, MA: Beacon Press.

Habermas, J. (1981). *Theorie des kommunikativen Handelns (Vols. 1 & 2).* Frankfurt, Germany: Suhrkamp.

Hutchings, P. (1999). *1999 Pew scholars institute.* Menlo Park, CA: The Carnegie Foundation for the Advancement of Teaching.

Knapper, C., & Cropley, A. (2000). *Lifelong learning in higher education.* London, England: Kogan Page.

Kreber, C. (2001). Designing a teaching portfolio based on a formal model of the scholarship of teaching. In D. Lieberman & C. Wehlburg (Eds.), *To improve the academy: Vol. 19. Resources for faculty, instructional, and organizational development* (pp. 268–285). Bolton, MA: Anker.

Kreber, C., & Cranton, P. A. (2000). Exploring the scholarship of teaching. *Journal of Higher Education, 71,* 476–495.

Lawson, K. H. (1991). Philosophical foundations. In P. Jarvis & J. M. Peters (Eds.), *Adult education* (pp. 282–301). San Francisco, CA: Jossey-Bass.

Lengrand, P. (1986). *Areas of learning basic to lifelong education.* Oxford, England: Pergamon.

Little, T. C. (1983). The institutional context for experiential learning. In T. C. Little (Ed.), *Making sponsored experiential learning standard practice.* San Francisco, CA: Jossey-Bass.

Marsick, V. (1990). Action learning and reflection in the workplace. In J. Mezirow (Ed.), *Fostering critical reflection in adulthood* (pp. 23–47). San Francisco: Jossey-Bass.

Mezirow, J. (Ed.). (1990). *Fostering critical reflection in adulthood.* San Francisco, CA: Jossey-Bass.

Mezirow, J. (1991). *Transformative dimensions of adult learning.* San Francisco, CA: Jossey-Bass.

Mezirow, J. (2001). *Learning as transformation.* San Francisco, CA: Jossey-Bass.

Ozmon, H., & Graver, S. (1990). *Philosophical foundations of education* (4th ed.). Toronto, Canada: Merrill Publishing Company.

Pratt, D. D., & Associates. (1998). *Five perspectives on teaching in adult and higher education.* Malabar, FL: Krieger.

Prosser, M., & Trigwell, K. (1996). Congruence between intention and strategy in science teachers; approach to teaching. *Higher Education, 32,* 77–87.

Schapiro, S. A. (1999). *Higher education for democracy.* New York, NY: Peter Lang.

Zinn, L. (1990). Identifying your philosophical orientation. In M. W. Galbraith (Ed.), *Adult learning methods: A guide to effective instruction* (pp. 60–74). Malabar, FL: Krieger.

NOTE

The ideas expressed in this chapter were developed as part of a larger study funded by the Social Sciences and Humanities Research Council of Canada.

Contact:

Carolin Kreber
Associate Professor of Adult and Higher Education
Department of Educational Policy Studies
University of Alberta
Edmonton, Alberta T6G 2G5 Canada
Voice   (780) 492 7623
Fax   (780) 492 2024
Email   carolin.kreber@ualberta.ca

Carolin Kreber has been a faculty member in the Adult and Higher Education Program of the Department of Educational Policy Studies at the University of Alberta since 1997. She teaches undergraduate and graduate courses on adult learning and development, instructional design, and current issues in postsecondary education. From 1993 to 1997, she worked as an educational development consultant at the Instructional Development Office at Brock University in Southern Ontario. Her present research focuses on faculty roles and responsibilities, higher education and lifelong learning, diversity and equity, and teaching and learning in higher education.

18

A Matrix for Reconsidering, Reassessing, and Shaping E-Learning Pedagogy and Curriculum

Laura Bush
Barry Maid
Duane Roen
Arizona State University

Educational stakeholders are increasingly engaged in discussions about the effective design, distribution, and evaluation of e-learning. We invite educators to build on already existing scholarship as they make future e-learning decisions. Specifically, we combine four categories of academic scholarship from Boyer (1990) with six assessment criteria from Glassick, Huber, and Maeroff (1997) to construct a matrix that may be applied to any post-secondary learning or teaching context. We argue that while each medium in which faculty might find themselves teaching differs from others, the teaching itself, and effective teaching in general, is definable and, therefore, can be evaluated using the matrix.

INTRODUCTION

A range of educational stakeholders (faculty, programs, departments, institutions, students, and the tax-paying public who support higher education) are increasingly engaged in important discussions about the effective design, distribution, and evaluation of e-learning (e.g., Graham, Cagiltay, Lim, Craner, & Duffy, 2001; Young & Young, 1999). With these discussions in mind, we invite educators to build on already existing scholarship in the field of teaching and learning to guide them as they make e-learning decisions for the future. We feel that while it is important to understand that each medium in which we might find ourselves teaching differs from others (e.g., teaching web-based or computer-mediated classes is very different from teaching classes with interactive video) the teaching itself, and effective teaching in general, is definable and, therefore, can be evaluated.

In our discussion here, for example, we revisit Ernest Boyer's (1990) four categories of academic scholarship in *Scholarship Reconsidered*. We then combine Boyer's categories with the six criteria from Glassick, Huber, and Maeroff's (1997) *Scholarship Assessed* to construct a matrix that may be applied to a wide range of postsecondary learning or teaching contexts. Using Laura's undergraduate teaching experience and her work in faculty development, we then explain and illustrate how the matrix can be used to assist a scholar-teacher as she evaluates and shapes e-learning and teaching for the benefit of diverse stakeholders.

ERNEST BOYER: *SCHOLARSHIP RECONSIDERED*

Rather than view scholarship as something distinct from service, teaching, and administration, Ernest Boyer (1990) argues we must, for the health of higher education, define scholarship broadly enough to embrace the full range of academic work—work that serves a wide range of stakeholders inside and outside the academy. In Boyer's (1990) scheme, the scholarly work of the professoriate has four interrelated functions: discovery, integration, application, and teaching. The scholarship of discovery is essentially what academics traditionally consider research to be—investigation for its own sake. The scholarship of integration consists of "making connections across the disciplines, placing the specialties in larger context, illuminating data in a revealing way, often educating nonspecialists, too" (Boyer, 1990, p.18). Boyer's (1990) third category, the scholarship of application, implies questions such as, "How can knowledge be responsibly applied to consequential problems?" and "Can social problems *themselves* (Boyer's emphasis) define an agenda for scholarly investigation?" (p. 21). What's exciting about Boyer's questions is that "[n]ew intellectual understandings can arise out of the very act of application. . . . In such activities as these, theory and practice vitally interact, and one renews the other" (p. 23). Boyer's (1990) fourth category, the scholarship of teaching, describes our crucial work with students and our responsibility to remain life-long learners. Boyer (1990) reminds us that "good teaching means that faculty, as scholars, are also learners" (p. 24). Among other things, effective teaching—with or without technology—requires that "[p]edagogical procedures must be carefully planned, continuously examined, and relate directly to the subject taught" (Boyer, 1990, pp. 23–24).

GLASSICK, HUBER, AND MAEROFF: *SCHOLARSHIP ASSESSED*

Extending Boyer's reconsideration of what it means to be engaged in scholarly work, Charles Glassick, Mary Huber, and Gene Maeroff explicate six criteria for assessing scholarship in their 1997 publication, *Scholarship Assessed*. After surveying nearly 900 chief academic officers of United States postsecondary institutions, Glassick, Huber, and Maeroff (1997) inductively constructed the six criteria: clear goals, adequate preparation, appropriate methods, significant results, effective presentation, and reflective critique. We specifically apply these criteria to the work of faculty in e-learning environments. To do that, we show how Boyer's (1990) four categories of scholarship and Glassick, Huber, and Maeroff's (1997) six criteria for assessing scholarship intersect to form a matrix that faculty can use to reconsider, reassess, and ultimately, shape or re-shape e-learning pedagogies (Figure 18.1).

FIGURE 18.1
Matrix Combining
Scholarship Reconsidered and Scholarship Assessed

	Four Categories of Academic Scholarship Boyer 1990			
	Teaching	*Integration*	*Application*	*Discovery*
Clear Goals				
Adequate Preparation				
Appropriate Methods				
Significant Results				
Effective Presentation				
Reflective Critique				

Six Criteria for Assessing Scholarship, Glasick, Huber, Maeroff, 1997.
Note: Faculty may use this matrix to guide them as they assess the full range of their scholarly work.

Before looking at the matrix, itself, we feel it is important to recognize the oppositional pull of the two axes. Boyer's (1990) expansion of the definition of scholarship tends to be open and heuristic in nature. Glassick, Huber, and Maeroff's (1997) assessment criteria tend to be focused and strategic. By creating a matrix with axes pulling in different directions, we hope faculty and administrators will be able to understand that while e-learning opportunities and pedagogies might open many new doors, we must still respond to the real, concrete need to assess what we do.

Clear Goals

Glassick, Huber, and Maeroff (1997) pose three questions to determine whether the scholar has established clear goals: "Does the scholar state the basic purposes of his or her work clearly? Does the scholar define objectives that are realistic and achievable? Does the scholar identify important questions in the field?" (p. 25). We have recast those questions to account for the decisions that faculty need to make when considering teaching with technology: How can I state the basic purposes of my teaching with technology? What are some realistic and achievable objectives for my teaching with technology? What are some important questions for students to explore with technology? And perhaps most important, is technology even an issue?

In Laura's business communication course, for example, her main objective is to expand and improve business students' reading, writing, speaking (or presentational), and computer literacies. In the course syllabus, Laura outlines the specific information and competencies students should expect to acquire throughout the semester by completing learning activities that depend on students' effective use of technologies such as Blackboard course management software, discussion forums, email messages, Microsoft Word, PowerPoint, and the Internet. In brief, students should be able to 1) identify three basic purposes of business communication, 2) organize information to fit their audiences, purposes, and the situation, 3) construct documents that are clear, complete, correct, visually inviting, save the reader's time, and build good will by creating a friendly, businesslike, positive style, 4) work effectively in groups by understanding strategies for responding to individual's differing styles, overcoming barriers to success, resolving conflict, and completing assignments on time, 5) understand the effect of verbal and nonverbal communication in business settings, and 6) make short oral presentations that are clear, well organized, stay within time limits, and demonstrate good audience awareness.

Laura's six outcomes are fairly standard for a course in business communication. What is different is that she includes computer literacies for students as an area that needs to be expanded and improved upon. What Laura has done is move the technological aspects of the classroom into the mainstream. Being able to effectively communicate with email, research on the web, use PowerPoint as a presentation tool, and the like are skills that need to be refined in the same way as other literacy skills have traditionally been refined. Throughout Laura's course, she has *not* included technology as something special or as a mere add-on to course requirements and assignments, but rather, she has integrated technology so that it becomes the norm.

Adequate Preparation

As a result of their survey, Glassick, Huber, and Maeroff (1997) offer the following questions to assess the scholar's preparation: "Does the scholar show an understanding of existing scholarship in the field? Does the scholar bring the necessary skills to his or her work? Does the scholar bring together the resources necessary to move the project forward?" (p. 27). Again, we have recast these questions: What is my understanding of existing scholarship on teaching with technology? What skills do I bring my teaching with technology? What resources can I use to promote learning, or, more specifically, to promote learning with the aid of technology?

Whether a teacher is a compassionate pioneer of the past or a wary or resistant adopter of the present, all scholar-teachers who choose to enhance their course with some form of technology should at least become familiar with the growing body of research on e-learning. Best practices, guidelines, and research are increasingly available on the Internet and in online, peer-reviewed journals such as *The Technology Source, The National Teaching and Learning Forum, The Journal of Scholarship of Teaching and Learning, Journal on Excellence in College Teaching,* and *Educational Researcher Online.* In addition, teachers can participate in national movements to support excellence in teaching with technology as well as in assisting faculty as they learn to adapt new technologies to promote learning. Such movements and organizations include, for example, the Teaching, Learning, and Technology Group (TLT), Multimedia Educational Resource for Learning and Online Teaching (MERLOT), the Flashlight Project for evaluating teaching with technology, and various grant-funded projects such as Preparing Teachers to Use Technology (PT 3 Grants) to support faculty integration of technology into K–12 and postsecondary programs and courses. Satellite broadcasts on key subjects such as intellectual property, copyright, and effective instructional design using technology are also available to faculty wishing to understand the issues, problems, and solutions to e-learning challenges. At many colleges and universities, in-house workshops and small-group or one-to-one consultations are also available to faculty who seek support, teaching tips, or guidelines for the effective integration of technology into their courses.

At our institution, for example, three campus units—the center for learning and teaching excellence, distance learning and technology, and instruction technology instruction support—have co-sponsored and designed week-long summer institute courses to assist faculty as they retool and redesign their own courses for fully online or technology-enhanced instruction. Summer institute courses available to all university faculty and other college teachers include, for example, "Enhancing Instruction Through Technology," "Teaching, Learning, and Assessment in Distance Education," "Active Learning with Technology," "Introduction to Marcromedia Flash," "Digital Video for Instruction and Research," and "Teaching, Learning, and Assessment in Distance Education." Faculty participation in such workshops gives evidence of postsecondary teachers' growing awareness and desire to prepare adequately for teaching in technology-enhanced environments. Glassick, Huber, and Maeroff's (1997) particular question about adequate preparation also shows us how important it is to embrace Boyer's (1990) taxonomy. In other words, once we accept that a scholarship of teaching exists, reviewing the literature, keeping up with current scholarship, and contributing to the scholarly conversation become a norm.

Appropriate Methods
Here, Glassick, Huber, and Maeroff's (1997) defining questions are straightforward: "Does the scholar use methods appropriate to the goals? Does the scholar apply effectively the methods selected? Does the scholar modify procedures in response to changing circumstances?" (p. 28). Here are our revisions: What methods of teaching with technology can I use to achieve the learning goals for the course? How can I effectively apply the selected e-learning teaching methods? How can I modify my use of technology in response to changing circumstances? These particular questions must be viewed as central to teaching with technology. Too often, newcomers to e-learning tend to see appropriate methods as one whole. They, wrongfully, assume that one pedagogy works for every e-learning situation. To make such an erroneous assumption is equivalent to assuming that instructors who are accustomed to lecturing to 250 students will use that same pedagogy when they teach a seminar to 15 students.

In the undergraduate classes and faculty development workshops that Laura conducts, she works to promote active learning by structuring lessons aided by various technologies. For example, Laura often uses short PowerPoint presentations to facilitate interactive discussions that encourage student/participants' active involvement using questions, hyperlinks to interactive Internet resources, time for reading and reflection, and engagement or exchange with peers. She also facilitates active/cooperative learning techniques using a "cooperative learning randomizer," a simple Excel spreadsheet designed to ensure individual accountability and encourage positive interdependence—two important features of effective cooperative learning. The randomizer is designed to be easily modified for both large lecture settings or small classes, depending on the number of assigned groups/teams and the number of student members in those groups/teams. In other words, a teacher can readily and appropriately modify the technology for varied teaching situations. For example, when Laura presented on teaching with technology to a large group of 75 faculty members at the University of Texas, San Antonio, she modified the randomizer so that teams of five faculty members would be randomly called upon as they were seated at 15 round tables. In contrast, when she teaches undergraduate students in computer-mediated classrooms, Laura modifies the randomizer to call individually upon 20 to 25 students working together in a corresponding number of teams, usually five to seven. In a computer-mediated classroom setting, she also prefers to use the cooperative learning technique of write-pair-square by partnering students sitting next to one another at computers and then creating teams composed of four by joining paired partners who are, ideally, located near one another throughout the room.

Significant Results

Pragmatic considerations are the focus of Glassick, Huber, and Maeroff (1997) in posing questions that assess the results of the scholar's work: "Does the scholar achieve the goals? Does the scholar's work add consequentially to the field? Does the scholar's work open additional areas for further exploration?" (p. 29). Our revisions: When using technology, how am I achieving the intended learning goals for students? How is my work with technology adding consequentially to students' learning and to the field? How is my work with technology opening additional areas for further exploration for students?

An extension of Glassick, Huber, and Maeroff's (1997) pragmatism here may lead us to the realization that though it may be difficult to assess that any particular technology specifically leads to an increase in student learning (Joy, II & Garcia, 2000; Russell, 1999; Twigg, 2001), to not incorporate certain technologies will unequivocally leave students disadvantaged. When word processing was a new technology, for instance, researchers asked whether word processing made one a better writer. That question became irrelevant once word processing became the "normal" way to write. As other technologies such as email, using the web for reference, and presentation software become the "normal" way to do business, we would be failing our students if we did not incorporate pedagogies using these tools into our curriculum.

Effective Presentation

Glassick, Huber, and Maeroff (1997) also don their rhetorical hats to examine the effectiveness of the scholar's work: "Does the scholar use a suitable style and effective organization to present his or her work? Does the scholar use appropriate forums for communicating work to its intended audiences? Does the scholar present his or her message with clarity and integrity?" (p. 32). Here are our revisions: How are my style and organization for teaching with technology affecting students' learning? What e-learning forums are most appropriate for communicating with students and others? With which technologies can I enhance the clarity and integrity of my communication with students and others?

Laura works to use technology to facilitate interactive, rather than passive, learning and to take advantage of its ability to appeal to diverse learning styles. She increases interaction and aids students who learn in a variety of ways through 1) well-designed PowerPoint presentations that encourage interaction between herself as a presenter and her students; such interactive presentations presumably appeal to students who learn best through both aural and visual means, 2) online discussions designed to stimulate deeper level thinking and broader participation by a majority of students, and where some students who may have traditionally felt reticent in class or some how silenced by the larger group, now feel comfortable to be active participants, and 3) interactive web sites or simulations that enable students to more readily engage with course content or ideas. Although little research has been done to prove it, the web has the potential to offer students the rare opportunity of appealing to all three learning styles. The use of text in a web site, for example, likely appeals to aural learners, its use of graphics to visual learners, and its necessary use of the mouse and "point and click" interface engages kinesthetic learners. Furthermore, while significant barriers to web accessibility are ongoing and legitimate concerns for users with a variety of physical or economic challenges, the Internet has also opened up possibilities for their access to higher education previously unimagined or unavailable (Schmetzke, 2001; U.S. Department of Commerce, 2000).

Reflective Critique
The last criterion in Glassick, Huber, and Maeroff's (1997) list implies the following questions: "Does the scholar critically evaluate his or her own work? Does the scholar bring an appropriate breadth of evidence to his or her critique? Does the scholar use evaluation to improve the quality of future work?" (p. 34). Our questions are: How can I critically evaluate my teaching with (or without) technology? What breadth of evidence do I need to bring to my critique? How can I best use evaluation to improve the quality of future teaching with (or without) technology?

Teachers can initiate formative and summative evaluations of their teaching with technology in a variety of ways. As in any course, they may begin by gathering information from students' perspectives using student evaluations or surveys that ask specific questions about students' experience in a web-enhanced course or program. Classes supported by course management software such as Blackboard conveniently allow Laura to construct online surveys that invite students to offer feedback about their learning experience. Blackboard's online survey capability also provides Laura the ability to survey faculty members about their technology skills, level of comfort, and opinions with regard to technology-enhanced learning before and after they participate in summer institute courses. This information helps shape and reshape the ways Laura uses technology to enhance learning in faculty development workshops. Following a workshop or activity, she also uses more conventional assessments like the *Plus/Delta* Classroom Assessment Technique (Angelo & Cross, 1993) to discover what participants thought worked well and what they would suggest she modify about the workshop or activity for future participants. In addition to gaining information from students or faculty participants' perspectives, Laura relies on her own experience during the lesson, writing notes to herself on her outlined lesson plans about what worked, what did not, and what she will revise for the future. As a scholar-teacher, she also works to discuss and write about her methods for teaching with technology in order to share what she has learned and receive feedback about her methods. This chapter itself is an example of three scholar-teachers making their work public and available for critique. By publishing and distributing the matrix that combines the work of Boyer (1990) and Glassick, Huber, and Maeroff (1997), we invite other scholar-teachers to investigate, replicate, and/or adapt our work in teaching, and, more specifically, in teaching with technology.

We close by returning to the matrix that we have now modified into three additional matrices that focus faculty attention on only one of Boyer's (1990) four scholarly categories: teaching (with technology). The first of three modified versions of the matrix includes a blank matrix that faculty may fill out and use to assist them as they make the transition from teaching in nondigital to digital environments (Figure 18.2). The second is a blank matrix that faculty may fill out and use to guide them as they work to ensure quality learning and teaching with or without technology (Figure 18.3). The third is an example matrix that Laura filled out to guide her as she developed and conducted a day-long workshop on teaching with technology for 75 cross-disciplinary faculty members at the University of Texas, San Antonio, on May 15, 2001 (Figure 18.4).

FIGURE 18.2
Transitioning Matrix

Criterion for Assessment	Teaching in a Nondigital Environment	Teaching in a Digital Environment
Clear Goals		
Adequate Preparation		
Appropriate Methods		
Significant Results		
Effective Communication		
Reflective Critique		

Note: Faculty may use this matrix to help them make the transition from teaching in nondigital to digital environments.

FIGURE 18.3

Blank Matrix Focused on the Scholarship of Teaching

	One of Boyer's (1990) Categories of Scholarship: Teaching (with or without technology)
Clear Goals	
Adequate Preparation	
Appropriate Methods	
Significant Results	
Effective Communication	
Reflective Critique	

Six Criteria for Assessing Scholarship, Glassick, Hueber, Maeroff, 1997.

Note: Faculty may use this matrix to assess their teaching with or without technology.

FIGURE 18.4

Completed Matrix
Faculty Development Workshop, May 15, 2001

	One of Boyer's (1990) Categories of Scholarship: Teaching (with technology)
Clear Goals	At the end of this day-long workshop, faculty will be able to

- *Articulate* an increased understanding of teaching and technology issues and *participate* more fully in the global discussion about e-learning

- *Use* already existing scholarship in teaching and learning to reconsider, reassess, and shape or reshape their own methods for using technology to enhance instruction in f-2-f, mixed, or distance learning courses

- *Formulate* clear goals for student learning in a defined context and select appropriate technologies to support and enhance active learning inside or outside any post-secondary classroom

Adequate Preparation	To prepare for teaching with technology, I:

- *Study* print and online articles or resources on teaching with technology and best practices in the field

- *Subscribe* to mailing lists on teaching, distance learning, and professional development for teaching

- *Expand* my technical toolbox through interaction with peer colleagues, summer institute courses, self-study, software/hardware/online help, and tutorials

- *Participate* in TLTR, AAHE, MERLOT, and/or other discipline specific conferences addressing e-learning

- *Attend* workshops/satellite broadcasts on e-learning

- *Challenge* myself to improve, innovate, or attempt new methods of teaching with technology after training and exploring teaching, learning, and technical resources

Appropriate Methods	This workshop will use the following teaching methods:

- *Interactive discussion* facilitated by a well-designed PPT presentation that encourages active involvement using questions, time for reading and reflection, and engagement and exchange with peer colleagues

- *Active/cooperative learning* techniques supported by CL randomizer (Excel), individual accountability, positive interdependence, and tent cards on tables

- *Resources* available on the Internet and made available as a printed booklet with URLS and as handouts for workshop participants' future reference

- *Example lesson plans,* matrix, and faculty inventory for use during the day-long institute. The workshop will attempt to simulate the use and benefits of technology (value added) in a technology-enhanced course

- *Hardware and software:* PC laptop, Internet access, streaming media and projection capabilities, mobile microphone system, Microsoft Office

Significant Results	To evaluate the effectiveness of this workshop and the effectiveness of my work in teaching with technology, I will:

- *Conduct* a plus/delta assessment at the end of the workshop

- *Share* my work in e-learning on and off campus, including at conferences or by request from individuals or groups in educational settings

- *Contribute* to the scholarship of teaching and learning with technology by co-writing, publishing, and distributing "A Matrix for Reconsidering, Reassessing, and Shaping E-Learning Pedagogy and Curriculum"

- *Provide* rationale and motivation to other faculty to contribute to the discussion and shape instructional or curriculum design decisions for e-learning

- *Participate* on various committees and advisory boards for e-learning

Effective Presentation	To increase the likelihood of an effective presentation for this workshop, I will:

- *Facilitate* interactive, rather than passive, learning

- *Appeal* to diverse learning styles through technology enhancements, cooperative learning methods, and appropriate handouts or visuals

- *Distribute* model lesson plans for teaching with technology in a printed booklet. Invite workshop participants, at times, to act as students in my business communication classroom and complete portions of the lesson plans I designed for that course to gain hands-on experience in a simulated technology-enhanced classroom

Reflective Critique	To evaluate my performance and the effectiveness of the workshop, I will:

- *Study* the plus/delta evaluations from participants
- *Make* notes on lesson plans about what worked well and what I need to modify for future workshops
- *Discuss and write* about effective methods for teaching with technology based on this and other technology-focused workshops. Make work public and available for critique through peer-reviewed journals, inviting other teacher scholars to critique, replicate, and/or adapt ideas on the scholarship of teaching and learning with technology

Six Criteria for Assessing Scholarship, Glassick, Huber, Maeroff, 1997.

CONCLUSION

The effective design and implementation of technology-enhanced courses, curricula, and programs are two of the most compelling and pervasive forces shaping teaching and learning in the 21st century. We suggest that faculty would do well to consult already existing scholarship on teaching and learning—such as that articulated by Boyer (1990) and Glassick, Huber, and Maeroff (1997)—to assist them as they make pedagogical decisions for the future of e-learning.

REFERENCES

Angelo, T. A., & Cross, K. P. (1993). *Classroom assessment techniques: A handbook for college teachers* (2nd ed.). San Francisco, CA: Jossey-Bass.

Boyer, E. (1990). *Scholarship reconsidered: Priorities of the professoriate.* Princeton, NJ: The Carnegie Foundation for the Advancement of Teaching.

Glassick, C., Huber, M., & Maeroff, G. (1997). *Scholarship assessed: Evaluation of the professoriate.* San Francisco, CA: Jossey-Bass.

Graham, C., Cagiltay, K., Lim, B., Craner, J., & Duffy, T. M. (2001). Seven principles of effective teaching: A practical lens for evaluating online courses. *The Technology Source.* Retrieved December 10, 2001, from http://horizon.unc.edu/TS/default.asp?show=article&id=839

Joy II, E. H., & Garcia, F. E. (2000). Measuring learning effectiveness: A new look at no-significant-difference findings. *Journal of Asynchronous Learning Networks, 4* (1). Retrieved December 11, 2001, from http://www.aln.org/alnweb/journal/jaln-vol4issue1.htm

Russell, T. L. (1999). *No significant difference phenomenon.* Raleigh, NC: North Carolina State University Press.

Schmetzke, A. (2001). Online distance education: "Anytime, anywhere" but not for everyone. *Information Technology and Disabilities, 7* (2). Retrieved December 10, 2001, from http://www.rit.edu/~easi/itd/itdv07n2/axel.htm

Twigg, C. (2001). *Innovations in online learning: Moving beyond no significant difference.* Troy, NY: Center for Academic Transformation Rensselaer Polytechnic Institute. Retrieved December 11, 2001, from http://www.center.rpi.edu/PewSym/mono4.html

U.S. Department of Commerce. (2000). *Falling through the net: Toward digital inclusion.* Washington, DC: U.S. Government Printing Office. Retrieved December 10, 2001, http://www.ntia.doc.gov/ntiahome/fttn00/contents00.html

Young, C., & Young, L. (1999). Assessing learning in interactive courses. *Journal on Excellence in College Teaching, 10* (1), 63–76. Retrieved December 10, 2001, from http://ject.lib.muohio.edu/contents/article.php?article=186

Contact:

Laura Bush
Center for Learning and Teaching Excellence
Arizona State University
PO Box 870101
Tempe, AZ 85287-0101
Voice   (480) 965-5620
Fax   (480) 727-7068
Email   L.Bush@asu.edu

Barry Maid
East College
Arizona State University East
7001 E. Williams Field Road
Mesa, AZ 85212
Voice   (480) 727-1190
Fax   (480) 727-1777
Email   Barry.Maid@asu.edu

Duane Roen
Center for Learning and Teaching Excellence
Arizona State University
Tempe, AZ 85287-0101
Voice   (480) 965-3555
Fax   (480) 727-7068
Email   duane.roen@asu.edu

Laura Bush is an Instructional Professional at Arizona State University's Center for Learning and Teaching Excellence (CLTE). In addition to teaching the undergraduate course Business Communications, she regularly facilitates faculty workshops in active learning and the use of computers and the Internet to aid student learning. She also designed the CLTE and Wakonse web sites and now oversees their maintenance and further development. Before earning her PhD in English with an emphasis in American literature, autobiography theory, and computer-mediated writing classrooms, Laura taught composition and literature for five years as a faculty member in the Department of English at Ricks College in Rexburg, Idaho.

Barry Maid is Professor and Head Faculty of Technical Communication at Arizona State University East (ASU) where he led the development of a new program in Multimedia Writing and Technical Communication. Before coming to ASU, he taught at the University of Arkansas, Little Rock, where, among other duties, he directed the Writing Center and the First Year Composition Program, chaired the Department of English, and helped in the creation of the Department of Rhetoric and Writing.

Though most of his time is now spent building his second independent writing department, he tries to keep in touch with his professional interests of computers and writing, writing program administration, and academic/industry partnerships.

Duane Roen, Professor of English, currently directs the Center for Learning and Teaching Excellence at Arizona State University. Previously, he directed the Composition Program there, as well as the Writing Program at Syracuse University. Serving as Coordinator of Graduate Studies in English at the University of Arizona from 1990 to 1992, he also worked as Director of Rhetoric, Composition, and the Teaching of English from 1988 to 1992. He has published six books and has written more than 130 articles, chapters, and conference papers—mostly on various aspects of teaching and learning.

Bibliography

Achterberg, C. (2002). Providing a global perspective. *About Campus, 6*(6), 17–24.

Addison, W. (1978). *Helping others learn: Designing programs for adults.* Reading, MA: McLagan.

Ahern-Rindell, A. J. (1999). Apply inquiry-based and cooperative group learning strategies to promote critical thinking. *Journal of College Science Teaching, 28*(3), 203–207.

Aksamit, D., Leuenberger, J., & Morris, M. (1987). Preparation of student services professionals and faculty for serving learning-disabled college students. *Journal of College Student Personnel, 28,* 53–59.

Alexander, C., & Strain, P. (1978). A review of educator's attitudes toward handicapped children and the concept of mainstreaming. *Psychology in the Schools, 15,* 390–396.

American Political Science Association (APSA). (1998). Task force on civic education in the 21st century: Expanded articulation statement: A call for reactions and contributions. *PS: Politics and political science, 31* (3), 636.

Anderson, B. J., & Miezitis, S. (1999). Stress and life satisfaction in mature female graduate students. *Initiatives, 59*(1), 33–43.

Anderson-Inman, L., Knox-Quinn, C., & Szymanski, M. (1999). Computer-supported studying: Stories of successful transition to postsecondary education. *Career Development for Exceptional Individuals, 22*(2), 185–212.

Angelo, T. A. (2000, November). *Twenty years of teaching and learning: Tracing trends, teasing out lessons, and looking ahead.* Paper presented as Part II of the closing plenary at the 20th annual Lilly Conference on College Teaching, Oxford, OH.

Angelo, T. A. (2001). Doing faculty development as if we value learning most: Transformative guidelines from research to practice. In D. Lieberman & C. Wehlburg (Eds.), *To Improve the Academy: Vol. 19. Resources for faculty, instructional, and organizational development* (pp. 97–112). Bolton, MA: Anker.

Angelo, T. A., & Cross, K. P. (1993). *Classroom assessment techniques: A handbook for college teachers* (2nd ed.). San Francisco, CA: Jossey-Bass.

Arnsten, A. F. (1998, June 12). The biology of being frazzled. *Science, 280,* 1711–1712.

Asmussen, K. J., & Creswell, J. W. (1995). Campus response to a student gunman. *Journal of Higher Education, 66* (5), 575–591.

Astin, A. W. (1992). What really matters in general education: Provocative findings from a national study of student outcomes. *Perspectives, 22* (1), 23–46.

Astin, A. W. (1993). *What matters in college: Four critical years revisited.* San Francisco, CA: Jossey-Bass.

Astin, W. A., Vogelgesang, L. J., Ikeda, E. K., & Yee, J. A. (2000). *How service learning affects students.* Los Angeles, CA: University of California at Los Angeles, Higher Education Research Institute.

Austin, A. E. (1990). *To leave an indelible mark: Encouraging good teaching in research universities through faculty development. A study of the Lilly Endowment's teaching fellows program 1974–1988.* Nashville, TN: Vanderbilt University, Peabody College.

Austin, A. E. (1992). Supporting junior faculty through a teaching fellows program. In M. D. Sorcinelli & A. E. Austin (Eds.), *Developing new and junior faculty* (pp. 73–86). New Directions for Teaching and Learning, No. 50. San Francisco, CA: Jossey-Bass.

Baird, J. S. (1987). Perceived learning in relation to student evaluation of university instruction. *Journal of Educational Psychology, 79* (1), 90–91.

Bakos, J. D., Jr. (1997). Communication skills for the 21st century. *Journal of Professional Issues in Engineering Education and Practice, 123* (1), 14–16.

Baldwin, R. G. (1998). Technology's impact on faculty life and work. In K. Herr Gillespie (Ed.), *The impact of technology on faculty development, life and work* (pp. 7–21). New Directions for Teaching and Learning, No. 76. San Francisco, CA: Jossey-Bass.

Bandura, A. (Ed.). (1997). *Self-efficacy in changing schools.* Cambridge, MA: Cambridge University Press.

Barr, R. B., & Tagg, J. (1995). From learning to teaching: A new paradigm for undergraduate education. *Change, 27* (6), 13–25.

Baxter-Magolda, M. B. (1992). *Knowing and reasoning in college: Gender-related patterns in students' intellectual development.* San Francisco, CA: Jossey-Bass.

Belenky, M. B., Clinchy, B. M., Goldberger, N. R., & Tarule, J. M. (1986). *Women's ways of knowing: The development of self, voice, and mind.* New York, NY: Basic Books.

Bennett, J. (1999). Learning communities, academic advising, and other support programs. In J. H. Levine (Ed.), *Learning communities: New structures, new partnerships for learning*. Columbia, SC: National Center for the First-Year Experience and Students in Transition.

Berk, R. A. (1996). Student rating of 10 strategies for using humor in college teaching. *Journal on Excellence in College Teaching, 7*(3), 71–92.

Beutell, N. J., & O'Hare, M. M. (1987). Coping with role conflict among returning students: Professional versus nonprofessional women. *Journal of College Student Personnel, 28*(2), 141–145.

Blackburn, R. T., & Lawrence, J. H. (1995). *Faculty at work: Motivation, expectation, satisfaction*. Baltimore, MD: The Johns Hopkins University Press.

Blackhurst, A. E., Lahm, E. A., Harrison, E. M., & Chandler, W. G. (1999). A framework for aligning technology with transition competencies. *Career Development for Exceptional Individuals, 22*(2), 131–151.

Blackorby, J., & Wagner, M. (1996). Longitudinal post-school outcomes of youth with disabilities: Findings from the national longitudinal transition study. *Exceptional Children, 62*(5), 399–413.

Blake, W. (1963). *The marriage of heaven and hell*. Coral Gables, FL: University of Miami Press.

Bloom, B. S. (1956). *Taxonomy of educational objectives—The classification of educational goals: Handbook I—cognitive domain*. New York, NY: David McKay.

Boice, R. (1992). Lessons learned about mentoring. In M. D. Sorcinelli & A. E. Austin (Eds.), *Developing new and junior faculty* (pp. 51–61). New Directions for Teaching and Learning, No. 50. San Francisco, CA: Jossey-Bass.

Bonk, C. J. (2001). *Online teaching in an online world*. Bloomington, IN: CourseSHare.com.

Boud, D. (1997). *Providing for lifelong learning through work-based study. Challenges for policy and practice*. Paper presented at the International conference on lifelong Learning, Guildford, Surrey.

Boud, D., & Feletti, G. (1991). Introduction. In D. Boud & G. Feletti (Eds.), *The challenge of problem-based learning* (p. 12). New York, NY: St. Martin's Press.

Bowe, F. G. (2000). *Universal design in education: Teaching nontraditional students*. Westport, CT: Bergin & Garvey.

Boyer, E. L. (1987). *College: The undergraduate experience in America*. New York, NY: HarperCollins.

Boyer, E. L. (1990). *Scholarship reconsidered: Priorities of the professoriate.* Princeton, NJ: The Carnegie Foundation for the Advancement of Teaching.

Boyer, E. L. (1994, March 9). Creating the new American college. *The Chronicle of Higher Education,* p. A48.

Boyer, E. L. (1996). The scholarship of engagement. *Journal of Public Service & Outreach, 1* (1), 11–20.

Boyte, H. C. (2000). The struggle against positivism. *Academe, 86,* 46–51.

Bransford, J. D., Brown, A. L., & Cocking, R. R. (Eds.). (2000). *How people learn: Brain, mind, experience, and school.* Commission on Behavioral and Social Sciences and Education National Research Council. Washington, DC: National Academy Press.

Bredehoft, D. J. (1991). Cooperative controversies in the classroom. *College Teaching, 39* (3), 122–125.

Bringle, R. G., & Hatcher, J. A. (1995). A service-learning curriculum for faculty. *Michigan Journal of Community Service Learning, 2,* 112–122.

Brookfield, S. D. (1990). *The skillful teacher: On technique, trust, and responsiveness in the classroom.* San Francisco, CA: Jossey-Bass.

Brookfield, S. D. (1993). Self-directed learning, political clarity and the critical practice of adult education. *Adult Education Quarterly, 43* (4), 227–242.

Brown, J. S., Collins, A., & Duguid, P. (1989). Situated cognition and the culture of learning. *Educational Researcher, 13,* 32–41.

Brownstein, A. (2001, October 29). College board conference reflects a new concern for colleges and students: Terrorism. *The Chronicle of Higher Education Career Network.* Retrieved November 4, 2001, from http://chronicle.com/free/2001/10/2001102904n.htm

Burgstahler, S. (2000). *Universal design of instruction.* Seattle, WA: University of Washington, DO-IT.

Burgstahler, S., Duclos, R., & Turcotte, M. (1999). *Preliminary findings: Faculty, teaching assistant, and student perceptions regarding accommodating students with disabilities in postsecondary environments.* Seattle, WA: University of Washington, DO-IT.

Burroughs, C. B. (1990). The new professionalism: Teaching and/or scholarship. *Liberal Education, 76* (5), 14–17.

Caffarella, S., & Zinn, L. (1999). Professional development for faculty in higher education: A conceptual framework of barriers and supports. *Innovative Higher Education, 23* (3), 241–254.

Cambridge, B. L. (2000). The scholarship of teaching and learning: A national initiative. In M. Kaplan & D. Lieberman (Eds.), *To Improve the Academy: Vol. 18. Resources for faculty, instructional, and organizational development* (pp. 55–68). Bolton, MA: Anker.

Cambridge, B. L. (2001). Fostering the scholarship of teaching and learning: Communities of practice. In D. Lieberman & C. Wehlburg (Eds.), *To improve the academy: Vol. 19. Resources for faculty, instructional, and organizational development* (pp. 3–16). Bolton, MA: Anker.

Campus Compact. (2001). *A conceptual framework for building the pyramid of service-learning and civic engagement: Creating an engaged campus.* Providence, RI: Campus Compact.

Candy, P. (1991). *Self-direction for lifelong learning.* San Francisco, CA: Jossey-Bass.

Cannon, J. R. (1997). The constructivist learning environment survey may help halt student exodus from college science courses. *Journal of College Science Teaching, 27* (1), 67–71.

Carnegie Academy for the Scholarship of Teaching and Learning (CASTL). (n.d.). Available: http://www.middlesex.cc.ma.us/carnegie/

Cherif, A. H. (1994). Instructional strategies that never fail us. *Journal of College Science Teaching, 24* (1), 55–58.

Chickering, A. W., & Gamson, Z. (1987). Seven principles for good practice in undergraduate education. *AAHE Bulletin, 39,* 3–7.

Chickering, A. W., & Reisser, L. (1993). *Education and identity.* San Francisco, CA: Jossey-Bass.

Child, M., & Williams, D. D. (1996). College learning and teaching: Struggling with/in the tensions. *Studies in Higher Education, 21* (1), 31–45.

Chism, N. V. N., Fraser, J. M., & Arnold R. L. (1996). Teaching academies: Honoring and promoting teaching through a community of expertise. *New directions for teaching and learning: Honoring exemplary teaching.* San Francisco, CA: Jossey-Bass.

Claxton, C. S., & Ralston, Y. (1978). *Learning styles: Their impact on teaching and administration.* Washington, DC: American Association for Higher Education.

Clouder, L. (1997). Women's ways of coping with continuing education. *Adult Learning, 8* (6), 146–148.

Cohen, P. A. (1981). Student ratings of instruction and student achievement: a meta-analysis of multisection validity studies. *Review of Educational Research, 51,* 281–309.

Cohen, S. A. (1987). Instructional alignment: Searching for a magic bullet. *Educational Researcher, 16* (8), 16–20.

Coles, R. (1993). *The call to service: A witness to idealism.* Boston, MA: Houghton Mifflin.

Commission on International Education. (1997). *Educating for global competence: America's passport to the future.* Washington, DC: American Council on Education.

Conti, G. J. (1998). Identifying your teaching style. In M. W. Galbraith (Ed.), *Adult learning methods* (pp. 73–77). Malabar, FL: Kreiger.

Cook, C. E. (2001, November 18). Center gives teachers guidelines for discussing terrorism. *Ann Arbor News,* p. B2.

Cornwell, G. H., & Stoddard, E. W. (1999). *Globalizing knowledge: Connecting international and intercultural studies.* Washington, DC: Association of American Colleges and Universities.

Costa, A. L., & O'Leary, P. W. (1992). Co-cognition: The cooperative development of the intellect. In N. Davidson & T. Worsham (Eds.), *Enhancing thinking through cooperative learning.* New York, NY: Teachers College Press.

Costello, M. J. (1991). *The greatest games of all times.* New York, NY: John Wiley and Sons.

Cox, M. D. (1995). The development of new and junior faculty. In W. A. Wright & Associates (Eds.), *Teaching improvement practices: Successful strategies for higher education* (pp. 283–310). Bolton, MA: Anker.

Cox, M. D. (1997). Long-term patterns in a mentoring program for junior faculty: Recommendations for practice. In D. DeZure & M. Kaplan (Eds.), *To improve the academy: Vol. 16. Resources for faculty, instructional, and organizational development* (pp. 225–268). Stillwater, OK: New Forums Press.

Cox, M. D. (1999, November). *The teacher as scholar of teaching: What, how, why?* Paper presented at the Faculty Development Seminar for the College of Nursing at the University of Cincinnati, Cincinnati, OH.

Cox, M. D. (1999). Peer consultation and faculty learning communities. In C. Knapper & S. Piccinin (Eds.), *Using consultants to improve teaching* (pp. 39–49). New Directions for Teaching and Learning, No. 79. San Francisco, CA: Jossey-Bass.

Cox, M. D. (2001). Faculty learning communities: Change agents for transforming institutions into learning organizations. In D. Lieberman & C. Wehlburg (Eds.), *To improve the academy: Vol. 19. Resources for faculty, instructional, and organizational development* (pp. 69–96). Bolton, MA: Anker.

Cox, M. D. (Ed.). (2001). *Teaching communities, grants, resources, and events: 2001–2002.* Oxford, OH: Miami University.

Cox, M. D. (2001). *Sourcebook 2001: Designing, implementing, and leading faculty learning communities.* Oxford, OH: Miami University.

Cox, M. D. (in press). Fostering the scholarship of teaching and learning through faculty learning communities. *Journal on Excellence in College Teaching.*

Cox, M. D., & Blaisdell, M. (1995, October). *Teaching development for senior faculty: Searching for fresh solutions in a salty sea.* Paper presented at the 20th annual Conference of the Professional and Organizational Development Network in Higher Education, North Falmouth, MA.

Cranton, P. A. (1994). *Understanding and promoting transformative learning.* San Francisco, CA: Jossey-Bass.

Cranton, P. A. (1996). *Professional development as transformative learning.* San Francisco, CA: Jossey-Bass.

Cross, K. P. (1998). Classroom research: Implementing the scholarship of teaching. In T. Angelo (Ed.), *Classroom assessment and research: An update on uses, approaches and research findings* (pp. 5–12). New Directions for Teaching and Learning, No. 75. San Francisco, CA: Jossey-Bass.

Cross, K. P., & Steadman, M. H. (1996). *Classroom research: Implementing the scholarship of teaching.* San Francisco, CA: Jossey-Bass.

Daiker, D., Fuller, M., & Wallace, J. (Eds.). (1989). *Literature: Options for reading and writing* (2nd ed.). New York: Harper & Row.

Daloz, L. A. (1986). *Effective teaching and mentoring: Realizing the transformational power of adult learning experiences.* San Francisco, CA: Jossey-Bass.

Dalton, J. C. (1999). Beyond borders: How international developments are changing student affairs practice. *New Directions for Student Services, No. 86.* San Francisco, CA: Jossey-Bass.

Darling-Hammond, L. (1998). Teacher learning that supports student learning. *Educational Leadership, 55* (5), 6–12.

Davis, J. R. (1995). *Interdisciplinary courses and team teaching: New arrangements for learning.* Phoenix, AZ: American Council on Education/Oryx Press.

Derek Bok Center for Teaching and Learning, Harvard University (Producer). (1993). *Thinking Together: Collaborative Learning in Science* [Videotape]. Boston, MA: Derek Bok Center for Teaching and Learning, Harvard University.

DeZure, D. (1996). Closer to the disciplines: A model for improving teaching within departments. *AAHE Bulletin, 48* (6), 9–12.

DeZure, D. (1998–1999). Interdisciplinary teaching and learning. *Teaching Excellence Essays: Toward the Best in the Academy, 10* (3). Stillwater, OK: Professional and Organizational Development Network in Higher Education.

DeZure, D. (Ed.). (2000). *Learning from Change: Landmarks in teaching nd learning in higher education from Change magazine (1969–1999).* Sterling, VA: Stylus.

Diamond, R. M. (1998). *Designing and assessing courses and curricula: A practical guide.* San Francisco, CA: Jossey-Bass.

Dobbert, M. L. L. (1998). The impossibility of internationalizing students by adding materials to courses. In J. A. Mestenhauser & B. J. Ellingboe (Eds.), *Reforming the higher education curriculum: Internationalizing the campus* (pp. 53–68). Phoenix, AZ: American Council on Education/Oryx Press.

Dodd, J. M., Fischer, J., Hermanson, M., & Nelson, J. R. (1990). Tribal college faculty willingness to provide accommodations to students with learning disabilities. *Journal of American Indian Education, 30* (1), 8–16.

DO-IT. (2001). *DO-IT Prof Annual Report.* Seattle, WA: University of Washington, DO-IT.

DO-IT, University of Washington (Producer), & Burgstahler, S. (Director). (2001). *Building the team: Faculty, staff, and students working together* [Videotape]. Seattle, WA: University of Washington, DO-IT.

DO-IT, University of Washington (Producer), & Burgstahler, S. (Director). (2001). *Working together: Faculty and students with disabilities* [Videotape]. Seattle, WA: University of Washington, DO-IT.

Dona, J., & Edmister, J. H. (2001). An examination of community college faculty members' knowledge of the Americans with Disabilities Act of 1990 at the fifteen community colleges in Mississippi. *Journal of Postsecondary Education and Disability, 14* (2), 91–103.

Dreyfus, H. L., & Dreyfus, S. E. (1986). *Mind over machine: The power of human intuition and expertise in the era of the computer.* New York, NY: Free Press.

Driscoll, A. (1998). Comprehensive design of community service: New understanding, options, and vitality in student learning at Portland State University. In E. Zlotkowski (Ed.), *Successful service-learning programs: New models of excellence in higher education* (pp. 150–168). Bolton, MA: Anker.

Duch, B. J., Allen, D. E., & White, H. B. (2000, October). Problem-based learning: Preparing students in the 21st century. In *Teaching at UNL, 22* (2). The newsletter of the UNL Teaching and Learning Center. Used with permission of *Teaching Excellence,* a service of POD member services.

Dyer, T. G. (1985). *The University of Georgia: A bicentennial history 1785–1985.* Athens, GA: The University of Georgia Press.

Eaton, M. (2002). Searching for the 'new university': Changing faculty roles. *Project on the Future of Higher Education.* Available: http://www.antioch.edu/pfhe

Edwards, A. F., Jr. (1996). *Interdisciplinary undergraduate programs: A directory* (2nd ed.). Acton, MA: Copley.

Ehrlich, C. (2001, November 9). Engineers evaluate their responsibilities. *The Michigan Daily,* p. 3.

El-Shamy, S. (in press). *Training games: Everything you need to know about using games to reinforce learning.* New York, NY: Stylus Press.

Engineering Accreditation Commission of the Accreditation Board for Engineering and Technology (ABET). (1995). *ABET engineering criteria 2000.* Baltimore, MD: Author.

Erdle, S., & Murray, H. G. (1986). Interfaculty differences in classroom teaching behaviors and their relationship to student instructional ratings. *Research in Higher Education, 24* (2), 115–127.

Ewell, P. (2002). Three dialectics in higher education's future. *Project on the Future of Higher Education.* Available: http://www.antioch.edu/pfhe

Ewell, P. T., Jones, D. P., & Lenth, C. S. (1996). What research says about improving undergraduate education: Twelve attributes of good practice. *AAHE Bulletin,* 5–8.

Eyler, J., & Giles, D. E., Jr. (1999). *Where's the learning in service-learning?* San Francisco, CA: Jossey-Bass.

Fabry, V. J., Eisenbach, R., Curry, R. R., & Golich, V. L. (1997). Thank you for asking: Classroom assessment techniques and students' perceptions of learning. *Journal on Excellence in College Teaching, 8* (1), 3–21.

Feldman, K. A. (1998). Identifying exemplary teachers and teaching: evidence from student ratings. In K. A. Feldman & M. B. Paulsen (Eds.), *Teaching and learning in the college classroom* (2nd ed., pp. 391–414). Needham Heights, MA: Simon & Schuster.

Fichten, C. S., Amsel, R., Bourdon, C. V., & Creti, L. (1988). Interaction between college students with a physical disability and their professors. *Journal of Applied Rehabilitation Counseling, 19,* 13–21.

Fichten, C., Barile, M., & Asuncion, J.V. (1999). *Learning technologies: Students with disabilities in postsecondary education.* Office of Learning Technologies. Montreal, Canada: Dawson College, Adaptech Project.

Fitzgerald, F. S. (1945). *The crack-up.* New York, NY: New Directions.

Flow of Scientific Information. (n.d.). Retrieved December 12, 2001 from http://www.lib.uwaterloo.ca/usered/grad/researchskills/flow_of_info.htm

Freire, P. (1993). *Pedagogy of the oppressed* (rev. ed., M. B. Ramos, Trans.). New York, NY: Continuum.

Fonosch, G. G., & Schwab, L. O. (1981). Attitudes of selected university faculty members toward disabled students. *Journal of College Student Personnel, 22,* 229–235.

Frank, K., & Wade, P. (1993). Disabled student services in postsecondary education: Who's responsible for what? *Journal of College Student Development, 34* (1), 26–30.

Frijda, N. H. (1988). The laws of emotion. *American Psychologist, 43,* 349–358.

Gaff, J. G. (1999). *General education: The changing agenda.* Washington, DC: Association of American Colleges and Universities.

Gaff, J. G., Ratcliff, J. L., & Associates. (1997). *Handbook of the undergraduate curriculum: A comprehensive guide to purposes, structures, practices and change.* San Francisco, CA: Jossey-Bass.

Gajar, A. (1998). Postsecondary education. In F. Rusch & J. Chadsey (Eds.), *Beyond high school: Transition from school to work* (pp. 383–405). Belmont, CA: Wadsworth.

Gardiner, L. F. (1994). *Redesigning higher education: Producing dramatic gains in student learning.* (Higher Education Report No. 7). Washington, DC: ASHE-ERIC. (ERIC Document Reproduction Service No. ED 394 442)

Giampetro-Meyer, A., & Holc, J. (1997). Encouraging students to demonstrate intellectual behavior that professors respect. *College Teaching, 45* (3), 92–96.

Gillespie, F. (1998). Instructional design for the new technologies. In K. Herr Gillespie (Ed.), *The impact of technology on faculty development, life and work* (pp. 39–52). New Directions for Teaching and Learning, No. 76. San Francisco, CA: Jossey-Bass.

Gilligan, C. (1982). *In a different voice: Psychological theory and women's development.* Cambridge, MA: Harvard University Press.

Glaser, B., & Strauss, A. L. (1967). *The discovery of grounded theory: Strategies for qualitative research.* Chicago, IL: Aldine.

Glassick, C. E., Huber, M. T., & Maeroff, G. I. (1997). *Scholarship assessed: Evaluation of the professoriate.* San Francisco, CA: Jossey-Bass.

Goode, W. J. (1960). A theory of role strain. *American Sociological Review, 25* (4), 483–496.

Goodyear, G. E., & Allchin, D. (1998). Statements of teaching philosophy. In M. Kaplan (Ed.), *To improve the academy: Vol.17. Resources for faculty, instructional, and organizational development* (pp.103–122), Stillwater, OK: New Forums Press.

Graham, C., Cagiltay, K., Lim, B., Craner, J., & Duffy, T. M. (2001). Seven principles of effective teaching: A practical lens for evaluating online courses. *The Technology Source.* Retrieved December 10, 2001, from http://horizon.unc.edu/TS/default.asp?show=article&id=839

Grasha, A. (1984). Learning styles: The journey from Greenwich Observatory to the college classroom. *Improving College and University Teaching, 22,* 46–53.

Grigg, N. S. (1998). Universities and professional associations: Partnerships for civil engineering careers. *Journal of Management in Engineering, 14* (2), 45–55.

Guskin, A., & Marcy, M. (2001). Facing the future: Faculty work, student learning and fundamental reform. *Project on the future of higher education.* Available: http://www.antioch.edu/pfhe

Guskin, A., & Marcy, M. (in press). Pressures for fundamental reform: Creating a viable academic future. In R. Diamond (Ed.), *Field guide to academic leadership.* San Francisco, CA: Jossey-Bass.

Grunert, J. (1997). *The course syllabus: A learner-centered approach.* Bolton, MA: Anker.

Haas, P. F., & Keely, S. M. (1998). Coping with faculty resistance to teaching critical thinking. *College Teaching, 46* (2), 63–68.

Habermas, J. (1971). *Knowledge and human interests.* Boston, MA: Beacon Press.

Habermas, J. (1981). *Theorie des kommunikativen Handelns (Vols. 1 & 2).* Frankfurt, Germany: Suhrkamp.

Hall, D. T. (1972). A model of coping with role conflict: The role behavior of college educated women. *Administrative Science Quarterly, 17* (4), 471–486.

Hall, E. T. (1976). *Beyond culture.* New York, NY: Doubleday.

Hall, F. S. (1994). Management education by design. *Journal of Management Education, 18* (2), 182–198.

Hamilton, V. (1982). Cognition and stress: An information processing model. In L. Goldberger & S. Breznitz (Eds.), *Handbook of stress: Theoretical and clinical aspects* (pp. 105–120). New York, NY: Free Press.

Hammond, K. R. (2000). *Judgments under stress.* New York, NY: Oxford University Press.

Hannah, M., & Pliner, S. (1983). Teacher attitudes toward handicapped children: A review and synthesis. *School Psychology Review, 12,* 12–25.

Hanson, K. H., & Meyerson, J. W. (1994). *International challenges to American colleges and universities: Looking ahead.* Washington, DC: American Council on Education/Oryx Press.

Harkavy, I., Puckett, J., & Romer, D. (2000). Action research: Bridging action and Research. *Michigan Journal of Community Service Learning,* special issue, 113–118.

Harr, J. (1995). *A civil action.* New York, NY: Vintage Books.

Harvey, C. D., & Wiebe, B. S. (1997). "I'm going to make the effort": How mothers become successful university students. *Canadian Home Economics Journal, 47* (4), 155–159.

Havanek, J. E., & Brodwin, M. G. (1998). Restructuring university and colleges: The student-focused paradigm. *Education, 119* (1), 115–119.

Hayward, F. M. (2000). *Internationalization of U.S. higher education: Preliminary status report 2000.* Washington, DC: American Council on Education.

Hayward, F. M., & Siaya, L. M. (2001). Public experience, attitudes, and knowledge: A report of two national surveys about international education. Washington, DC: American Council on Education.

Healey, M. (2000). Developing the scholarship of teaching in higher education: A discipline-based approach. *Higher Education Research & Development, 19* (2), 169–189.

Henderson, C. (2001). *College freshmen with disabilities: A biennial statistical profile.* Washington, DC: American Council on Education.

Higher Education Research Institute (HERI). (1999). *National norms: 1998–1999 HERI faculty survey report.* Los Angeles, CA: University of California at Los Angeles Graduate School of Education and Information Studies. Retrieved April 16, 2001 from http://www.gseis.ucla.edu/heri/heri.html

Hill, J. L. (1996). Speaking out: Perceptions of students with disabilities regarding adequacy of services and willingness of faculty to make accommodations. *Journal of Postsecondary Education and Disability, 12* (1), 22–43.

Hoffa, W., & Pearson, J. (1997). *NAFSA's guide to education abroad for advisers and administrators.* Washington, DC: NAFSA Association of International Educators.

Holly, C. (1990). The new professionalism: Changes and challenges. *Liberal Education, 76* (5), 17–19.

Home, A. M. (1998). Predicting role conflict, overload and contagion in adult women university students with families and jobs. *Adult Education Quarterly, 48,* 85–97.

hooks, b. (1994). *Teaching to transgress: Education as the practice of freedom.* New York, NY: Routledge.

Horn, L., & Berktold, J. (1999). Students with disabilities in postsecondary education: A profile of preparation, participation, and outcomes. *Education Statistics Quarterly, 1* (3), 59–64.

Houck, C., Asselin, S., Troutman, G., & Arrington, J. (1992). Students with learning disabilities in the university environment: A study of faculty and student perceptions. *Journal of Learning Disabilities, 25* (10), 678–684.

Howard, D. L. (2001, September 20). Teaching through tragedy. *The Chronicle of Higher Education Career Network.* Retrieved September 22, 2001, from http://chronicle.com/jobs/2001/09/2001092001c.htm

Humphreys, D. (2000). National survey finds diversity requirements common around the country. *Diversity Digest.* Retrieved from http://www.diversityweb.org/Digest/f00/survey.html

Hurst, J. C. (1999). The Matthew Shepard tragedy: Management of a crisis. *About Campus, 43,* 5–11.

Hutchings, P. (Ed.). (1998). *The course portfolio: How faculty can examine their teaching to advance practice and improve student learning.* Washington, DC: American Association for Higher Education.

Hutchings, P. (1999). *1999 Pew scholars institute.* Menlo Park, CA: The Carnegie Foundation for the Advancement of Teaching.

Hutchings, P. (Ed.). (2000). *Opening lines: Approaches to the scholarship of teaching and learning.* Menlo Park, CA: The Carnegie Foundation for the Advancement of Teaching.

Hutchings, P., & Shulman, L. S. (1999). The scholarship of teaching: New elaborations, new developments. *Change, 31* (5), 11–15.

Ikponmwosa, O. S. H. (1986). Knowledge of grades and student evaluation of university instruction. *Indian Journal of Psychometry and Education, 17* (1–2), 47–52.

Institute of International Education. (2000). *Open doors 2000.* New York, NY: Institute of International Education.

Irby, D. M. (1994). What clinical teachers in medicine need to know. *Academic Medicine, 69,* 333–342.

Jamieson, J. (1984). Attitudes of educators toward the handicapped. In R. Jones (Ed.), *Attitudes and attitude change in special education: Theory and practice* (pp. 206–222). Arlington, VA: The Council for Exceptional Children.

Johnson, D. W., Johnson, R. T., & Smith, K. A. (1991). *Active learning: Cooperation in the college classroom.* Edina, MN: Interaction Book Co.

Johnston, J. S., Jr., & Edelstein, R. J. (1993*). Beyond borders: Profiles in international education.* Washington, DC: Association of American Colleges and Universities.

Joy II, E. H., & Garcia, F. E. (2000). Measuring learning effectiveness: A new look at no-significant-difference findings. *Journal of Asynchronous Learning Networks, 4* (1). Retrieved December 11, 2001 from http://www.aln.org/alnweb/journal/jaln-vol4issue1.htm

Kabat-Zinn, J. (1990). *Full catastrophe living: Using the wisdom of your body and mind to face stress, pain, and illness.* New York, NY: Delta Press.

Kardia, D. (1998). Becoming a multicultural faculty developer: Reflections from the field. In M. Kaplan & D. Lieberman (Eds.), *To Improve the Academy: Vol. 17. Resources for faculty, instructional, and organizational development* (pp. 15–33). Stillwater, OK: New Forums Press.

Kardia, D., Bierwert, C., Cook, C. E., Miller, A.T ., & Kaplan, M. L. (2002, February/January). Discussing the unfathomable: Classroom-based responses to tragedy. *Change, 34* (1), 18–23.

Kegan, R. (1994). *In over our heads: The mental demands of modern life.* Cambridge, MA: Harvard University Press.

Kennedy, M. (1987). Inexact sciences: Professional education and the development of expertise. *Review of Research in Education, 14,* 133–167.

Kerr, C. (1963, 1994). *The uses of the university.* Cambridge, MA: Harvard University Press.

King, P. M., & Kitchener, K. S. (1994). *Developing reflective judgment.* San Francisco, CA: Jossey-Bass.

Klein, J. T. (1999). *Mapping interdisciplinary studies.* Washington, DC: Association of American Colleges and Universities.

Knapper, C., & Cropley, A. (2000). *Lifelong learning in higher education.* London, England: Kogan Page.

Knipp, D. (2001, Spring). Knowledge surveys: What do students bring to and take from a class? *United States Air Force Academy Educator.* Retrieved March 18, 2002 from http://www.usafa.af.mil/dfe/educator/S01/knipp0401.htm

Knowles, M. S. (1975). *Self-directed learning: A guide for learners and teachers.* Chicago, IL: Association/Follett.

Knowles, M. S. (1980). *The modern practice of adult education: From pedagogy to andragogy.* New York, NY: Cambridge Books.

Knowles, M. S. (1989). *The making of an adult educator: An autobiographical journey.* San Francisco, CA: Jossey-Bass.

Knowles, M. S., & Associates (1984). *Andragogy in action: Applying modern principles of adult learning.* San Francisco, CA: Jossey-Bass.

Kolvenbach, Rev. S. J. (2000, October). *The service of faith and the promotion of justice in American Jesuit higher education.* Paper presented at the Conference on Commitment to Justice in Jesuit Higher Education, Santa Clara University, CA.

Krause, L. B. (1998). The cognitive profile model of learning styles. *Journal of College Science Teaching, 28* (1), 57–61.

Kreber, C. (2001). Designing teaching portfolios based on a formal model of the scholarship of teaching. In D. Lieberman & C. Wehlburg (Eds.), *To improve the academy: Vol. 19. Resources for faculty, instructional, and organizational development* (pp. 285–305). Bolton, MA: Anker.

Kreber, C. (2001). The scholarship of teaching and its implementation in faculty development and graduate education. In C. Kreber (Ed.), *Scholarship revisited: Perspectives on the scholarship of teaching* (pp. 79–88). New Directions for Teaching and Learning, No. 86. San Francisco, CA: Jossey-Bass.

Kreber, C. (Ed.). (2001). Scholarship revisited: Perspectives on the scholarship of teaching. *New Directions for Teaching and Learning, No. 86.* San Francisco, CA: Jossey-Bass.

Kreber, C., & Cranton, P. A. (2000). Exploring the scholarship of teaching. *The Journal of Higher Education, 71* (4), 476–495.

Kronberg, J. R., & Griffin, M. S. (2000). Analysis problems: A means to developing students' critical-thinking skills. *Journal of College Science Teaching, 29,* 348–352.

Larson, W. A. (Ed.). (1994). *When crisis strikes on campus.* Washington, DC: Council for Advancement and Support of Education.

Laurillard, D. (1993). *Rethinking university teaching: A framework for the effective use of educational technology.* London, England: Routledge.

Lave, J. (1988). *Cognition in practice: Mind, mathematics and culture in everyday life.* New York, NY: Cambridge University Press.

Lawson, K. H. (1991). Philosophical foundations. In P. Jarvis & J. M. Peters (Eds.), *Adult education* (pp. 282–301). San Francisco, CA: Jossey-Bass.

Leamnson, R. (1999). *Thinking about teaching and learning: Developing habits of learning with first year college and university students.* Sterling, VA: Stylus.

Leonard, W. H. (2000). How do college students best learn? An assessment of popular teaching styles and their effectiveness. *Journal of College Science Teaching, 29* (6), 385–388.

Lengrand, P. (1986). *Areas of learning basic to lifelong education.* Oxford, England: Pergamon.

Levinson, D. J. (1959). Role, personality, and social structure in the organizational setting. *Journal of Abnormal and Social Psychology, 58* (2), 170–180.

Lewin, K. (1948). *Resolving social conflicts.* New York, NY: Harper Press.

Lewontin, R. C. (1997). The Cold War and the transformation of the academy. In A. Schiffrin (Ed.), *The Cold War and the university: Toward an intellectual history of the postwar years* (pp. 1–34). New York, NY: The New Press.

Leyser, Y. (1989). A survey of faculty attitudes and accommodations for students with disabilities. *Journal of Postsecondary Education and Disability, 7* (3 & 4), 97–108.

Leyser, Y., Vogel, S., Wyland, S., & Brulle, A. (1998). Faculty attitudes and practices regarding students with disabilities: Two decades after implementation of Section 504. *Journal of Postsecondary Education and Disability, 13* (3), 5–19.

Light, R. J., Singer, J. D., & Willett, J. B. (1990). *By design: Planning research on higher education.* Cambridge, MA: Harvard University Press.

Lind, M. (1995). To have and have not: Notes on the progress of the American class war. *Harper's, 250* (1741), 35–47.

Little, T. C. (1983). The institutional context for experiential learning. In T. C. Little (Ed.), *Making sponsored experiential learning standard practice.* San Francisco, CA: Jossey-Bass.

Loacker, G. (Ed.). (2000). *Self assessment at Alverno College.* Milwaukee, WI: Alverno College.

Lord, T. (1994). Using constructivism to enhance student learning in college biology. *Journal of College Science Teaching, 23,* 346–348.

Lowman, J. (1984). *Mastering the techniques of teaching.* San Francisco, CA: Jossey-Bass.

Lowman, J. (1996). Characteristics of exemplary teachers. In M. D. Svinicki & R. J. Menges (Eds.), *Honoring exemplary teaching* (pp. 33–40). San Francisco, CA: Jossey-Bass.

Majher, P., & Kuharevicz, N. L. (2001, January 15). Engineering's innovative global product development course taught simultaneously on three continents. *The University Record,* 1–2.

Mallinckrodt, B., & Leong, F. T. (1992). Social support in academic programs and family environments: Sex differences and role conflicts for graduate students. *Journal of Counseling and Development, 70* (6), 716–723.

Marincovich, M., Prostko, J., & Stout, F. (Eds.). (1998). *The professional development of graduate teaching assistants.* Bolton, MA: Anker.

Marsick, V. (1990). Action learning and reflection in the workplace. In J. Mezirow (Ed.), *Fostering critical reflection in adulthood* (pp. 23–47). San Francisco: Jossey-Bass.

Maskell, D. L., & Grabau, P. J. (1998). A multidisciplinary cooperative problem-based learning approach to embedded systems design. *IEEE Transactions on Education, 41* (2), 101–103.

Matthews, P., Anderson, D., & Skolnick, B. (1987). Faculty attitudes toward accommodations for college students with learning disabilities. *Learning Disabilities Focus, 3,* 46–52.

McBride, M. C. (1997). Counseling the superwoman: Helping university women cope with multiple roles. *Guidance and Counseling, 12,* 19–23.

McCusker, C. (1995). The Americans with Disabilities Act: Its potential for expanding the scope of reasonable academic accommodations. *Journal of College and University Law, 21* (4), 619–641.

McDonough, T., & Hayward, F. (2000, October 20). ACE, Carnegie select eight institutions with outstanding international programs. *ACENews*. Retrieved from http://www.acenet.edu/news/press_release/2000/10october/carnegie.html

McKeachie, W. J. (1994). *Teaching tips* (9th ed.). Lexington, MA: D. C. Heath.

McNeil, J. M. (2000). *Employment, earnings, and disability*. Prepared for the 75th annual Conference of the Western Economic Association International, Vancouver, Canada.

McPherson, M. (2001, December 9). International education. Now more than ever. *New York Times*, p. A30.

Menges, R. J. (1996). Experiences of newly hired faculty. In L. Richlin (Ed.), *To improve the academy: Vol. 15. Resources for faculty, instructional, and organizational development* (pp. 169–182), Stillwater, OK: New Forums Press.

Menges, R. J., Weimer, M., & Associates. (Eds.). (1996). *Teaching on solid ground: Using scholarship to improve practice* (pp. xi–xxii). San Francisco, CA: Jossey-Bass.

Merriam, S. B. (1988). *Case study research in education: A qualitative approach*. San Francisco, CA: Jossey-Bass.

Mestenhauser, J. A., & Ellingboe, B. (1998). *Reforming the higher education curriculum: Internationalizing the curriculum*. Phoenix, AZ: American Council on Education/Oryx Press.

Metheny, D., & Metheny, W. (1997). Enriching technical courses with learning teams. *College Teaching, 45* (1), 32–36.

Mezirow, J. (Ed.). (1990). *Fostering critical reflection in adulthood*. San Francisco, CA: Jossey-Bass.

Mezirow, J. (1991). *Transformative dimensions of adult learning*. San Francisco, CA: Jossey-Bass.

Mezirow, J. (2001). *Learning as transformation*. San Francisco, CA: Jossey-Bass.

Miami University. (1981). *Lilly post-doctoral teaching awards program end-of-the-year report, January 1–May 8, 1981*. Oxford, OH: Author.

Mikolaj, E. L., & Boggs, D. L. (1991). Intrapersonal role conflicts of adult women undergraduate students. *Journal of Continuing Higher Education, 39* (2), 13–19.

Millis, B. J., & Cottell, P. G. (1998). *Cooperative learning for higher education faculty*. Westport, CT: Greenwood.

Mills, J. (1998). Better teaching through provocation. *College Teaching, 46* (1), 21–26.

Minner, S., & Prater, G. (1984). College teachers' expectations of LD students. *Academic Therapy, 20* (2), 225–259.

Moore, C. J., Newlon, B. J., & Nye, N. (1986). Faculty awareness of needs of physically disabled students in the college classroom. *Bulletin of the Association on Handicapped Student Services Programs in Postsecondary Education, 4,* 137–145.

Morrison, D. E. (1997). Overview of instructional consultation in North America. In K. T. Brinko & R. J. Menges (Eds.), *Practically speaking: A sourcebook for instructional consultants in higher education* (pp. 121–129). Stillwater, OK: New Forums Press.

Nantz, K. S., & Lundgren, T. D. (1998). Lecturing with technology. *College Teaching, 46* (2), 53–57.

National Center for the Study of Postsecondary Educational Supports (NCSPES). (2000a). *National survey of educational support provision to students with disabilities in postsecondary education settings.* Honolulu, HI: University of Hawaii at Manoa.

National Center for the Study of Postsecondary Educational Supports (NCSPES). (2000b). *Postsecondary education and employment for students with disabilities: Focus group discussions on supports and barriers in lifelong learning.* Honolulu, HI: University of Hawaii at Manoa.

National Council on Disability. (2000). *Transition and post-school outcomes for youth with disabilities: Closing the gaps to post-secondary education and employment.* Washington, DC: Author.

Nelson, C. E. (1996). Students diversity requires different approaches to college teaching, even in math and science. *American Behavioral Scientist, 40* (2), 165–177.

Nelson, J., Dodd, J., & Smith, D. (1990). Faculty willingness to accommodate students with learning disabilities: A comparison among academic divisions. *Journal of Learning Disabilities, 23* (3), 185–189.

New England Resource Center for Higher Education. (n.d.). *Program on faculty professional service and academic outreach.* Boston, MA: University of Massachusetts, Boston.

Newman, F. (2000). Saving higher education's soul. *Change, 33,* 16–23.

Newman, F., & Scurry, J. (2001, July 13). Online technology pushes pedagogy to the forefront. *The Chronicle of Higher Education,* p. B7.

Nikolova Eddins, S. G., Willams, D.G., Bushek, D., Porter, D., & Kineke, G. (1997). Searching for a prominent role of research in undergraduate education: Project interface. *Journal on Excellence in College Teaching, 8* (1), 69–81.

Nuhfer, E. B. (1993). Bottom-line disclosure and assessment. *Teaching Professor, 7* (7), 8.

Nuhfer, E. B. (1996). The place of formative evaluations in assessment and ways to reap their benefits. *Journal of Geoscience Education, 44* (4), 385–394.

Nuhfer, E. B., & Pavelich, M. (2001). Levels of thinking and educational outcomes. *National Teaching and Learning Forum, 11* (1) 5–8.

Oweini, A. (1998). How students coped with the war: The experience of Lebanon. *Journal of Higher Education, 69* (4), 406–423.

Ozmon, H., & Graver, S. (1990). *Philosophical foundations of education* (4th ed.). Toronto, Canada: Merrill Publishing Company.

Palmer, P. J. (1998). *The courage to teach: Exploring the inner landscape of a teacher's life.* San Francisco, CA: Jossey-Bass.

Palomba, C. A., & Banta, T. W. (1999). *Assessment essentials: Planning, implementing, and improving assessment in higher education.* San Francisco, CA: Jossey-Bass.

Pascarella, E. T. (2001). Cognitive growth in college. *Change, 33* (1), 21–27.

Patrick, D. L. (1996). Correspondence to Senator Tom Harkin, September 9, 1996. Retrieved March 16, 2002, from www.usdoj.gov/crt/foia/cltr204.txt

Paul, R. W., Elder, L., & Bartell, T. (1997). *California teacher preparation for instruction in critical thinking: Research findings and policy recommendations.* Sacramento, CA: California Commission on Teacher Credentialing.

Perry, W. G., Jr. (1999). *Forms of ethical and intellectual development in the college years.* San Francisco, CA: Jossey-Bass (a reprint of the original 1968 work with minor updating).

Perry, W. J. (1999). *Forms of intellectual and ethical development in the college years* (Reprint). San Francisco, CA: Jossey-Bass.

Phelps, L. A., & Hanley-Maxwell, C. (1997). School-to-work transitions for youth with disabilities: A review of outcomes and practices. *Review of Educational Research, 67* (2), 197–226.

Pierce, G. (1998, Spring). Teaching teachers: A model for the professional development of new faculty. *Adult Learning,* 17–20.

Pratt, D. D., & Associates. (1998). *Five perspectives on teaching in adult and higher education.* Malabar, FL: Krieger.

Prosser, M., & Trigwell, K. (1996). Congruence between intention and strategy in science teachers; approach to teaching. *Higher Education, 32,* 77–87.

Quinlan, K. M. (1998). Promoting faculty learning about collaborative teaching. *College Teaching, 46* (2), 43–47.

Ramaley, J. A. (2000). Embracing civic responsibility. *AAHE Bulletin, 52* (7), 9–13.

Ratcliff, J. L., Johnson, L. D., La Nasa, S. M., & Gaff, J. G. (2001). *The status of general education in the year 2000: Summary of a national survey.* Washington, DC: Association of American Colleges and Universities.

Reskin, B., & Roos, P. (1990). *Job queues. Gender queues.* Philadelphia, PA: Temple University Press.

Rhem, J. (1996). Urgings and cautions in student-centered teaching. *The National Teaching & Learning Forum, 5* (4), 1–5.

Rhodes, T. (2002). Could it be that it does make sense? A program review process for integrating activities. In D. Lieberman & C. Wehlburg (Eds.), *To Improve the Academy: Vol. 20. Resources for faculty, instructional, and organizational development* (pp. 49–64). Bolton, MA: Anker.

Rice, E. (1990). Rethinking what it means to be a scholar. In L. Ekroth (Ed.), *Teaching excellence: Toward the best in the academy.* Stillwater, OK: POD Network.

Rice, E. (1991). The new American scholar: Scholarship and the purposes of the university. *Metropolitan Universities, 1* (4), 7–18.

Rice, D., & Stacey, K. (1997). Small group dynamics as a catalyst for change: A faculty development model for academic service-learning. *Michigan Journal of Community Service Learning, 4,* 64–71.

Richlin, L. (1993, November). *The ongoing cycle of scholarly teaching and the scholarship of teaching.* Paper presented at the 13th annual Lilly Conference on College Teaching, Oxford, OH.

Richlin, L. (2001a). Scholarly teaching and the scholarship of teaching. In C. Kreber (Ed.), *Scholarship revisited: Perspectives on the scholarship of teaching* (pp. 57–68). New Directions for Teaching and Learning, No. 86. San Francisco, CA: Jossey-Bass.

Richlin, L. (2001b, November). *Making public the scholarship of teaching. Part 1: Designing publishable projects. Part 2: Presenting and publishing the scholarship of teaching.* Paper presented at the 21st annual Lilly Conference on College Teaching, Oxford, OH.

Robertson, D. L. (1988). *Self-directed growth.* Muncie, IN: Accelerated Development.

Robertson, D. L. (1996). Facilitating transformative learning: Attending to the dynamics of the education helping relationship. *Adult Education Quarterly, 47* (1),
41–53.

Robertson, D. L. (1997). Transformative learning and transition theory: Toward developing the ability to facilitate insight. *Journal on Excellence in College Teaching,
8* (1), 105–125.

Robertson, D. L. (1999a). Unconscious displacements in college teacher and student
relationships: Conceptualizing, identifying, and managing transference. *Innovative Higher Education, 23* (3), 151–169.

Robertson, D. L. (1999b). Professors' perspectives on their teaching: A new construct
and developmental model. *Innovative Higher Education, 23* (4), 271–294.

Robertson, D. L. (2000a). College teaching as an educational helping relationship.
Toward the Best in the Academy, 13 (1).

Robertson, D. L. (2000b). Enriching the scholarship of teaching: Determining appropriate cross-professional applications among teaching, counseling, and psychotherapy. *Innovative Higher Education, 25* (2), 111–125.

Robertson, D. R. (2000c). Professors in space and time: Four utilities of a new
metaphor and developmental model for professors-as-teachers. *Journal on Excellence in College Teaching, 11* (1), 117–132.

Robertson, D. R. (2001). Beyond learner-centeredness: Close encounters of the systemocentric kind. *Journal of Faculty Development, 18* (1), 7–13.

Ronkowski, S. A. (1993). Scholarly teaching: Developmental stages of pedagogical
scholarship. In L. Richlin (Ed.), *Preparing faculty for new conceptions of scholarship*
(pp. 79–90). New Directions for Teaching and Learning, No. 54. San Francisco,
CA: Jossey-Bass.

Russell, T. L. (1999). *No significant difference phenomenon.* Raleigh, NC: North Carolina State University Press.

Sarton, M. (1961). *The small room.* New York, NY: Norton.

Schapiro, S. A. (1999). *Higher education for democracy.* New York, NY: Peter Lang.

Schmetzke, A. (2001). Online distance education: "Anytime, anywhere" but not for
everyone. *Information Technology and Disabilities, 7* (2). Retrieved December 10,
2001, from http://www.rit.edu/~easi/itd/itdv07n2/axel.htm

Schneider, C. G., & Shoenberg, R. (1998). *Contemporary understandings of liberal education.* Washington, DC: Association of American Colleges and Universities.

Schon, D. A. (1995). The new scholarship requires a new epistemology. *Change, 27* (6), 27–34.

Shadid, A. (2002, February 26). 'Arc of crisis' study funds hiked: U.S. adding language training centers for strategically important areas. *Ann Arbor News,* p. A4.

Shapiro, N. S., & Levine, J. H. (1999). *Creating learning communities: A practical guide to winning support, organizing for change, and implementing programs.* San Francisco, CA: Jossey-Bass.

Shea, T. P., Sherer, P. D., & Kristensen, E. W. (2002). Harnessing the potential of online faculty development: Challenges and opportunities. In D. Lieberman & C. Wehlburg (Eds.), *To improve the academy: Vol. 20. Resources for faculty, instructional, and organizational development* (pp. 162–178). Bolton, MA: Anker.

Shoenberg, R. E., & Turlington, B. (1998). *Next steps for languages across the curriculum: Prospects, problems, and promise.* Phoenix, AZ: American Council on Education/Oryx Press.

Siegel, D. (1994). *Campuses respond to violent tragedy.* Phoenix, AZ: Oryx.

Simpson, R. D., & Smith, K. S. (1993, Winter). Validating teaching competencies for graduate teaching assistants: A national study using the Delphi method. *Innovative Higher Education, 18* (2), 133–146.

Smith, B. L., & McCann, J. (2001). *Reinventing ourselves: Interdisciplinary education, collaborative learning, and experimentation in higher education.* Bolton, MA: Anker.

Smith, K. S. (1993, Spring). Investment in teaching: Mentoring for teaching assistants. *The Journal of Graduate Teaching Assistant Development, 1* (1), 43–48.

Smith, K. S. (in press). Pivotal events in graduate teacher preparation for a faculty career. *The Journal of Graduate Teaching Assistant Development.*

Smith, K. S., & Simpson R. D. (1995, Spring). Validating teaching competencies for faculty members in higher education: A national study using the Delphi method. *Innovative Higher Education, 19* (3), 223–233.

Smith, R. (2001). Expertise and the scholarship of teaching. In C. Kreber (Ed.), *Scholarship revisited: Perspectives on the scholarship of teaching* (pp. 69–78). New Directions for Teaching and Learning, No. 86. San Francisco, CA: Jossey-Bass.

Smith, R. M., Byrd, P., Nelson, G. L., Barrett, R. P., & Constantinides, J. C. (1992). Crossing pedagogical oceans: International teaching assistants in U.S. undergraduate education. *ASHE-ERIC Research Reports, Vol. 21, No. 8.* Washington DC: ERIC Clearinghouse on Higher Education.

Solla, L. (2000). *Chem 602: Lecture, week one.* Retrieved December 10, 2001, from http://www.library.cornell.edu/psl/chem602/lectures/lecture1.htm

Spradley, J. P. (1979). *The ethnographic interview.* Chicago, IL: Holt, Rinehart and Winston.

Spradley, J. P. (1980). *Participant observation.* Chicago, IL: Holt, Rinehart and Winston.

Stanton, T. K. (1990). *Integrating public service with academic study: The faculty role.* Providence, RI: Campus Compact.

Stark, J. S. (1986). Administrator and faculty views of scholarly performance. *New Directions for Institutional Research, No. 50,* 59–74.

Stern, D. N., Sander, L. W., Nahum, J. P., Harrison, A. M., Lyons-Ruth, K., Morgan, A. C., Bruschweiler-Stern, N., & Tronick, E. Z. (1998). Non-interpretive mechanisms in psychoanalytic therapy: The "something more" than interpretation. *International Journal of Psycho-Analysis, 79,* 903–921.

Sternberg, R. J. (1998). Principles of teaching for successful intelligence. *Educational Psychologist, 33,* 65–72.

Stephenson, F. J. (2001). *Extraordinary teachers: The essence of excellent teaching.* Kansas City, MO: Andrews McMeel Publishing.

Stiggins, R. (2001, November 8). *Assessment and state performance standards.* Workshop presented by the Nebraska State Department of Education, University of Nebraska, Lincoln.

Stodden, R. A. (1998). School-to-work transition: Overview of disability legislation. In F. Rusch & J. Chadsey (Eds.), *Beyond high school: Transition from school to work.* Belmont, CA: Wadsworth Publishing.

Stodden, R. A., & Dowrick, P. W. (2001). Postsecondary education and employment of adults with disabilities. *American Rehabilitation, 25* (3), 19–23.

Strauss, A. L. (1987). *Qualitative analysis for social scientists.* New York, NY: Cambridge University Press.

Sugar, S. (1998). *Games that teach: Experiential activities for reinforcing learning.* San Francisco, CA: Jossey-Bass.

Sullivan, W. M. (n.d.). *Institutional identity and social responsibility.* Washington, DC: Council on Public Policy Education.

Tang, T. L. (1997). Teaching evaluation at a public institution of higher education: Factors related to the overall teaching effectiveness. *Public Personnel Management, 26* (3), 379–390.

Taylor, K., & Marienau, C. (1997). Constructive development theory as a framework for assessment in higher education. *Assessment and Evaluation in Higher Education, 22* (2), 233–244.

Teasdale, J. D., Segal, Z., & Williams, J. M. G. (1995). How does cognitive therapy prevent depressive relapse and why should attentional control (mindfulness) training help? *Behavior Research and Therapy, 33* (1), 25–39.

Theall, M., & Centra, J. A. (2001). Assessing the scholarship of teaching: Valid decisions from valid evidence. In C. Kreber (Ed.), *Scholarship revisited: Perspectives on the scholarship of teaching* (pp. 31–43). New Directions for Teaching and Learning, No. 86. San Francisco, CA: Jossey-Bass.

Thomas, A. M. (1991). *Beyond education: A new perspective on society's management of learning.* San Francisco, CA: Jossey-Bass.

Thompson, A., Bethea, L., & Turner, J. (1997). Faculty knowledge of disability laws in high education: A survey. *Rehabilitation Counseling Bulletin, 40,* 166–180.

Thompson, S., & Nelson, C. (2000, November). *Scholarship of teaching and learning (SOTL): Programs, progress, problems, and prospects.* Paper presented at the 20th annual Lilly Conference on College Teaching, Oxford, OH.

Thiagarajan, S. (1999). *Teamwork and teamplay: Games and activities for building and training teams.* San Francisco, CA: Jossey-Bass.

Tiberius, R. G. (2001). A brief history of educational development: Implications for teachers and developers. In D. Lieberman & C. Wehlburg (Eds.), *To improve the academy: Vol. 20. Resources for faculty, instructional, and organizational development* (pp. 20–37). Bolton, MA: Anker.

Tiberius, R. G., & Billson, J. M (1991). The social context of teaching and learning. In R. J. Menges & M. Svinicki (Eds.) *College teaching: From theory to practice* (pp. 67–86). New Directions for Teaching and Learning, No. 45. San Francisco, CA: Jossey-Bass.

Tight, M. (Ed.). (1981). *Adult learning and education.* Kent, England: Croom Helm.

Tinto, V., & Goodsell, A. (1993). *A longitudinal study of freshman interest groups at the University of Washington.* University Park, PA: National Center for Postsecondary Teaching, Learning, and Assessment.

Tobias, S., & Raphael, J. (1997). *The hidden curriculum: Faculty-made tests in science, Part I lower-division courses.* New York, NY: Plenum.

Twigg, C. (2001). *Innovations in online learning: Moving beyond no significant difference.* Troy, NY: Center for Academic Transformation Rensselaer Polytechnic Institute. Retrieved December 11, 2001, from http://www.center.rpi.edu/PewSym/mono4.html

U.S. Department of Commerce. (2000). *Falling through the net: Toward digital inclusion.* Washington, DC: U.S. Government Printing Office. Retrieved December 10, 2001, from http://www.ntia.doc.gov/ntiahome/fttn00/contents00.html

Vaz, R. F. (2000). Connected learning: Interdisciplinary projects in international settings. *Liberal Education, 86* (1), 2–9.

Vogel, S., Leyser, Y., Wyland, S., & Brulle, A. (1999). Students with learning disabilities in higher education: Faculty attitude and practices. *Learning Disabilities Research & Practice, 14* (3), 173–186.

Vygotsky, L. (1986). *Thought and language.* Cambridge, MA: MIT Press.

Waddell, C. D. (1999). *The growing digital divide in access for people with disabilities: Overcoming barriers to participation in the digital economy.* Retrieved from http://www.icdri.org/the_digital_divide.htm

Wagner, M., & Blackorby, J. (1996). Transition from high school to work or college: How special education students fare. *The future of children: Special education for students with disabilities, 6* (1), 103–120.

Webster's third new international dictionary of the English language, unabridged. (1966). Springfield, MA: Merriam.

Weimer, M. (1993, November/December). The disciplinary journals of pedagogy. *Change, 25* (6), 45–51.

Weimer, M. (1997). Integration of teaching and research: Myth, reality, and possibility. *New Directions for Teaching and Learning, No. 72,* 53–62.

Weimer, M. (2001). Learning more from the wisdom of practice. In C. Kreber (Ed.), *Scholarship revisited: Perspectives on the scholarship of teaching* (pp. 45–56). New Directions for Teaching and Learning, No. 86. San Francisco, CA: Jossey-Bass.

Wergin, J. F. (2001). Beyond carrots: What really motivates faculty. *Liberal education, 87* (1), 50–53.

West, M., Kregel, J., Getzel, E., Zhu, M., Ipsen, S., & Martin, E. (1993). Beyond Section 504: Satisfaction and empowerment of students with disabilities in higher education. *Exceptional Children, 59* (5), 456–467.

Western Interstate Commission for Higher Education. (1992). *Bringing into focus the factors affecting faculty supply and demand: A primer for higher education and state policy makers.* Boulder, CO: Author.

Weston, C. B., & McAlpine, L. (2001). Making explicit the development toward the scholarship of teaching. In C. Kreber (Ed.), *Scholarship revisited: Perspectives on the scholarship of teaching* (pp. 89–97). New Directions for Teaching and Learning, No. 86. San Francisco, CA: Jossey-Bass.

White, C. R. (1994). A model for comprehensive reform in general education: Portland State University. *The Journal of General Education, 43* (3), 167–228.

White, C. R. (1998). Placing community-building at the center of the curriculum, *Metropolitan Universities, 9* (1), 55–62.

Widoff, J. C. (1999). The adult male undergraduate student experience: Real men do return to school. *Journal of Continuing Higher Education, 47* (2), 15–24.

Wingspread Group in Higher Education. (1993). *An American imperative: Higher expectations for higher education.* Racine, WI: Johnson Foundation.

Wladkowski, R. J., & Westover, T. (1999). Accelerated courses as a learning format for adults. *The Canadian Journal for the Study of Adult Education, 13* (1), 1–20.

Wong, E. D. (1995). Challenges confronting the researcher/teacher: A rejoinder to Wilson. *Educational Researcher, 24* (8), 2–23.

Wooldridge, B. (1995). Increasing the effectiveness of university/college instruction: Integrating the results of learning style research into course design and delivery. In R. R. Sims & S. J. Sims (Eds.), *The importance of learning styles* (pp. 49–68). Westport, CT: Greenwood.

Wright, W. A., & O'Neil, M. C. (1994). Teaching improvement practices: New perspectives. In E. C. Wadsworth (Ed.), *To improve the academy: Vol. 13. Resources for faculty, instructional, and organizational development* (pp. 5–38). Stillwater, OK: New Forums Press.

Yelin, E., & Katz, P. (1994). Labor force trends of persons with and without disabilities. *Monthly Labor Review, 117,* 36–42.

Young, C., & Young, L. (1999). Assessing learning in interactive courses. *Journal on Excellence in College Teaching, 10* (1), 63–76. Retrieved December 10, 2001, from http://ject.lib.muohio.edu/contents/article.php?article=186

Youtz, B. (1984). The Evergreen State College: An experiment maturing. In R. M. Jones & B. L. Smith (Eds.), *Against the current.* Cambridge, MA: Schenkman.

Yuker, H. (1994). Variables that influence attitudes toward people with disabilities. *Psychosocial Perspectives on Disability, 9* (5), 3–22.

Zinn, L. (1990). Identifying your philosophical orientation. In M. W. Galbraith (Ed.), *Adult learning methods: A guide to effective instruction* (pp. 60–74). Malabar, FL: Krieger.

Zlotkowski, E. (Ed.). (1997–2000). *AAHE series on service-learning in the disciplines.* Washington, DC: American Association for Higher Education.

Zlotkowski, E. (1998). A service learning approach to faculty development. In J. P. Howard & R. Rhodes (Eds.), *Service learning pedagogy and research* (pp. 81–89). San Francisco, CA: Jossey-Bass.

Zoller, U. (2000). Teaching tomorrow's college science courses: Are we getting it right. *Journal of College Science Teaching, 29* (6), 409–414.